Florence Foster Jenkins

NICHOLAS MARTIN has worked as a croupier, a labourer, a bouncer and a barman. In his early twenties he worked at sea as a deck hand and later as a yacht captain. He then worked as a journalist, contributing to *The Sunday Times*, the *Guardian* and various magazines, before graduating from the National Film and Television School as a screenwriter in 1992. He wrote extensively for TV before writing *Florence Foster Jenkins* for Pathé. He lives in London.

JASPER REES is an arts journalist and author who has contributed regularly to many British publications. His books include *I Found My Horn: One Man's Struggle with the Orchestra's Most Difficult Instrument* (published in the US as *A Devil to Play*) and *Bred of Heaven: One Man's Quest to Reclaim His Welsh Roots*. He lives in London.

EAST SUSSEX COUNTY COUNCIL
WITHDRAWN
2 7 JUN 2023

17

04401325

FLORENCE FOSTER JENKINS

The remarkable story of America's best-known
and least-talented soprano

Biography by Jasper Rees
Screenplay by Nicholas Martin

PAN BOOKS

First published 2016 by Pan Books
an imprint of Pan Macmillan
20 New Wharf Road, London N1 9RR
Associated companies throughout the world
www.panmacmillan.com

ISBN 978-1-5098-2468-7

Biography © Big Hat Stories Ltd and Jasper Rees, 2016
Screenplay © Big Hat Stories Ltd, 2016

The right of Nicholas Martin and Jasper Rees to be identified as the
authors of this work has been asserted by them in accordance
with the Copyright, Designs and Patents Act 1988.

Florence Foster Jenkins film artwork and photographs © Pathé Productions Limited, 2016

Grateful acknowledgement is made to the following for permission to reproduce
the images herein: The Library of Congress; Billy Rose Theatre Division,
The New York Public Library; Museum of the City of New York; Byron Collection;
Getty Images; Margaret Bourke-White; The LIFE Picture Collection; Gregor Benko;
NYC Municipal Archives; Carnegie Hall Archives.

All rights reserved. No part of this publication may be reproduced,
stored in a retrieval system, or transmitted, in any form, or by any means
(electronic, mechanical, photocopying, recording or otherwise)
without the prior written permission of the publisher.

Pan Macmillan does not have any control over, or any responsibility for,
any author or third-party websites referred to in or on this book.

1 3 5 7 9 8 6 4 2

A CIP catalogue record for this book is available from the British Library.

Printed and bound by CPI Group (UK) Ltd, Croydon, CR0 4YY

This book is sold subject to the condition that it shall not, by way of
trade or otherwise, be lent, hired out, or otherwise circulated without
the publisher's prior consent in any form of binding or cover other than
that in which it is published and without a similar condition including
this condition being imposed on the subsequent purchaser.

Visit www.panmacmillan.com to read more about all our books
and to buy them. You will also find features, author interviews and
news of any author events, and you can sign up for e-newsletters
so that you're always first to hear about our new releases.

Contents

Prologue *1*

1: Wilkes-Barre, Pa *11*

2: Mrs Dr Jenkins *27*

3: Philadelphian *43*

4: Chairman of Music *58*

5: Mrs St Clair Bayfield *72*

6: Legatee *87*

7: Club Woman *102*

8: The Singing President *122*

9: Lady Florence *150*

10: Queen of the Night *180*

11: Prima Donna of Carnegie Hall *197*

12: Like Father, Like Daughter *212*

Epilogue *228*

Acknowledgements and Bibliography 233

FLORENCE FOSTER JENKINS
Screenplay by Nicholas Martin
239

PROLOGUE

On the evening of Wednesday 25 October 1944 something like two thousand people were shut out of Carnegie Hall. Crowded onto the New York City sidewalk, some waved $20 bills in an effort to persuade their way in, even though the most expensive tickets, long since sold out, officially cost $3. They could only watch as Cole Porter walked through the doors of the most hallowed concert hall in America, there to be joined by the much-loved superstar soprano Lily Pons, and the queen of burlesque Gypsy Rose Lee. Some say they saw Tallulah Bankhead swan in too. The old hall also swarmed with journalists eager to witness a phenomenon.

The night before, Frank Sinatra was on the same stage at an election rally in support of President F. D. Roosevelt. The night after, the New York Philharmonic Orchestra performed under the baton of Artur Rodziński. But on 25 October it was the turn of Florence Foster Jenkins, a sizeable woman in her mid-seventies who had recently released a series of recordings. It was these – including her versions of Mozart's Queen of the Night aria and Delibes's 'Indian Bell Song' – which had created such a feverish thirst to be there.

The evening has no real right to be remembered on so important a day in the history of the world: 25 October 1944 is such a pivotal date that there is a whole book about it – *One Day in a Very Long War* by John Ellis. In the Philippines the Battle of Leyte Gulf became the largest naval conflict in history, in which for the first time the Imperial Japanese Navy deployed kamikaze suicide bombers against US warships. In Europe, the last Romanian city under German occupation was liberated by Romanian and Soviet forces, who also pushed the Wehrmacht from their Norwegian base in Kirkenes, while Bomber Command and the US Air Force took part in daylight raids against Essen, Homberg and Hamburg.

Meanwhile, back in New York, the cover of the recital programme featured a photograph of a stately lady wearing, over short permed brown hair, a tiara with a diadem mounted in the centre. A heavy necklace plunged past her low neckline towards two tentatively clasped hands. On her left hand was a thumb ring. Her eyes were beady and her jaw firm. On a mid-blue background, and under black capitals blazing her name, were the words 'Coloratura Soprano'.

Inside the programme, bona fides advised of previous triumphs. Madame Jenkins, as she liked to be known, 'possesses a marked individuality in style and piquancy in her interpretations'. So reported the *New York Journal-American*. A Dr B. B. James (publication unattributed) confirmed that a recent audience in the federal capital 'included persons in the political, cultural and intellectual society of Washington', all of them 'critically minded hearers'. The *New York Daily Mirror* hailed 'a personage of authority and indescribable charm' whose annual recitals 'bring unbounded joy'.

These notices were in accordance with more or less everything that had ever been written about 'Lady Florence' (another of her preferred modes of address). She had been singing to select audiences since the 1910s, mostly in the protected world of the women's clubs which flourished in great profusion in New York City from the turn of the century. In 1917 she founded her own society and called it the Verdi Club, to whose members she later began singing in an annual

recital in the ballroom of the Ritz-Carlton Hotel. Press coverage was not solicited, other than from the *Musical Courier*, a
trade paper whose friendly discretion could be relied upon,
indeed bought. The recitals acquired a cult following and,
apart from the odd exuberant heckler, for years no one publicly said the salient and obvious thing about Florence Foster
Jenkins: that she was a remarkably talentless singer. Instead
they cheered and clapped and stifled their guffaws by stuffing
handkerchiefs in their mouths.

In 1941 those recordings introduced her feeble voice and
drastic pitching to a wider public, and word started to travel.
Then came Carnegie Hall. Supported by a pianist, a flautist
and a string quartet, she proceeded to massacre a variety of
tunes in a variety of outlandish costumes. The three thousand
who crammed Carnegie Hall as it had never been crammed
before raised such a commotion that her accompanist Cosme
McMoon judged the recital 'the most remarkable thing that
has happened there'. Her assault on the famous aria from *The
Magic Flute* had all the trappings of a brilliant comedic tour
de force as she persistently failed to reach the stipulated
notes. But it wasn't meant to be funny, any more than her
rendition of 'Clavelitos', a short, flirtatious song in the Hispanic idiom which pushed the audience to fresh peaks of
hysteria. As Florence lobbed rosebuds into the audience from
a basket on her arm, one uncontrollable actress had to be
removed from her box. In such a frenzied atmosphere it is
hard to imagine anyone creating enough of a disturbance to
warrant ejection, and yet apparently it happened. The instant
demand for an encore meant that poor McMoon had to make
his way down into the stalls to retrieve the flowers. The pleasure – and the pain – was even more intense the second time
round. And throughout the evening Madame Jenkins interpreted the gales of laughter and waves of applause as a genuine

acknowledgement of her art. Afterwards, her guests mingled with her onstage. 'Don't you think I had real courage to sing the Queen of the Night again,' she said to one of them, 'after that wonderful recording I made of it at the studio?'

The next morning news spread far across the United States. 'Mme Jenkins, if you haven't heard, and the chances are you haven't, is a lady who gives song recitals because there's no law against it.' That was the *Milwaukee Journal*. 'She takes the songs that bring out the best in Lily Pons and permits them to bring out her worst. And the worst of Mme Jenkins, you are herewith assured, is something awful.' Earl Wilson of the *New York Post* reported that Florence Foster Jenkins could 'sing anything but notes'. 'Hey, You Music Lovers!' ran the headline above his report. 'I Heard Madame Jenkins.' Describing her recital as 'one of the weirdest mass jokes New York has ever seen', his column – he was not a music journalist – pondered the discrepancy between the serious demeanour of the performer and the unbridled jollity of the audience. On the way out Wilson bumped into a man he described as the singer's personal representative, whose name he transcribed as Sinclair Bayfield.

'Why?' Wilson asked.

'She loves music,' said St Clair Bayfield, an Englishman in his late sixties who for many years had been a minor Broadway actor. There was only one question Wilson could ask next.

'If she loves music, why does she do this?'

'People may say I couldn't sing, but no one can ever say I didn't sing.' That's what Florence Foster Jenkins is reported to have said towards the end of her life. It certainly sounds like her. She lived for music and she loved to perform. She refused, utterly and triumphantly, to dwell on her limitations as a singer or to be cowed by those who mocked her. Indeed there is a poignant possibility that Florence simply could not hear those limitations. Audiences certainly rejoiced in her sincerity, and the pleasure she derived from entertaining them. Her performances, by dint of sheer charisma, some-how transcended technique. So inspirational is her example that even the greatest singers have found a place in their hearts for her. In 1968 the young Barbra Streisand was asked by *New York* magazine which other singers she'd like to be: 'Ray Charles and Florence Foster Jenkins,' she said. For *Vanity Fair* in 2003 David Bowie nominated *The Glory (????) of the Human Voice*, the RCA album of Florence's recordings released in 1962, as one of the 25 LPs that he counted as his greatest discoveries. (The only other soprano listed among all the blues, jazz and rock was Gundula Janowitz singing Strauss's *Four Last Songs*.)

Nowadays Florence is not alone. One of the reasons why her extraordinary story resonates, long after the great prima donnas to whom she absurdly compared herself have been forgotten, is that there are Florences all around us: less than entirely talented performers who nonetheless have a yearning to be heard. Latter-day incarnations of Florence audition on *The X Factor* or *America's Got Talent* and, like her, are mysti-fied by the howls of ridicule. Florence is their patron saint. As Cosme McMoon explained, 'She thought she was great.'

And yet Florence was also a complete one-off. It is almost always overlooked that she was a passionate, serious and hugely knowledgeable lover of music, and an impresario who for thirty-five years was a very significant patron of young talent in New York. Some of the burgeoning stars of opera were grateful for her friendship. If her pursuit of audience approval manifested an unconscious need to heal some sort of psychic wound – and it certainly looks that way – the cause lies somewhere in what went before. Earl Wilson passed on a story he heard that Florence's musical ambitions were blocked by her parents and then her husband, only to be liberated after all of them had died. It's a neat fairy tale. But is it a true fairy tale?

In general terms, hers is a story of her time: about an American woman's quest for an education, about a Darwinian urge to clamber up the ladder of society, about the stigma of divorce in the nineteenth century, about female empowerment embodied in the rise of women's clubs, and about the value of culture. Her progress through a boom society ruled by money is archetypal but it is also profoundly personal. She was born just after the Civil War, played her part in one world war and survived into another. Early on, her marriage took her to the heart of America's military establishment, where she found much to admire in her principled female in-laws while the males made for a grim array of the arrant, the psychotic and the morally spineless. Her husband's failings, she claimed with some justification, scarred her physically, and lastingly. And then there is the melodrama of her own family squabbles, which not once but twice necessitated the intervention of the law.

From the early years of Florence's life, when the human psyche is malleable clay, primary sources are scarce. It's not even clear whether she was born in Pennsylvania or New Jersey. Her elusiveness is written in the many variations of her name in the newspapers which later reported on her movements: Miss Florence Foster, Mrs Dr Jenkins, Mrs F. F. Jenkins, Madame Foster Jenkins, Mrs Florence Foster Jenkins, Mme Jenkins, Lady Florence – plus any number of typographical misnomers: Mrs F. E. Jenkins, Mrs Florence Foster Jekins, Florence Foster Jones and, the name she would have loved best of all, Florence Verdi Jenkins. It doesn't feel

like a coincidence that an elderly woman celebrated for
having no voice was vouchsafed none in the first half of her
life story. Nothing that she actually said was written down and
remembered until she was past the age of forty. Averse to
self-examination, she left no diary and gave only two interviews. The biographer's task is further frustrated by the
disappearance of all but four of the five hundred letters which
passed between Florence and St Clair Bayfield over thirty
years of common-law marriage.

This is, secondarily, his story too. By the time St Clair
arrived in New York as a young man, he had already enjoyed
a great many adventures of his own. In his career he spent
vastly more hours on stage than Florence, but her two hours
in Carnegie Hall eclipse them all. He didn't seem to mind
because he was utterly devoted to her. Instead, posterity has
made him the principal conduit for her life story. One of the
main sources is a biography which he embarked on after her
death and which was continued after his by his widow Kathleen. It was never published, and most of it has been lost, but
in 1971 Mrs Bayfield read out a substantial chunk in a joint
interview alongside two Verdi Club members who had known
Florence personally. Even here caution is advisable: it is ne-
cessary to scrape away the accretions from what Florence told
St Clair, what St Clair told Kathleen, and what Kathleen
wrote down, each narrator being guided by their own agenda.
Florence was certainly an unreliable narrator who moulded
her memories into a shape that made sense to her. She preferred to project an inspiring image of herself. The climax of
the Verdi Club's annual ball always featured its president
appearing in the guise of the great women of myth or history.
One year she dressed up as a winged Angel of Inspiration.
Another she was revealed proudly trussed up in the armour of
Brünnhilde, the Wagnerian Valkyrie. The image, with horned

helmet and spear, suggested spellbinding potency. But what was she protecting behind that awesome breastplate?

The essential unknowability of a historical figure is attractive to speculators. Wherever there is no final key to the inner life of an enigma, writers, film-makers and artists are to be found clustering like thirsty herds at a watering hole. Increasingly this has been true of Florence. There have been several plays about her, and each has earned more attention than the last. The first was Terry Sneed's *Precious Few*, premiered in Little Rock, Arkansas, in 1994. Charles Fourie's *Goddess of Song* was seen in Cape Town in 1999. Her story graduated to the Edinburgh Festival Fringe in 2001 in a play called *Viva La Diva* by Chris Ballance. In 2005 Florence made it to Broadway in Stephen Temperley's *Souvenir*. That same year *Glorious!* by Peter Quilter opened in the West End in London and has gone on to be performed in over forty countries and in twenty-seven languages.

Now a celebratory film brings the name of Florence Foster Jenkins to wider attention than ever before. The script by Nicholas Martin, which concentrates on the climactic final years of her musical odyssey, has attracted some of the highest achievers in cinema. Meryl Streep, who has earned more Academy Award nominations than any actor in history (nineteen and counting, of which she has won three), charmingly embodies an indomitable woman who inspires devotion by blithely turning a blind eye – and a deaf ear – to any hurdles planted in her path. Her Florence makes the world a brighter place. Hugh Grant gives the most touching performance of his career as the debonair but sensitive St Clair Bayfield. The film also offers a hugely engaging performance from Simon Helberg as Cosme McMoon. The director is Stephen Frears, whose previous studies of fascinating women include

Dangerous Liaisons, *The Queen* and *Philomena*. Madame Jenkins would have been thrilled with all the attention.

It is rare – maybe unprecedented – for a biography and the script of a biopic to be published in harness. Florence Foster Jenkins feels like an ideal fit for such treatment, being a figure with a splendid flair for self-dramatisation. The film, as films should and must, takes the facts and fashions them into an entertainment that, in this case, rejoices in the comic and innocent side of her personality. The script alludes to many of Florence's delightful eccentricities – her collection of dining chairs in which great Americans had supposedly died, her phobia of sharp objects, the limitless supply of potato salad stored in the bathtub when she entertained. Along the way many of the supporting players in her life pop up in Nicholas Martin's script – Carlo Edwards, who secretly gave her singing lessons; Kathleen, the mistress of St Clair Bayfield; Earl Wilson, the author of that Carnegie Hall review the morning after. There are even cameos for the great maestro Toscanini and for Tallulah Bankhead, who, at least in the film, definitely makes it to Carnegie Hall.

While film-goers discover Florence on film, this biography attempts to spool back to the beginning and unpick the complexities of an unusual life which held back the moment of highest drama till the end.

1: WILKES-BARRE, PA

What does the world know about Wilkes-Barre? All American eyes have turned on the Pennsylvania coal town only once. In 1926 the celebrated baseball slugger Babe Ruth hit what was then thought to be the longest ever home run. The ball flew so far he asked for it to be measured. It came out at around 217 yards. For the rest of its history, Wilkes-Barre has tended not to hit the ball out of the park.

It has tiptoed into the purview of American culture as a byword for Ordinaryville, USA. Listen closely in *All About Eve* and at one point Bette Davis can be heard dropping the name. 'The evil that men do – how does it go? Something about the good they leave behind. I played it once in Wilkes-Barre.' She's quoting Mark Antony in *Julius Caesar*. Wilkes-Barre was a very long way from ancient Rome, which is why the great writer-director Joseph Mankiewicz, multiple winner of Academy Awards and a Wilkes-Barre native, dropped a joke into the script.

Wilkes-Barre is memorialised in a long-forgotten Broadway musical romcom from 1963 called *Tovarich*. Adapted from a Thirties play and film which made light of communism, the show includes a song called 'Wilkes-Barre, Pa'. It's sung by a young man who has fallen in love with the maid, who happens to be a countess on the run from the Russian revolution. He paints his home town as an all-American heaven.

Take me back where I belong
Tell my baby I was wrong,
Never should have gone away
Wilkes-Barre, Pa!

In the role of the countess, Vivien Leigh won a Tony award for best actress in a musical. It can't have been for her singing. Like Wilkes-Barre's most celebrated daughter, she could barely hit a note.

The city's name is rooted in the journey to independence. John Wilkes was a member of the British parliament who was such a zealous reformer he was imprisoned for sedition. Later he championed the cause of the American rebels. So did Isaac Barré, a Dublin-born son of a French Huguenot, who was blinded in one eye at the Battle of Quebec – he is among the group immortalised in Benjamin West's epic painting *The Death of General Wolfe*. A fiery orator, he dubbed the colonists 'sons of liberty'. Yoked by a hyphen, and in the nineteenth century often lumped together in the single word Wilkesbarre, these two men gave their names to Florence Foster's home town.

The city sits on the southern bank of the Susquehanna river in the Wyoming valley. The first white men reached there in 1769. The skirmishes and conflagrations which soon took place in the valley floor offer a microcosm of the struggles that shaped the nation, between settlers and Native Americans, colonists and royalists. The first newspaper was published in Wilkes-Barre in 1795. The following year *The Herald of the Times* had its first major story when the exiled Duc d'Orléans, later to become King Louis Philippe of France, passed through. In 1806 there was another notable visitation in the form of a travelling elephant show. A bridge was built over the Susquehanna, which variously flooded or froze but was soon navigated by steamboat. In 1831 the first canal boat left Wilkes-Barre bound for Philadelphia bearing, among other necessities, the mineral which would make the valley rich.

The discovery of anthracite coal caused Wilkes-Barre to grow at speed, its workforce swollen above all by immigrants from the mining communities of Wales. It is thought to be the first place on earth where anthracite was burned to generate domestic heat. Wilkes-Barre acquired a moniker: the Diamond City. In the 1860s alone its population doubled to more than ten thousand (it eventually peaked at 87,000 in 1930). By the time Florence Foster was born, Wilkes-Barre was a force in the state. And her forebears had planted their feet near the summit of Pennsylvania society.

Genealogy was the source of fascinated one-upmanship among the descendants of settlers. In such a young country, roots mattered. Florence and her mother were life members of the city's Genealogical and Biographical Society among numerous other patriotic clubs. A profile of Florence in the *New York Times* in 1916 described her as 'born in Pennsylvania of distinguished American ancestry'. She was the product, on both sides of her family tree, of settlers who had sailed for the American colonies in the 1630s. But the claim to pure blood and high-born roots stretched many centuries further into the past. Her father's branch traced a direct line all the way back to the Norman Conquest. Sir Richard Forester was claimed by his descendants as the brother-in-law of William of Normandy, though genealogists and historians dispute his paternity. But at sixteen he certainly fought at the Battle of Hastings. Another forebear is said to have saved Richard the Lionheart's life on the Third Crusade. On the strength of the connection, Florence would later join a society called the Order of the Three Crusades.

Her father, Charles Dorrance Foster, was born in 1836,

the only child of the marriage between Phineas Nash Foster, a farmer in Jackson County, and Mary Bailey Bulford (née Johnson), a widow with three much older children. As a schoolboy he spent his vacations on the family farm. Later he dabbled as a teacher both locally and all the way off in Illinois. When the United States was convulsed by Civil War in 1861, he did not serve, instead gaining admittance to the Bar of Pennsylvania. He soon had a large practice. In 1870, when he was thirty-three, his wealth was listed as $42,000 in real estate and $10,000 in personal estate. When Foster's father died in 1878 he inherited two farms in Dallas and Jackson Townships just to the north-west of Wilkes-Barre. His father's step-children, Charles's older half-siblings whose surname was Bulford, were left to fend for themselves. The windfall had a demotivating impact on his professional life. A mere five years on, a contemporary history of Luzerne County reported that 'clients soon came to him, but . . . he found that possession sufficient to occupy most of his time and for all of his wants, so he gave only incidental attention to legal practice'. Instead he involved himself in buying and selling real estate, farmland and livestock and litigating bullishly on large matters and small: from the distribution of coal board revenues to pesky opera house billboards that sprouted in the street outside his home. '$3 REWARD,' he once offered in a small newspaper announcement. 'For the name of the person who broke the glass out of my window, Wednesday afternoon, playing ball.'

Foster's portion of Wilkes-Barre's wealth and splendour drew a tart portrait from another local historian: 'He is the possessor of wealth ample enough to gratify anything short of sordid avarice. Few men enjoy, at so early an age, such complete physical, financial, and social advantages.'

Charles D. Foster was a prominent Episcopalian and

staunch Republican. He acquired a property at 124 South Franklin Street, in a district where Wilkes-Barre's conservative elite tended to cluster in elegant and spaciously arranged mansions. Not far away was the St Stephen's Episcopal church, another few doors down the Westmoreland Club. Foster was a member of both. He was the sort of wealthy pillar of the community whom people wanted on their boards. Thus he was president of the first street railway in Wilkes-Barre, director of one turnpike company, treasurer of another, director of the Wyoming National Bank, a member of sundry Masonic, banking, genealogical and historical associations. To these local accomplishments he added electoral success. He was defeated in his first tilt at the Lower House of the Pennsylvania legislature in 1882, then voted in two years later; he served for a single term.

Photographs of Foster show a well-dressed figure with fair hair atop a heavy brow and a full face rounded off by a forthright jaw. The eyebrows are dense and the moustache substantial. In one portrait of Foster as a younger man it droops either side of his mouth. In a later image it twirls upwards.

Charles D. Foster married Mary Jane Hoagland from Hunterdon, New Jersey, on 4 October 1865. Precisely when she entered the world is uncertain. Four censuses give four different versions, suggesting a streak of vanity. In 1860, when she was still living with her parents, the year of her birth was written down as 1838. A decade later, by which time she was married, she had somehow shed seven years and her birth year was now 1845. Ten years on she was only nine years older, the birth date having been dropped to 1846. There were no further alterations in the following two censuses. Then, after her husband's death, she suddenly lost another four years.

A photograph of Mary Foster in middle age shows a hand-some woman in a high-necked dress, brunette hair piled above a well-proportioned face and a strong mouth. As to what came out of that mouth, the evidence is in short supply. But she was clearly proud of her English and Dutch ancestry. She joined a prodigious number of the lineage associations which abounded in the United States. At some point she came into or acquired a property that was of some signifi-cance in American folklore. This was the so-called Fleming's Castle in Hunterton County, where her grandfather had been a judge. In reality it was a modest clapperboard tavern built in 1756 by Irish-born Samuel Fleming; its importance derived from a reference to 'stopping at Fleming's' in General George Washington's journal.

Mary Foster gave birth on 19 July 1868 to a daughter, although it's not clear where as no birth certificate has been unearthed. Florence's death certificate put her place of birth as Wilkes-Barre, while St Clair Bayfield submitted a legal petition in 1945 stating that Florence was born in Fleming-ton, New Jersey, which is not unlikely: quite often, before hospital birth, women would go home for their confinement. The child was christened Narcissa Florence. Narcissa was not a common name; in 1868 newspapers across the whole of America refer to only eleven women called Narcissa. She was named, perhaps, after Narcissa Whitman, the pioneering mis-sionary who in 1836 became the first white woman to traverse the Rockies. More probably her blonde hair and blue eyes put her mother in mind of a member of the daffodil family. It was not the name by which Florence Foster Jenkins would later be known, but it aptly encapsulated something of her person-ality.

During Florence's early years, her father made frequent excursions to the farm to oversee the running of the land but also to drop in on his mother. She was still living in the modest farmhouse where he grew up and which she professed to favour over 'all the wealth and splendor that a city can afford'. A keen equestrian, Foster drove out in a Portland cutter pulled by a pair of horses he stabled by his house, and he took his daughter with him to visit her grandmother. When the snow came they would wrap up in rugs for enchanting rides in the sleigh through the Luzerne countryside.

Florence was raised as a daughter of the age. She applied herself to crochet and the piano. When she fell in love with the latter, the die was cast. The stories about her early musical career must be taken on trust. In an interview Florence gave in 1927 she said she was a piano soloist at the age of ten, performing in many public concerts, on one occasion 'facing undismayed an audience numbering ten thousand persons'. St Clair Bayfield dated her debut to an even earlier age, telling an interviewer that she'd first performed in Philadelphia at eight. Neither of these stories has the ring of truth. Florence did later perform in front of thousands in Philadelphia but, while musical ability was a valuable social asset in a young girl, there is room for doubt that Foster would have tolerated the spectacle of his accomplished young daughter playing for anyone but drawing-room guests.

And yet the environment in which she grew up was learned and cultured. Her father was widely read and poly-mathic in his interests. Students and other Wilkes-Barreans often heard him give amusing and informed talks on a vast range of subjects: Roman history, the superiority of the American school system, the impact of Magna Carta, the US Mint, the hieroglyphs of the Rosetta Stone, the cardinal virtues of business, the music of the ancients, contemporary literature, the structure of banks, the influence of the solar system on the turn of the seasons, American history in the colonial epoch and, more than once, temperance. Mary Foster was a keen and increasingly accomplished painter of landscapes and portraits in oil. Later in life Florence hung two large portraits of herself side by side over her Steinway in her New York apartment. One showed her as a child, the other as a woman in early middle age. Both were very probably the work of her mother.

The most character-forming event in Florence's childhood was the birth, in 1875, of a sister. After such a long wait the arrival of a baby girl, whom her parents named Lillian Blanche, will have been the cause of much celebrating. Older siblings very often have more conflicted feelings about the sudden appearance of a rival. Seven years is a long time for a child to rejoice in the undivided love of her mother and father. Even if only on an unconscious level, Florence now had to work harder for her parents' attention. Soon after this event the accomplished little pianist seems to have begun performing for domestic audiences in Wilkes-Barre. It is possible to speculate that the uncritical applause provided her with an alternative source of approval and validation.

As a child she would have been taken on the train for jaunts in Philadelphia, just over a hundred miles to the southeast of Wilkes-Barre. It was a city to excite the imagination of a young girl. Its burgeoning wealth manifested itself in the streets and gardens. A seated bronze likeness of Lincoln was commissioned in 1866, the year after his assassination, and unveiled in 1871. (Florence's parents may well have been among the three hundred thousand who viewed Lincoln's body as its funeral train passed through the city in the thousand-mile journey from Washington, DC back to Springfield, Illinois.) The Association for Public Art effected an improving face-lift of the city's public spaces. Sculpture sprouted in the parks and avenues. When she walked through the botanical

wonderland of Bartram's Garden, Florence would have encountered a pair of Medici lions – two of many big cats to
prowl the city. These cast-iron copies were emissaries from
the cradle of the Renaissance with which Florence shared her
name. In 1874, when Florence was six, America's first zoo
opened its doors in Philadelphia, its completion much delayed
by the Civil War. For the price of twenty-five cents visitors
could view a thousand animals. A century on from the Declaration of Independence, a statue of England's patron saint
George slaying the dragon appeared in Fairmount Park, while
the Columbus monument commemorated in marble the Italian who found the Americas. That same year Philadelphia
became the first American city to host the World Fair. Across
six months, nearly ten million people visited two hundred
specially erected pavilions on the site of the Centennial Exposition to marvel at a giant celebration of America's commercial
and industrial prowess. On Pennsylvania Day alone, a quarter
of a million people flooded the site. It seems probable that
Foster took his eight-year-old daughter to the first public display of such revolutionary concepts as the Remington
typographic machine, the Wallace-Farmer electric dynamo,
Alexander Graham Bell's telephone, and Heinz ketchup. The
US Navy's pavilion was overseen by the man, appointed by
President Ulysses S. Grant himself, who would one day be
her father-in-law.

In July 1878, when Florence had just turned ten, she went
with her sister and father to observe a total eclipse of the sun
from a hotel at the nearby Harveys Lake, the largest natural
body of water in Pennsylvania. She had her father to herself
in the summer of 1881 on a ten-day visit to Niagara Falls;
a trip taken, so the *Wilkes-Barre Record* reported, 'for their
health'. This was a period of upheaval for Florence. That
autumn she was cast out of the family home to be enrolled at

the Moravian Seminary in Bethlehem, Pennsylvania: America's first ever boarding school for young women.

Founded in 1785 by a branch of the Protestant Church that had its roots in the fifteenth-century Hussite movement in Bohemia, the school's education was steeped in religion. A prospectus published in 1876 explained that 'the moral and religious training of the young is shaped after the teachings of Christ, and by no means subordinated to the acquisition of mere human knowledge'. The principal was appointed from the clergy and, on a strictly non-sectarian footing, there were daily visits to the chapel to cleanse the soul before the day started. The majority of pupils were drawn from Pennsylvania, New York and New Jersey but others came from further-flung states in the Union – California, Texas, Louisiana – and some came from beyond the country's borders: Canada, Central and South America, England. As for the academic schooling on offer, twenty resident tutors alongside specialist teachers between them taught several subjects that would one day stand Florence in good stead (German, French, rhetoric, mythology, book-keeping, vocal and instrumental music, painting, drawing, elocution and – given her later obsession with birdsong – ornithology). There were also quite a few that wouldn't (mineralogy, astronomy, wax-work, natural sciences, logic). Florence doubtless baulked at the restricted opportunities for freedom of movement. Even in their leisure hours, she and her schoolmates were constantly under the eye of a tutoress, who would accompany them everywhere: the refectory, the dormitory, the school grounds for walks. There were plenty of pianos for her to practise on: the school boasted forty-six of them, plus two cabinet organs. But musical attainment was secondary to the overall emphasis on producing young women with an instinct for good behaviour. 'The government of the household aims at instilling right principles and forming good habits,' explained the prospectus. 'Hence the pupils are amenable to a code of rules touching their moral obligations as individuals and their duties as members of a family; while the constant supervision which character-izes the daily regime enables the tutoresses to exercise an influence for good over their charge, which otherwise might not be done. The method of instruction is patient, laborious and hence likely to be thorough.' For three terms of Moravian improvement to his daughter, Charles Foster paid a fee of around $300 (it was $280 in 1876). The bill encompassed such sundries as washing and choir singing, use of the library and cutlery, access to stationery, medical care from a house physician, fuel, baths and pew rents.

The school record does not indicate if she stayed any longer than a year; two years seems more probable. There were other changes afoot. In September 1882 Florence's father was nominated to stand as a Republican for Luzerne County in the assembly in Philadelphia. And it was around this time that the Fosters moved house to 27 South Franklin Street, which was even closer to the church.

Another story told by St Clair Bayfield is that as a girl Florence expressed a desire to study music in Europe. To a young pianist it may have seemed a logical ambition. When her fingers touched the keyboard, they produced sounds of European civilisation. This was the music America listened to. *Tannhäuser* had just been performed at the recently opened Metropolitan Opera in New York while the repertoire of the newly formed Boston Symphony Orchestra was overwhelm-ingly European. The city's much older orchestra clarified its allegiance in its name: the Handel and Haydn Society. When the Strasbourg-born émigré composer F. L. Ritter pub-lished the first major history of American music in 1883, he found it still heavily under European influence and in only the early stages of self-discovery. In the first half of the 1880s, several important events separately heralded a distinct identity for American music: Marshall W. Taylor published the first anthology of negro spirituals, while a choir of black singers sang at the White House; a chorded zither was patented in the US; and Scott Joplin sat down at a piano in the Silver Dollar Saloon in St Louis, Missouri, and invented ragtime.

Events which may have been more closely observed by Florence, all of them reported in the newspapers, showed that women could play a significant part in the musical life of the nation. In 1882 an opera called *The Joust* was premiered in Omaha, Nebraska. Its music was composed by one G. Estabrook, whose real name was Gussie Clowry. When she died in 1897, one of her songs was reported by the *Philadelphia Inquirer* to have sold over a million copies. Closer to home was the creation in Potsdam, New York, of what is now known as the Crane School of Music. Its remit was to train public-school music teachers, and it was the brainchild of a thirty-year-old woman, Julia Ettie Crane. 'Is there any one thing more universally demanded by mankind than music?' she wrote. 'Nothing brings greater return in real understanding and development, for the time spent, than music.'

In her own way Florence would come to embody that principle. Charles D. Foster will have needed some persuading on the point. As a domestic accomplishment, Florence's abilities were to be cherished. But Europe was another matter. Kathleen Bayfield described him as 'the old-fashioned type who thought girls should stay home, play the piano, paint and be a lady of leisure'. There is no suggestion that Foster had been anywhere near the place, though he will have known the stories of Americans lured to Europe by the siren wail of an older culture. The novels of Henry James – written after prolonged experience of the fleshpots – made cautionary noises about young Americans of an artistic bent venturing into the European lair. James discoursed frankly on children sired out of wedlock, radical politics and terrorist foment, all flavoured with a soupçon of aristocratic hauteur. *Roderick Hudson* (1875) traced the tragic corruption of Rome on an American artist. *The Europeans* (1878) told of sober New Englanders 'exposed to peculiar influences' when Americans raised across the Atlantic came home. A specifically dire warning was embedded in *The Portrait of a Lady* (1881) in which beautiful young heiress Isabel Archer is pursued by unscrupulous suitors in Europe; she plumps for the worst of the lot, a louche and cold-hearted American expatriate who condemns her to a life of unhappiness.

Florence is more likely to have taken her inspiration from tales of female empowerment and self-expression in Louisa May Alcott's *Little Women*, the vastly successful first volume of which was published in the year of her birth. She may have imagined a future for herself conflated in the fates of the more artistic of the four March sisters. On the one hand Beth is a talented pianist whose life is cut short when she contracts scarlet fever. On the other, Amy is the most selfish and vain of the four, but burgeons as a writer whose ambitions of self-fulfilment and growth are fully realised only when she is taken to Europe. Glimpsed in the full flower of adulthood, she offered a satisfactory template for a creative young American woman with wanderlust: 'Time seemed to have stood still with Amy, for happiness had kept her young and prosperity given her the culture she needed. A stately, graceful woman, who showed how elegant simplicity could be made by the taste with which she chose her dress and the grace with which she wore it.'

Meanwhile, the concept of young women studying piano and singing was gaining acceptance in Europe. The Guildhall School of Music and the Royal College of Music were both established in 1880. In the first round of scholarships offered by the latter to young students of the piano, fourteen out of seventeen went to women.

While it is conceivable that Florence's stories of thwarted musical ambition were exaggerated, there are enough different sources which talk of her parents banning her from singing to confirm that, in later life, Florence at least believed she had been held back. But there was a far more immediate cause of devastation. In 1883, the eight-year-old Lilly fell ill with diphtheria.

If the infection developed in the standard way, she would at first have complained of a mild sore throat and developed a fever. Then came the alarming whelps of a croup-like cough and, when she opened her mouth, white patches would be seen forming at the back of her throat. Her neck started to swell, her skin turned blue and she found it excruciatingly painful to swallow, then began to have difficulty breathing. Child mortality rates from diphtheria had been slowly declining from around the year of Lilly's birth, but there was still no treatment. In New York a physician called Joseph O'Dwyer was developing a system of intubation that could be used on children as young as one to stop them asphyxiating. He did not present his findings for another two years and the apparatus would not be adopted for another five. As the Fosters well knew, diphtheria did not discriminate. Foster was infected too, though as he had survived it earlier in life he was not in danger. But epidemics in America had cut a swathe through populations in New England and, more recently, California. Only five years earlier it attacked the progeny of Queen Victoria, killing Princess Alice and her four-year-old daughter.

On 29 June 1883, it claimed another victim. 'Yesterday evening about six o'clock,' reported the *Wilkes-Barre Record*,

> the angel of death visited the home of our esteemed townsman, C. D. Foster, Esq., and removed his youngest daughter, Lilly, a little girl only nine [sic] years of age. She fell a victim to that dire disease, diphtheria, after a brief sickness. The little one, so suddenly called away in the very midst of the bright days of childhood, had won her way deep into the hearts of all who knew her. She was of a joyous and kindly disposition, and had given ample evidence of the possession of still nobler qualities which would have made her after life one of great promise. In their deep affliction the sorrowing parents have the sympathy of every one. Their grief, however, is one that cannot soon be overcome, but must be left to the gentle hand of all-healing time to assuage.

While this was hardly an unusual tragedy – a Bulford cousin born in the same year as Florence died at the age of seven – the impact of the death of a child on her parents need not be imagined. For an older sibling it may have been a more complex event. What is known of Florence in later life is that she craved attention. Any such need tends to be established in the earliest days of childhood. After Lilly's birth Florence experienced the small needling grief of the older sibling nudged out of the parental spotlight. Now in her sister's death she was consigned to the margins all over again. In her own grief there lurked a quiet unconscious triumph, the intensified sense of her uniqueness as the sole survivor in whom all hopes rested. This time her spell in the sidelines occurred when – as a very young woman shortly to turn fifteen – she had more power to act.

The funeral cortege left Wilkes-Barre at six in the morning

on 1 July, bound for the cemetery eight miles away in Hunts-ville, near the family farm. The party included Lilly's parents, Foster's mother and his Bulford siblings Olive and John, as well as other Bulford cousins, and Florence.

Ten days after her sister was buried, the fourteen-year-old Florence Foster eloped.

2: Mrs Dr Jenkins

According to the 1901 edition of the *Catalogue of Pupils at the Moravian Seminary for Young Ladies*, Florence Foster married Dr Frank Thornton Jenkins on 11 July 1883, ten days after the funeral of her sister and eight days before her fifteenth birthday. Her father was still recovering from diphtheria.

How did this happen? The circumstances of their meeting are not known. A sister of Frank Jenkins had been at the Moravian Seminary several years earlier, and perhaps that was how a connection was made. Later in life Florence kept the dance cards of the balls she'd attended as a young woman, and they may have met at one of those. At thirty, Frank was sixteen years her senior and so, in this moment of crisis, would inevitably have played the role of a surrogate father figure.

In 1880 the age of consent in Pennsylvania was ten (a small minority of states put the legal age at twelve). And yet the cusp of fifteen seems extraordinarily young. Many years later Florence would testify in court that she left home at sixteen, while she told St Clair Bayfield that she eloped at seventeen. In the echelons of society in which both newlyweds had been brought up, she married far younger than anyone in her family circle or his. Frank's youngest sister married the previous year at nineteen. Frank's late mother was eighteen at her wedding, and Florence's mother, depending on which census is to be credited, was either twenty-seven, twenty or nineteen. Only once the newly widowed Mary Foster altered her date of birth to 1850 would she have been fifteen on the day of her wedding. Might the school catalogue be wrong? The same page lists five other marriages of pupils from Florence's year. There are no records for two of them, but the dates given for the three others are corroborated by a newspaper report in one case and in the other two by the US census.

Frank Thornton was the son of a distinguished American naval officer. Rear Admiral Thornton Alexander Jenkins was born in Orange County, Virginia, in 1811 and, sponsored by the wife of President Madison, by the age of sixteen had joined the navy, in which he remained for forty-five years. He fought pirates in Cuba, helped suppress a slave rebellion in Virginia, served in the coastal survey and the lighthouse service, and patrolled the seas in the war with Mexico. His moment arrived in the Civil War. He came under considerable pressure from an elderly relative who was congressman for Virginia to side with his native slave-owning state. Instead, he performed secret work for President Lincoln before, despite being wounded, taking a significant commanding role in the defeat of the Confederate navy in the Gulf of Mexico. Admiral Farragut, under whom he served, praised his zeal and fidelity. He was promoted to rear admiral in 1870 and retired three years later.

Like Florence's father, such a man of substance measured out his position in memberships, and they reveal the pattern of his interests. Rear Admiral Jenkins was a member of the Naval Lyceum, the historical societies of America, Virginia and Sioux City, Iowa, societies in Washington devoted to philosophy, biology and anthropology, and Boston's Economic Society. A photograph taken in later life shows a much-decorated figure in uniform, wearing a white beard and with a stern look to his deeply shaded eyes. In his later years he was content to read omnivorously and correspond with distant cousins in Wales.

The rear admiral had been through more than one marital campaign too. Jenkins's first wife died soon after bearing him a second child in 1840. Her family was wealthy enough for Jenkins, inheriting his wife's portion upon his father-in-law's death in the same year, to buy a significant property in Maryland. (His association with her relatives turned vexatious. In 1858 he was opposed by them in a Baltimore court.)

In 1848 he married well again. Elizabeth Gwynn was the daughter of Gilbert R. Thornton, who during the Civil War would act as the Massachusetts paymaster-general responsible for remunerating soldiers in the state. Florence's future husband was the second issue of the marriage, born four years later. Frank and his younger brother Presley were outflanked by sisters. There were three above them and three more below.

As he grew up Frank saw little of his father, who was at sea and, by the time Frank was nine, at war. Just after the Civil War his mother died in her mid-forties, when Frank was thirteen. He was the oldest young male in an overwhelmingly feminine household. Naturally he had no other destiny but the US Navy. In 1869 at the age of seventeen he was appointed by President Grant himself as a cadet to the Naval Academy in Annapolis, Maryland. Three months later he passed his examination and entered the Academy proper as a midshipman. But then another nine months on he went absent without leave and was dropped from the rolls of the Academy. The story of his ejection travelled from Maryland to Washington to Philadelphia where it made the front page of the *Evening Telegraph*. His failure could not have been made more humiliatingly public. Even the US census seemed to disapprove: when the enumerator visited the home of the rear admiral that August, Francis became one of the teeming sorority himself: he was listed as female.

He went back to school. As a safer option he chose to study medicine at the University of Pennsylvania but he was a slow student and it took him a whole decade to qualify. He graduated in 1880, when the census found him restored to his correct gender and able finally to describe himself as a physician. He was living in a boarding house along with a dentist and a carpenter (although, curiously, when the census was completed for his father's house in Washington a week later he was also listed there, alongside four sisters and three female servants). Not that he managed to find any sort of employment in the medical profession. Instead he clambered onto a low rung of the Lighthouse Engineers of Philadelphia, a job he almost certainly secured via paternal influence.

While Frank's younger brother Presley attended the United States Military Academy at West Point, the sisters busied themselves in marrying into the military. Virginia's husband was the eminent military engineer Colonel (later General) Peter Hains, who was much lauded for designing the Tidal Basin, which helped control the flow of the Potomac into the heart of Washington, DC. He had just taken on this appointment in 1882. An interview in the *National Republican* talked admiringly of his spare build, broad shoulders, clean-cut features and clear blue eyes. In the same year Frank's youngest sister Nettie married a hero. Lieutenant George Converse, the son of an Ohio congressman, had lost an eye in a skirmish with the Apaches in Arizona (a 'splendid fight', said the *National Republican*). In the same encounter one of the groomsmen had suffered a severe wound to the arm. The guests at the private wedding, an Episcopalian ceremony conducted by a cousin of the bride, were officers of the infantry, cavalry and navy. When he went up for early retirement two years later, Converse was described as 'a gallant young officer who lost his eye, and almost his life, from an Apache bullet'. At this grand society wedding, Frank must have felt like the only young male neither togged up in a glamorous uniform nor gloriously wounded in the service of his country.

A year later, as he audited his first thirty years, he found little cause for pride. Thrown out of the navy, unwanted in the medical profession and bundled into a clerical job, his chances of basking in the triumph of a great public wedding to a society bride were minuscule. A vulnerable, grief-stricken fourteen-year-old girl was far less likely to discern in him the lineaments of failure. Perhaps her father's position and wealth increased Florence's attractiveness. It's possible that Florence hurled herself at Frank, and demanded that he rescue her. But the responsibility for what happened next lies with him. The logistics of arranging an elopement of such a young girl – by post, or by personal messenger, and at such a time – suggest that Frank was adept at conniving but incapable of imagining the consequences of such a drastic breach in the etiquette of courting.

There was no public announcement of the wedding. It was highly unusual for newspapers, eagle-eyed in their cataloguing of movements in society, to overlook the union of an admiral's son and the daughter of a prominent barrister. The marriage has an impetuous and furtive look. As Florence later told the story, her father promptly disinherited her. She certainly wasn't seen in Wilkes-Barre for a year.

She was more welcome at the rear admiral's grand household on 2115 Pennsylvania Avenue – 'America's main street'. Under its roof Florence found an abundance of new in-laws. Two of her new sisters-in-law were a whole generation older than her, but she had one new relative who was closer in age and, more importantly, in spirit. Alice, five years Frank's junior, had attended the Moravian Seminary, and she was musical. At that moment she was thriving as a composer. Three of her works – a waltz titled 'Contentment', a serenade for a tenor ('Parting') dedicated to a young naval ensign, and a lively galop named after a fast young thing called 'Carolyn' – all went to press in 1883. 'The character of the work,' purred the *National Republican*, 'speaks well for the musical culture of this city.' There were also three boys closer to her own age: the young Hains brothers John, Thornton and Peter, who were the sons of Colonel Hains and Frank's much older half-sister Virginia.

The newly-weds settled in Philadelpia. Florence's new metropolitan home had rather more to excite the fantasies of a cultured young woman than Wilkes-Barre. Philadelphia was conscious of its history. It was in Philadelphia that the Founding Fathers met to sign the Declaration of Independence by which thirteen American colonies seceded from the British Empire. The text was ratified by the Continental Congress in the city on 4 July 1776. Eleven years later the US Constitution was drafted in Philadelphia. Its deep revolutionary roots were visible in the largest concentration of eighteenth-century architecture to survive anywhere in America. Among them were the country's oldest hospital and oldest theatre and, in the Academy of Music, the US's long-surviving opera house. Then there was Independence Hall, host to the great events of the country's foundation, where the cracked Liberty Bell resided on the ground floor, with the inscription from Leviticus incised into its flank: 'Proclaim Liberty Throughout All the Land Unto All the Inhabitants thereof.'

Philadelphia's wealth, founded on coal, shipbuilding and trade in sugar and molasses from the West Indies, had long been rooted in the confluence of two rivers, and further riches travelled in on the railroad tracks. After the Civil War the city boasted of its status as the 'workshop of the world', home to thousands of looms and lathes, forges and steam engines in mills and plants which operated in almost all of the three hundred industrial activities charted by the US census.

And yet in due course Florence was lured home. A year on from her runaway wedding she returned to South Franklin Street, less to mark her sixteenth birthday than to be present at the last illness of her grandmother, who was eighty-seven. Frank joined her and made himself as useful as an employee of the Lighthouse Engineers could by assisting in the care of Foster's mother. She died that same month and after the funeral Foster took his family on a healing trip to the sea. When they returned Frank came to stay again for the weekend, and again a month later for the day. Death, initially the cause of a rift with her parents, now brought Florence back into the fold.

She was restored to her father's affection during, for him, a period of intense importance. Having failed to win election as a Republican candidate for the state legislature two years previously, he was standing again in the autumn. As the election approached, throughout October the *Wilkes-Barre Record* encouraged its readers to give him their vote. 'There is scarcely any doubt about the election of Mr Foster,' affirmed one short item. 'He will make a creditable Representative.' 'Charles D. Foster should receive every intelligent man's vote irrespective of party affiliations. He will.' 'He will not fail.' He didn't, although the district very nearly had to find another candidate when he was involved in a terrifying accident driving a pair of inexperienced horses in the countryside outside Wilkes-Barre. Florence and her mother were on board too. The scene was described in detail by another of the passengers, who happened to be the editor of the *Wilkes-Barre Record*.

One of the animals gave a mischievous kick and got his
hind leg over the pole, at once rendering him uncontrollable. A mad plunge was made for a bridge which spans
the creek . . . and the carriage narrowly escaped going
over the side. By this time the weight of the horse had
snapped the pole off and the carriage went against the
heels of the animals and started them off again. In order
to prevent a collision with some teams just ahead Mr
Foster endeavored to run his horses against a stone wall,
but in doing so the carriage careened and scattered the
occupants along the road, the wreck finally going over on
its side, with Mr Foster out of sight, and the animals
plunging furiously. The spectators expected to find Mr
Foster killed, but he was found under the wreck still
hanging to the ribbons and only slightly bruised. His wife
was found to have sustained a compound fracture of the
left forearm, their daughter, Mrs Dr Jenkins and Dr Johnson, escaping with insignificant bruises.

Foster was duly elected to serve a two-year term. His legis-
lative duties taking him to Philadelphia, he will have seen
his daughter and son-in-law often. In 1895 Frank earned a
promotion at work which was hailed as good news in Wilkes-
Barre. 'His friends will be pleased to learn,' it was reported,
'that Dr Frank T. Jenkins, son-in-law of our townsman, Hon.
C. D. Foster, has been promoted in the office of the Lighthouse Engineers of Philadelphia.' It attributed his success
not only to his abilities 'but to the fact that his habits have
always been strictly temperate, and in consequence could
endure more fatigue than those who held positions above
him'.

Frank's avoidance of drink earned the approval of his
father-in-law, who was several times invited to address the

Temperance Union. Posterity has nonetheless planted a question mark over Frank's moral rectitude. The story that is integral to the myth of Florence Foster Jenkins is that her husband infected her with syphilis. The venereal disease was relatively easy to contract in the latter part of the nineteenth century in America. Indeed, they married just as syphilis was becoming the cause of a public health disaster. The spread began around 1880 and would continue unabated for decades. By 1900 and for the following two decades, it is estimated that between 15 and 20 per cent of the general population was infected. Even towards the end of that period the disease was still more or less unmentionable. The *New York Times Index* didn't allude to it by name until 1917. In the 1880s, when there was no cure, the taboo was all the deeper. Syphilis thrived on public ignorance and spread fast in a climate of secrecy.

The problem was exacerbated by the fact that not every carrier knew they were infected. Its primary stage could bring genital sores, while in 50 per cent of cases the secondary stage involved lesions, a rash, or other symptoms which might last for months. But primary-stage symptoms did not always manifest themselves. In the early twentieth century syphilis came to be known as the great simulator because of its ability to mimic the symptoms of other ailments: headaches, aches in bones and joints, fever, rashes. And when physicians could see the signs, early on there was a prevailing tendency not to inform those infected. 'Even when you are positive that a person has syphilis,' advised the Baltimore physician Daniel W. Cathell, 'it is not always best to say so.' The conspiracy of silence spread into the general populace, for whom the disease brought with it the stigma of shame. Men, being the predominant carriers of syphilis, sought advice from doctors about whether to tell the women they were about to marry.

The physician, wrote Claude Quetel in his *History of Syphilis*, 'cannot escape the role of mediator, or arbiter, which is forced on him when a former syphilitic comes to his surgery and asks: "Doctor, is it safe for me to marry?" . . . [A] conflict arises, in which the interests of the patient and the public interest are opposed, for beyond this client stands a young girl, unborn children, a family, and society, and your prohibition will protect them all. What importance the doctor's mission assumes when he becomes the arbiter of so many common interests in this way!'

Being a qualified physician himself, albeit one who couldn't find work in medicine, Dr Frank Jenkins will have already known the answer. Because of the disease's congenital properties, sexual abstinence was insisted upon for anyone planning to have children, for between six months and five years. An article published in the *Boston Medical and Surgical Journal* in 1889 reported one doctor's estimate that 'a man with untreated syphilis who married and took no special precautions to protect his wife had a ninety-two percent chance of infecting his wife in the first year, a seventy-one percent chance in the second year, a twenty percent chance in the third year, and a negligible possibility every year thereafter'.

It seems unlikely that Frank would have kept himself pure for his future bride. It also seems unlikely that he would have had sexual relations with a woman of his own social standing. He would have gone to a brothel, and might even have done so after his marriage. A report published at the height of the epidemic found that men who contracted syphilis during marriage, as opposed to before, were more likely to infect their wives. In 1916, after a means of identifying the disease in carriers was developed, the Baltimore Vice Commission found syphilis in 64 per cent of the city's more than 250 prostitutes, and over 90 per cent were infected with gonorrhoea.

Nearly half had both, and less than 4 per cent had neither. There is no reason to suppose that Philadelphia, only a hundred miles to the north-east, was any different. Indeed, a paper referring to syphilis as the third great plague was published in the Quaker City in 1920.

There are three questions relating to Florence's syphilis. Did she actually suffer from it? And if she did, was she infected by her husband? Or was it a figment of her imagination which posterity has allowed to take root as an essential element in the melodrama of her life? The medical evidence is circumstantial. There may have been other reasons for her childlessness, but fear of passing the disease on to another generation is a possible factor. Then there is the physical impact of the treatment. Its incurability did not prevent snake-oil salesmen from marketing magic remedies. 'Primary, Secondary or Tertiary Syphilis permanently cured in thirty to ninety days,' ran one advertisement for a company based in Nebraska. 'We eliminate all poison from the system, so that there can never be a return of the disease in any form. Parties can be treated at home.' This was rampant profiteering. Until 1908, when a drug was developed which won its discoverer the Nobel Prize, the only treatment for syphilis was mercury, which had been around since Paracelsus recommended it to his patients in the mid-sixteenth century. A popular saying warned of 'a night with Venus, and a lifetime with Mercury'. Unlike the wing-heeled god from which the metallic element took its name, treatment by mercury was slow. Many more sufferers were killed by the mercury than the actual ailment it was supposed to cure. Side effects were many, various and gruesome. They included profuse sweating, corrosion of the membranes of the mouth, gum ulcerations, loosening and eventual loss of the teeth, kidney failure. Florence is not known to have complained of any of the above. But another of the side effects is hair loss. The many photographs of Florence in her pomp seem to display a woman with resplendent hair or, more often, a succession of voluminous hats. In fact she wore a wig, even as quite a young woman. Underneath, her hair thinned until she was completely bald.

Another side effect of mercury poisoning goes even further into the heart of Florence's story: prolonged exposure to mercury can cause tinnitus. Florence would prove to be a capable musician. While pianists rely on the instrument to be in tune, singers are at the mercy of their own hearing. St Clair Bayfield's theory was that in her own head she sounded in tune. The vast discrepancy between what Florence's audiences heard and what she believed they heard may perhaps be explained by the malign influence of mercury-induced tinnitus untuning the music in her ears. One of the indications of the disease's tertiary stage was 'the sensation of being serenaded by angels'.

The balance of probability is that Florence did suffer from a disease that could not be mentioned in polite society. That she received it from her husband is unprovable. But many years after her death, Kathleen Bayfield wrote that 'Florence's doctor husband had given her a dose of syphilis'. Kathleen had no incentive to present Florence as a victim so she must have considered it an incontrovertible fact.

The marriage certainly foundered, and quickly. Florence later described these years to St Clair Bayfield as a time of profound unhappiness, to the extent that it put her off marriage altogether. Frank may have soon repented of his clandestine seduction of a girl with whom he can have had little in common. But the evidence also suggests that the shining example of Rear Admiral Jenkins simply equipped his sons and grandsons for marital and/or moral failure, some of it far more dramatic than anything perpetrated by Frank.

Frank's brother Presley would bring dishonour on the family soon after he was appointed as a San Francisco forecast official in the Weather Bureau. Six months into the post he was suspended for 'neglect of duty and indiscretions in his private life', all to do with gambling debts and unpaid creditors who ratted on him to his employers in Washington. But his record was nothing compared to that of Frank's nephew Thornton Jenkins Hains. As a young man Hains, stationed at Fort Monroe in Virginia, had an altercation when out sailing with a lifelong friend and shot him through the heart. Although it wasn't revealed in court, the argument was over a woman. Hains awaited his trial with equanimity, chatting with friends in the street through his cell window, befriending jail officials who took him out for walks and even playing cards with a juror during the trial. The jury was swayed by an appeal from Hains's defence attorney not to 'shed the blood of a young Virginian whose grandfather served his country with honor – whose uncle fell in the Confederate cause'. His acquittal was described as 'the most puzzling and peculiar case that has interested Americans for many years'. There was far worse to come.

As for Florence's marriage, a trajectory of deteriorating relations is suggested by her and Frank's movements, annotated as ever by the Wilkes-Barre press. The Fosters were seen 'visiting Mrs Dr Jenkins' in Philadelphia in May 1886. She repaid the visit in the summer: on 13 July the *Wilkes-Barre Record* reported that the Fosters were 'having a visit from their daughter'. Frank was evidently there too because two days later he returned to Philadelphia 'after a brief visit with Representative Foster'. In late September Foster accompanied his daughter to Philadelphia. She visited them again in October, and again at Christmas. She was in Wilkes-Barre three times in 1887, and took a holiday with her parents in

Quebec and went on a late-summer outing with them to Harveys Lake, where she and her sister had been taken as children by their father. Frank Jenkins, on the other hand, was never seen in Wilkes-Barre again. The marriage, therefore, seems to have broken down some time in 1886.

Florence's uncertain marital status in this period was reflected in the papers' bewildering array of permutations on her name: she was variously Mrs Dr Jenkins, Mrs Florence Jenkins, Mrs N. Florence Jenkins and, in a musical context, Madame Foster Jenkins. If they made their separation a legal fact, they did not do so immediately. In a *History of Luzerne County* published in 1893, the entry on Charles Dorrance Foster alludes – with a misspelling of Frank's middle name – to 'one surviving child a daughter, Narcissa Florence, wife of Dr. Frank Hornto Jenkins, of Philadelphia, whose father, Hornto A. Jenkins is a rear admiral in the United States Navy'.

The question of whether Dr and Mrs Jenkins ever divorced was still of legal relevance more than sixty years later. St Clair Bayfield submitted a petition in 1945 which alluded to a divorce obtained on 24 March 1902, and to a decree which he believed had been found in a safe deposit box. That is the year given for the Jenkinses' divorce by the *Dictionary of American Biography*. But no such document has ever surfaced, and at the time it was in St Clair's interest to show that the Jenkins marriage had been legally terminated.

The divorce rate in the era of the Jenkins marriage was extremely low, even if marginally on the rise and a cause for alarm among religious and social conservatives who feared for the moral welfare of the nation. In 1885 the National Divorce Reform League was formed with the goal of counteracting 'individualism', seen as a tendency among wronged and battered women to place their own happiness above the wider interests of social cohesion built on the family. The opposing strain of thought was an integral element of the campaign for women's rights, as embodied by the pioneering activist Elizabeth Cady Stanton. 'I think divorce at the will of the parties,' she argued, 'is not only a right, but that it is a sin against nature, the family, and the state for man or woman to live together in the marriage relation in continual antagonism, indifference, and disgust.'

The other disincentive for both parties was that divorce could be enacted only in a courtroom, which enabled newspapers to feed a ravenous public appetite for salacious stories of marital discord and breakdown. The law furthermore called for some sort of 'causative reasoning': one party had to take the blame. In the majority of states, cause was usually desertion or infidelity, later supplemented by various forms of cruelty. Some physicians argued for syphilis to be legally accepted as grounds for divorce (partly proposed as a disincentive for infected spouses-to-be from entering into matrimony). By the early 1890s, after the antics of his brother and his nephew, Frank may have felt – or been encouraged to feel by his family – that the Jenkins name had been sullied in the public domain quite enough already.

Frank became gradually invisible. There was a rare sighting in January 1893 when he represented his father, who was too ill to travel, at the funeral of an admiral in Newport, Rhode Island. Then on 2 August Rear Admiral Thornton Alexander Jenkins suffered a heart attack and died. 'Sea Warrior Dead,' ran the headline in San Francisco's *Morning Call* (which a month later would report on his son Presley's suspension). The *Evening Star* in Washington praised his bravery, courtesy and generosity: 'his loss will be deeply felt by a large circle of friends and relatives, many of whom have been the recipients of his bounty and his influence.' He was buried in Arlington National Cemetery, founded during the

Civil War as a final resting place for Americans who gave their lives in military conflict. The funeral 'was conducted without military display and with unusual privacy for the obsequies of one so prominent as the deceased officer'. The *New York Times* obituary noted that among his surviving children was 'Dr. F. T. Jenkins of this city'. Frank had moved to New York. In this period he seems to have been of no fixed abode. As the male head of the family, he gave away his sister Carrie in December 1895, when he was described by the *Evening Times* in Washington DC as 'Dr Frank Thornton Jenkins, of Connecticut'. In 1898 he was living in Buffalo but that year moved to Niagara Falls where he opened a practice for the treatment of maladies relating to ears, nose and throat.

Charles D. Foster hadn't heard about a divorce. That year Florence's father drew up a will, which referred to Florence's 'present husband', simply for the purpose of specifically excluding him. 'The bequests to my said daughter shall not be subject to anticipation or any execution or attachment on any account whatever and the same shall be free from the control of her present or any future husband.' Although she had no means of knowing, it wasn't Florence who was cut out of the will; it was Frank. Florence's legacy from her relationship with the failed physician was a distrust of doctors, a wariness of marriage, and a surname which she would use for the rest of her life.

3: PHILADELPHIAN

Long after Florence Foster Jenkins's death, Cosme McMoon, her Carnegie Hall accompanist, gave a radio interview. Invited to describe what he knew of her early life, McMoon was casting back nearly seventy years to events which once upon a time had been related to him by an unreliable narrator. So on several levels, his recollections are unsafe.

'Very early she demonstrated this desire to sing,' he explained, 'and her parents objected to the excruciating quality of her voice, and in her early teens she ran away from home and went to Philadelphia to try to make her way. There she suffered great hardships and privations until her father, hearing of it, came down to town and took her back home. She was restored to her social and wealthy position, but with the proviso that she wouldn't sing anymore.'

The story of a total musical interdict, and the low parental opinion of her singing, is another essential element of the Florence legend. Indeed, St Clair Bayfield's testimony is that Frank Jenkins was no more sympathetic to her musical leanings than her parents. Unromantically, the evidence resists a full endorsement of this version of events. In 1886, the year she turned eighteen, Florence enrolled as a student at the Philadelphia Academy of Music for a two-year course. As to who paid her fees, it seems far more likely that it was her father rather than her husband, and that the break with Frank is what enabled her to return to music.

As a student Florence thrived. In February 1888 the *Wilkes-Barre Record* reported on her progress in a column on 'former Wilkes-Barreans'. 'Mrs Dr Jenkins, maiden name Miss Florence Foster, daughter of Hon. C. D. Foster . . . will graduate in May at the head of the class. She is now second in a class of over 800, and will probably take the highest honors.' Mrs Jenkins, it added, 'is a brilliant musician and is so considered in classical circles. She is very popular in social circles about Spruce and Pine Streets above Twentieth. Her many friends here will be glad to hear of her success.'

Spruce Street was home to the Academy. Its German principal was Richard Zeckwer, who took charge in 1876, bought the premises and ran it for the next forty years. Its classrooms were full of upright pianos and plastered in riotous flock wallpaper. Zeckwer's pedagogic style was trenchantly outlined in a prospectus for 1905–6. It offered twenty lessons for each ten-week term. Private half-hour lessons for finishing students cost $20, and it cost $5 to practise on a conservatory piano for an hour a day. The teachers for the high levels were all men, mostly with pendulous moustaches, none more than Zeckwer. The system of teaching large classes was to give as many people as possible access to a musical education. 'The masses must be educated thus or not at all,' explained the prospectus. Hence those eight hundred students. (In fact the Academy had room for two thousand.) One lesson a week focused on études, the other on pieces. 'Each pupil has the benefit of the entire hour, as the time not occupied in playing they are required to give attention to the performance of the other members of the class; to notice their errors; to endeavor to avoid a repetition of them.' Pupils were encouraged to correct, explain, criticise and approve as they listened to their peers, with the result that 'shyness, that bane of young performers, is cured or abated'. Florence's prediction of second place was not an idle boast. 'Having such a large number of scholars,' the rules and regulations made clear, 'it is possible to classify very exactly.'

To graduate Florence needed to perform before a neutral board of examiners. The course laid stress on conquering difficulty. In 1905 students had to present three Chopin études, a concerto, 'a difficult Beethoven sonata', a prelude and fugue from Bach's *Well-Tempered Clavier* as well as four other pieces from a list of difficult compositions, pass a course in theory, attend a year of sight-singing classes plus ensemble or symphony classes, and finally perform a difficult piece at the graduates' concert.

Florence's success was such that, a year after graduating, in the summer of 1889 she performed at one of Philadelphia's vast Sängerfests. The annual music festivals were a tradition brought over from Germany in the late seventeenth century by settlers who founded Germantown in Philadelphia. The first civic concerts, involving huge numbers of singers and instrumentalists, took place in 1835. A year later, women were allowed to participate in what evolved into public entertainments on an epic scale, always on a German theme. Appropriately, Florence chose German composers, and as a public performer was accorded for the first time the grand title of Madame Florence Foster Jenkins.

She warmed up for her appearance with a Fourth of July soirée in Wilkes-Barre where ninety guests listened to five soloists singing and performing on the piano. Florence undoubtedly practised what she would be unleashing on the Sängerfest in a few days. On 9 July in the cavernous auditorium of the Armory she walked alone onto a stage decorated with a few pot plants, and sat down at a Hardman grand piano to perform Schumann's Novelette No. 7. It was a ringing, forthright piece ideal for overcoming the intimidating conditions and a loud hubbub at the back. A twelve-strong male choir appearing just before her had struggled to make themselves audible and so did Florence. 'Most of the audience could not hear the finer effects at all,' recorded the *Wilkes-Barre Record*, 'although the artiste had a strong touch. Just as everyone was ready to listen the delightful music ceased.'

Florence had her chance again in the cooler evening concert when the audience had swollen to 2,500. She was on straight after one Madame Praetorius, a soprano from Buffalo who charmed both audience and reviewer ('she is said to be as lovely in private life as she appears to be when before the public gaze'). This time Florence's home-town reporter forgot to call her Madame, though he remembered to remind readers who her father was. In the first reported instance of Mrs Florence Foster Jenkins singing in public, she kept in mind that precept ingested at the Academy to aim high: she selected an excerpt from *Die Walküre*. Her Wagner was not a success. 'Mrs Jenkins could not entirely conceal a slight embarrassment at appearing before so large and critical a gathering,' it was said, 'but her performance was unmarred by a single break.' Afterwards she was showered with bouquets. Although intimidated by the occasion, Florence could be optimistic for the future. Her studies had made her 'an artist of great promise and she well deserved the plaudits and flowers accorded her'. (She was followed by a tenor from New York who elicited loud cheers of 'Bravo!' and many encores.) When years later she remembered performing nervelessly in front of ten thousand as a child, it seems likely she was alluding to her Sängerfest appearance in front of an audience a quarter that size when she was twenty-one. She went straight home to recover in Wilkes-Barre, where her father took his wife and daughter on a replenishing drive to Glen Summit, a local beauty spot.

The question arose, as for many a young woman, of what to do with a musical qualification if she was not to be a concert performer. The answer came in the less intimidating environment of the domestic musicale, a mainstay of American society in which, as the new decade dawned, Florence now found a niche. She gave an entertainment at her Philadelphia home in March 1890, then three months later another for guests of her parents back in South Franklin Street. She played Bach and Rubinstein (the paper didn't specify which of the two Rubinstein brothers, Anton or Nikolai) and delighted the audience 'with some excellent piano playing'. The presence of an accompanist suggests that Florence also sang. Florence ('the accomplished pianist') visited Wilkes-Barre again the next month. In 1891 her parents gave another musicale 'in honor of their daughter'. She played a Maskowsi minuet 'with fine delicacy and finish' to warm appreciation. This time she did not sing, but a married couple and a Miss Nellie Williams did. It was a long evening for early January; Mrs Foster served up refreshments at midnight.

But between these opportunities to perform Florence had to make a living. According to McMoon she put up with 'great hardships and privations' while St Clair Bayfield said she endured 'the life of *La Bohème*'. It seems possible that in later life Florence exaggerated the indigence of her twenties. But she did have a marketable skill to call on, and for much of the 1890s worked as a piano teacher in Philadelphia. This was an increasingly common pursuit for American women. In the first four decades of Florence's life there was a sharp rise in the proportion of women to men employed in music. By 1910 the figure stood at 66 per cent. The year before, the American journal *The Etude* published an article entitled 'Who's Who Among Famous Women Pianists and Violinists'. Most of them, far from famous, toiled in the shadows.

Announcements and advertisements from the same title allude to composers, concert pianists, movie pianists and accompanists, but also lecturers, teachers of all levels, tuners and women working in music shops. There was little shortage of potential customers. In America in the 1890s there were thought to be more pianos than bathtubs. In the following decade the sale of sheet music soared.

While Florence was a regular visitor back home throughout the early 1890s, she started to explore her independence by taking holidays elsewhere, doubtless in the company of other Philadelphians. She spent Easter in 1890 by the sea in Atlantic City, where she was one of hundreds of 'prominent sojourners', spotted by the *Times* of Philadelphia, who flocked to its many hotels to enjoy 'a tidal wave of festivity'. Excitements included euchre card parties, impromptu quadrilles and waltzes and, for one nature-seeking group of New Yorkers, wild-flower picking on the mainland. Florence was one of several Philadelphians staying at the 'home-like' (as in budget) Irvington. For the Fourth of July 1891, in the same month as Frank's nephew Thornton Jenkins Hains went on trial for murder, she was one of several 'interesting visitors' checking in at the Florida, 'a delightful little hotel' where there was an artistic chef and singing guests were encouraged. There was another holiday next month at Jamestown, Rhode Island, a honeypot for Philadelphians elbowed out of the neighbouring Newport by millionaires from New York. She was back there two years later in the same summer as her father-in-law's death and her brother-in-law's disgrace in San Francisco. In 1895 she stayed at the newly built Laurel-in-the-Pines in Lakewood, New Jersey, a resort set back from the ocean which was sufficiently fashionable in the 1890s for the *New York Times* to begin publishing a weekly dispatch in the summer season.

She also travelled in greater style with her parents. In October 1895 Florence accompanied them on a southern tour which took in the Atlanta Exposition in Georgia. The previous month the Exposition played host to a famous speech by African-American leader Booker T. Washington. The organisers were worried about giving him a platform but calculated that his appearance would throw favourable light on the South's racial progress.

Back in Pennsylvania, Charles Dorrance Foster pondered another tilt at political office, this time for Congress. Asked by a Democratic journalist if he would stand, he gnomically quoted from *David Copperfield*: 'Barkis is willin'.' The *Wilkes-Barre Evening News* described him as 'a formidable antagonist'. His oratory in this campaign was less inspiring than Booker T. Washington's. As the election loomed, he made a speech to an audience of five hundred at a Republican rally but was entirely upstaged by a fiery young speaker, aged only twenty-one, who attacked the Democrats on free trade and was 'cheered to the echo'. Foster failed to attract enough votes to be nominated for Congress.

Meanwhile Florence was becoming embedded in the musical life of Philadelphia. In January 1896 she and a Mrs Arthur Cleveland hosted an afternoon meeting of the Germantown Music Club. There were half a dozen participants, four men and two women. It's not clear that she sang, but this was the first time a newspaper reported her programming a musical gathering outside her or her parents' home. And while she taught, Florence was still learning. At some point she attended the Madame Kutz School in Philadelphia, perhaps to learn French – St Clair Bayfield would later say that one of her great strengths was an ability to sing in foreign languages. In 1896 she enrolled at the Heyl Dramatic School for a year's training. When she graduated in May 1897 her parents came to Philadelphia to attend. Florence was described as 'a talented elocutionist' by the *Philadelphia Inquirer*, which noted with approval her appearance in a shortened version of Richard Brinsley Sheridan's *The School for Scandal*. The performance took place in the drawing room of the New Century Club, one of the first women's clubs in the US, founded in the wake of the 1876 Centennial Exposition to support and promote science, literature and art. Florence did her bit for the cause in the character of Lady Teazle, a spendthrift young bride whose older husband fears being 'ruined by [her] extravagance'. The paper praised Mrs Jenkins's 'brilliant success' in greater detail three days later: 'her acting was easy, graceful and telling, while she read the lines with rare appreciation of their true meaning'. Did this cheekily imply that the actress understood what it meant to run through a husband's fortune? The paper certainly knew all about her family background: in the report Foster's career as a Wilkes-Barre attorney and active Republican in Luzerne County politics was detailed. It concluded with a further encomium for Foster's daughter: 'Besides her elocutionary gifts,' it said, 'she is a highly accomplished singer.' Back in her home town the *Evening News* picked up the story of her 'quite remarkable' talent, adding that her 'musical ability has been generally noted by her Wilkes-Barre friends'. She left the Heyl School in possession of something called the Murdock Prize.

As she entered her thirties there was a change in Florence's fortunes. Although she seems not to have known about it, her father made her the major beneficiary of a new will drawn up in 1898. He bequeathed her not only half of his considerable fortune but also his diamond stud and piano. This was hardly the act of a man who wished to thwart his daughter's music-making. In September 1899 she embarked on her most ambitious holiday yet, a summer trip to far-flung

Halifax in Nova Scotia; she returned via the Adirondacks in upstate New York, where she went camping. Her mother took Florence under her wing too. In April 1900, just after a trip home to Wilkes-Barre, she accompanied Mrs Foster to a meeting of the Daughters of the American Revolution in Atlantic City. The organisation, which that year celebrated its tenth anniversary, was set up in 1890 by a group of women after they were refused entry to the Sons of the American Revolution. Its aim was to raise funds for historic and patriotic preservation projects. Mary Hoagland Foster was a committed representative of the New Jersey chapter of the D.A.R. Florence and her mother were eligible to attend because they could trace their American lineage back to 1776.

Florence outstripped herself in August 1900 when she finally sailed for Europe. Presumably her father paid to have Florence conveyed in splendour across the Atlantic aboard the SS *Deutschland*, a newly commissioned steamship from the Hamburg America Line which that year broke the much-coveted record for the fastest ever Atlantic crossing. The luxury was nonpareil: the high-windowed first-class dining saloon was all caryatids and colonnades, stucco and gilt.

'For those desiring to cross the Atlantic as quickly as possible and with the greatest degree of comfort and luxury,' trumpeted a 1905 brochure, 'there can be no better choice than the great flyer of the Express Service.' This boast was not entirely borne out by the experience of those who nicknamed the *Deutschland* the 'cocktail shaker' owing to its tendency to vibrate at high speeds (causing part of its stern to fall off in 1902). The 23,000-ton, 37,500-horsepower, 200-metre leviathan delivered its passengers to Plymouth (for those wishing to alight for London) just over five days after leaving America. There is no record of Florence's itinerary once she arrived in Europe. Her other disembarkation options were Cherbourg or

Hamburg. Given her later devotion to the world of Italian opera, and support for the Italian Red Cross, it seems certain her European sojourn included a trip over the Alps to the home of Verdi. But she was apparently sick as a dog on both crossings. The experience terrified her and she never went near another ship for the rest of her life.

There were other signs of Florence's improving social status. In 1899 she was one of many private subscribers underwriting a pair of recitals in Germantown, and soon after her return from Europe she became a sponsor of the Philadelphia Orchestra. The life of Bohème was behind her. But much the most telling indication of her upward trajectory was her choice of holiday in the summer of 1902. Having kept away from the millionaires' playground in Rhode Island a decade earlier and opted instead for the quieter Jamestown, Florence checked in to the Casino in Newport, the oceanside watering hole where American wealth and European aristocracy annually convened. It was 'a town of paradoxes, contradictions, and amazing vanities and extravagances,' explained Mrs John King van Rensselaer in *The Social Ladder* (1925), whose 'chief industry . . . is the examination and appraisal of qualifications for Society'. Throughout the summer season the *New York Times*'s 'News from Newport' column gaily genuflected at the altar of new money as it commingled with old blood. Indeed the whole of America was kept informed of the comings and goings of various Vanderbilts and Astors, their arrivals and departures and even their routes to and fro – there were 1,600 daily newspapers in the US by 1900, consumed by twenty-four million readers. They were told who was throwing such and such a ball, giving lunch or dinner or a reception for whom, who was staying in which 'cottage', which was really no such thing. There being very few actual hotels in the town, the millionaires stayed instead in so-called 'cottages', which were vast edifices set in their own grounds. Up to the early 1900s these houses were simply transported in from elsewhere, and might be seen rolling along the street. Admiring descriptions of the bountiful table decor were meticulously vouchsafed. A slightly earlier version of the resort's golden era would later be memorialised by Edith Wharton in *The Age of Innocence,* published in 1920.

Into this world Florence boldly stepped on 22 August 1902. She was named in a list of people newly registered at the Casino, a rustic ivy-clad residence thrown up in 1880. Hotels were increasingly being built to cater for the fashionable women from up and down the East Coast who descended on Newport every summer but didn't have their own cottage. Greedy for social recognition, they greatly outnumbered the men. Florence arrived on the same day as two other married women. Also checking in were Viscount de Villeneuve Bargemon (spelled Bargemont in the *Times*), a couple of polo players, and Oliver Belmont, a vastly wealthy socialite known for a dissolute youth and a short-lived marriage, who was briefly serving as a Democrat in Congress. The day's round-up of news for eager readers took in a number of automobile speeding violations, a game of cricket proposed for Alfred G. Vanderbilt's nearby farm at Portsmouth, and a colonial ball to be hosted by Mrs Stuyvesant Fish in which members of the diplomatic corps would join in a minuet dressed in costumes of the Revolution. And the paper reported that 'the Dutchess [sic] of Marlborough appeared at the Casino to-day during the tennis match between the Englishmen and the Americans, and received a hearty reception from the large number of her friends who were there'.

The Duchess was a hugely symbolic figure in the westerly drift of power and influence across the Atlantic. She was the only daughter of railroad millionaire William K. Vanderbilt and had been more or less press-ganged by her formidably manipulative Alabaman mother into a loveless marriage with the ninth duke, Charles Spencer-Churchill, who until the month before Florence's visit had been Paymaster General in the government of Lord Salisbury. The duke, like many English aristocrats of the period, had married an American heiress on a strictly mercenary basis. His reward for making Consuelo a duchess was $2.5 million in railroad stock. Her charms had a greater impact on others, including the author of *Peter Pan*. 'I would wait all night in the rain,' J. M. Barrie once uttered, 'to see Consuelo Marlborough get into her carriage.' The duchess's mother had since divorced Vanderbilt and married his good friend, the aforesaid Oliver Belmont who was staying at the Casino. Later that week the Tsar's cousin Grand Duke Boris of Russia was in town.

At America's most exclusive resort, Florence found herself among this highfalutin nexus of US millionaires and European blue blood, all attended upon by elegant bounty hunters and fast-moving social climbers, of whom she was perhaps one: a free agent in a social milieu where marital collapse was more common and better tolerated than in the regular round. But it required persistence. 'It is an axiom of Newport that it takes at least four years to get in,' advised Mrs John King van Rensselaer. Alexander Graham Bell took many holidays there but he was ignored by Society. If Florence had ever been to Newport before for the season, the *Times*'s social correspondent hadn't noticed. Nor was she important enough for her departure to be reported.

Increasingly, too, she spent time with her parents outside Wilkes-Barre. In February 1903 she was in Washington, DC for a reception at the Elsmere honouring two of the founders of the Daughters of the American Revolution. One was Mary Smith Lockwood, a formidable septuagenarian in whose home the women first convened. She was a friend and associate of Elizabeth Cady Stanton, who championed a woman's right to divorce. The other D.A.R. founder was Mary Desha, who spent much of her life as a clerk in the civil service but came to government attention when, teaching in Alaska in the late 1880s, she sent a written protest about the living conditions of the natives back to Washington, sparking an investigation. Florence was moving in grand feminist circles. Of those women who helped decorate the drawing rooms of the Elsmere with palms and pink azaleas, some were described as wives or relatives of men. Florence was 'of Philadelphia'. In April she joined her parents at the Waldorf-Astoria in New York. The housand-room hotel, built in the German Renaissance style on the site of William Waldorf Astor's mansion on Fifth Avenue, was the largest hotel on the planet and had already given the world its own Waldorf salad as well as Eggs Benedict and Thousand Island dressing. Under its roof, afternoon tea became more than merely a symptom of Anglophile eccentricity. The hotel would become a landmark of great significance for Florence, even after it was demolished in 1929 to make way for the Empire State Building and re-opened on its current site two years later.

Florence renewed her campaign for acceptance in society's Olympian heights when she returned to Newport in the summer. The registrations at the Casino on 10 August 1903 included Marquis Torre Hermosa of Madrid and Count Conrad Hochberg of Dambran in Germany, who was a cousin of Kaiser Wilhelm II. Also in town was Count Kinsky, known by his fuller title as Ferdinand Bonaventura, 7th Prince Kinsky of Wchinitz and Tettau, who had only months to live. Florence just missed Mr and Mrs Alfred Vanderbilt, who had married in Newport two years earlier and would divorce in another five years, the woman named as Vanderbilt's mistress committing suicide, while he later went down with the *Lusi-tania*. The couple left town the day Florence arrived.

Newport in August was dedicated exclusively to pleasure. There was eating, dining and dancing, participating in or spectating at summer sports on land and sea. There were half a dozen beaches, albeit only one that counted socially. And there was music. If Florence entertained her fellow lotus-eaters in Newport at the piano, there is no record.

Later that autumn she accompanied her parents on a vacation to California. They travelled with a party from the East Coast courtesy of the Raymond & Whitcomb Company, an agency founded in 1879 by two enterprising Bostonians eager to capitalise on the opening up of the west created by the completion ten years earlier of the transcontinental railroad. New Englanders headed to California to escape the worst of the winter. The Fosters were among the first group of the season. The party comprised over fifty holiday-makers, nearly a quarter of them from Wilkes-Barre, all of them Americans apart from a doctor from Cologne in Germany. It's an indication of the lowly status of married women accompanying their husbands that unmarried women were mentioned by name while wives and children were not. The news item listed 'W. P. Billings, Miss Frinces [sic] Billings, Andrew Billings. G. H. Flanagan and wife. C. D. Foster and wife, Mrs Florence Jenkins . . .'

Riverside was a fashionable resort sixty miles inland from Los Angeles whose wealth was founded on citrus-fruit farming, the groves fanning out along the valley between low mountains. Orange trees were so central to Riverside's identity that when one of its two surviving navel orange trees from Bahía in Brazil, first planted in 1874, was moved to the famous Mission Inn hotel, the ceremonial task was undertaken by a top-hatted, shovel-wielding President Theodore

Roosevelt; this symbolic function being performed by the president in the year of Florence's visit.

The travelling party stayed at the New Glenwood. A photograph from 1903 shows a rustic colonnade flanking a white facade busy with wrought-iron balconies; sprigs of young palm sprouted from the terraced fourth floor and a ziggurat towered over the entrance. The party stayed for five days before moving on to Los Angeles.

During the trip Foster developed typhoid fever, a potentially fatal bacterial infection which had afflicted Florence's mother a year earlier. On such occasions he tended to draft a new will, which he did on returning east, though it barely differed from the 1898 version. Despite his illness, California whetted the Fosters' appetite for occasional long-distance travel and Florence had the chance to enjoy a great deal more of America and beyond. Straight after a summer holiday in Saratoga Springs in upstate New York, the family spent September 1905 in Oregon, where they visited Yellowstone Park and trespassed into British Columbia. Their most ambitious journey of all was to Mexico in early 1907, a round trip of ten thousand miles which took them as far as the border with Guatemala.

But Florence was contemplating a journey of a more permanent nature.

4: Chairman of Music

By her mid-thirties Florence had inherited some of her father's physical heft. Photographs of her as a youngish woman show a full face, a strong jaw and a big-boned frame. She had iridescent blue eyes and used a varying selection of wigs. Throughout her life those who knew Florence remarked on her beautiful speaking voice and her persuasive charm, which she was now about to unleash on the forbidding citadel of New York City high society.

There is no precise date for Florence's departure from Philadelphia. St Clair Bayfield thought it was in 1902, after the divorce he believed she'd obtained that year, but from 1903 to 1906 Florence continued to be reported as a resident of Philadelphia. The move seems to have happened over the summer of 1906. In the spring her home was described as 'the Quaker City'. But when she was staying in Washington in October, she was listed in the *Post* among other visitors from New York.

She joined one of the greatest tides of human history. In 1900 the city had 3.44 million inhabitants. Ten years later the figure had risen to 4.8 million. It was predicted in 1909 that Florence's new home town would outgrow London as the most populous city on earth within fifteen years. That year furnished the earliest known instance of the phrase 'big apple' in connection with the city. ('Kansas is apt to see in New York a greedy city,' wrote Edward S. Martin in *The Wayfarer in New*

York. 'It inclines to think that the big apple gets a dispropor-
tionate share of the national sap.') Most of the new arrivals
were European immigrants fleeing political upheaval and
economic hardship, and half of the city lived in poverty. But
by the turn of the century, when half the nation's wealth was
concentrated in the hands of 1 per cent of the population,
there were already four thousand millionaires in New York.

Florence swam in on the tide of fashion. New York was
Newport all the year round. She arrived just in time for the
publication of *The Metropolis*, Upton Sinclair's caustic satire
of the profligate, party-going, automobile-driving elite. 'One
heard of monkey dinners and pijama dinners at Newport,' he
wrote, 'of horseback dinners and vegetable dances in New
York.' It sold dismally: rich New Yorkers didn't wish to be
lectured, while the middle classes, avid for real scandal and
gossip, scoured the society pages rather than the bookshops
to feed their appetite. However great the inequality between
rich and poor, New York was where everyone was heading.
'I wouldn't dream of moving from New York to Philadelphia,
even,' drawled Maxine Elliott, the mistress of the banker J. P.
Morgan, 'unless it was in my private car.' Symbolically, 1908
was the year Philadelphia ceded to New York its claim to the
world's tallest building. The city hall, topped by a vast bronze
of the founder of the province of Pennsylvania, William Penn,
had been finished in 1894, surpassing Ulm Minster. Now the
Singer Building sailed past it towards the heavens.

As a New York neophyte, Florence had her mother's example to go on. As well as her activities in the capital and New
Jersey, where she frequently returned without her husband on
Daughters of the Revolution business, Mary Hoagland Foster
was a member of the Holland Dames, an organisation which
celebrated Dutch ancestry. They regularly convened in New
York and sometimes she dragged the Hon. C. D. Foster to

their annual luncheons at the Regis Hotel. She also made trips on her own to attend exhibitions and lectures.

Abandoning her home of nearly twenty-five years, Florence was attracted by two overlapping possibilities offered by New York. There was her desire, no different from everyone else's, to rise in society. But also in recent years she had been much less musically active in Philadelphia. Far greater opportunities awaited in New York, thanks to the phenomenal growth of societies formed by wealthy women with cultural tastes and time to indulge them.

One such club was the Euterpe. Several societies took their name from the Greek muse – there were Euterpes in Brooklyn and Poughkeepsie. As far back as 1870 a Euterpe Choral Society boasted a fifty-strong choir including, so it was claimed in the *New York Times*, 'some of the best talent in the country'. The Euterpe which Florence joined was a women's club devoted to social music-making. 'This society,' elucidated a volume called *Club Women of New York*, 'is mainly musical in its aims and work. The concerts and musical mornings which are given during the season at the Waldorf-Astoria are social events and are participated in by artists of high standing in the musical world. The club is also given luncheons by its members, and card parties, luncheons and outings are arranged at frequent intervals throughout the season.' A typical winter calendar would include musical mornings, a dinner dance and an evening concert. The outings might be to Long Island, or a trolley ride to Staten Island, where they'd have lunch and play bridge. As with other women's clubs, money was raised for deserving causes. 'This busy little musical and social club,' as the *Times* called it, differed from the city's many other clubs because it continued to meet through the summer for garden parties and al fresco gatherings. Although its activities were reported in the *Times*'s 'In the

Social Whirl' column, not all Euterpe members were quite elevated enough to whirl away to the summer fleshpots.

Florence's name was first linked to it in late 1906 when she attended a Thanksgiving luncheon for fifty at a tearoom called At the Sign of the Green Teapot. The menus were printed on little green teapots and like everyone she took home a souvenir of a bonbonnière mounted on a small pumpkin. The following week she joined several hundred guests at the club's annual afternoon reception, held at the home of its president in West 45th Street. Mrs Alcinous B. Jamison was known before marriage as Mary Ernestine Schmid. The daughter of a prosperous merchant, she owed some of her prominence to the career of her husband, a society proctologist and early proponent of colonic cleansing – a brochure of Dr Jamison's rejoiced in the title *Fourteen Reasons 'Why the Internal Bath'*. He also invented a prototype enema appliance and was a keen occultist. Mrs Jamison presided over a club that knew how to have fun. One bridge and euchre party which Florence, an inveterate dresser-up, enjoyed attending was on a Japanese theme. The committee wore Japanese costume, while unmarried younger members, dubbed Geisha Girls, distributed Japanese favours among the players. Prizes included kimonos and Japanese embroidered scarves. The first concert which Florence attended was the following week: an 'Annual Olde Folkes Concert of Sacrede and Worldly Musick will be helde at ye Waldorf', reported the *Times*, getting into the spirit.

Florence emerged from her chrysalis, aged forty, at a propitious moment in the empowerment of the New York female. An early symbol of emancipation was the establishment in 1903 – by Florence Jaffray Harriman – of the Colony Club, the first such place in New York created by women and for women. Not everyone in society was ready for this development. 'Denounced from the pulpits of the city and deplored by many eminent citizens in the newspapers,' writes Emily Katherine Bibby in *Making the American Aristocracy*, 'the outrageous enterprise persisted in flourishing, and ladies of the highest social standing happily identified themselves with its defiance of sanctified conventions.'

The advance of women was not always semaphored by a clenched fist. It happened too in the world of culture. In 1908, straight after her divorce, Maxine Elliott opened a theatre off Broadway which bore her name; she became the first woman to manage a theatre in America. On the streets of New York, women took up various enfranchising crazes for riding bicycles, wearing hobble-skirts, and in the New York afternoon even blameless middle-aged wives and spinsters made their way to the ever-expanding selection of grand hotels (including, from 1910, the Waldorf-Astoria) to take part in *thés dansants*.

The era of new possibilities for women would be marked by the death in 1908 of Mrs Astor, the monolith of old Manhattan. Her passing removed a formidable guardian from the doors of the establishment and offered fresh possibility for women determined to elbow a position for themselves that was not exclusively derived from fathers or husbands.

While in general it was men who made the money, it was women who made the rules in this new American aristocracy. They were the gatekeepers in whose power was the gift of access to the gilded inner sanctum, often blackballing those who aspired to entry for the merest sartorial solecism. They allowed some in and kept others out, and were committed to internecine scrapping. They were ruthlessly twitted in the waspish comedies of Clyde Fitch, who made up to $250,000 per play portraying fashionable heroines with a remorseless eye for social position and a gift for accumulating wealth. The titles told audiences what they were getting: *The Climbers*

(1901), *Her Own Way* (1903). *The Truth*, the hit of the 1907 season, told of a suspicious society matriarch who puts a tail on her husband while reserving for herself the right to lie as much as she sees fit.

Who was in or out could be learned from perusing the newspapers, in which there were daily reports during the season of invitations being sent out to receptions. The movements of wealthy women were the stuff of daily gossip, much of it taking place within the official framework of the women's clubs. The *New York Daily Tribune*'s 'Notes of the Club' column and the *New York Times*'s 'Activities in Clubland', in both of which Florence made increasingly regular appearances, reported the movements of these higher-ups, slaking the curiosity of the aspiring middle classes. 'Small luncheons, teas, and card parties by the dozen have been the popular entertainment this week,' chirruped one column. 'Not in months has there been such a number of cosy affairs given in people's homes rather than in hotel parlors.'

While not everyone was vouchsafed entry, Florence had a set of advantages on which she could draw. For a start, divorce – or its near equivalent, marital failure – at this social altitude was no longer a guarantee of banishment for an ex-wife. Not that Florence was necessarily divorced; she still deployed the distinguished name of Jenkins like the prow of an icebreaker. But her most important calling card was music. Her musical training earned her a status that floated free from distinction conferred by a man. In January 1907 she was on the bill of an entertainment put on by the Society of the Daughters of Indiana. There were solos for voice and for cello, an address on art student life in Paris, and 'a piano solo by Mrs Florence Foster Jenkins'. Such gatherings often took place in the morning. The venue was chosen from any one of the vast hotels that had sprouted all over midtown Manhattan, each of which had reception rooms for hire. In this case she performed in the Hotel Astor. (The Mexico trip came straight afterwards.)

In order to perform, Florence kept up her study of the piano. An extensive résumé of schools she attended, published in *Town Topics* in 1918, included something she called the Virgil Conservatory in New York. In fact there were two rival Virgil schools, set up by a pair of divorcees after their acrimonious split. Neither of them had this name. Almon and Antha Virgil were eminences in piano education who met over their shared interest in methods of teaching the instrument in groups. She founded the Virgil Piano School in 1891 while a decade later he retaliated with the Virgil School of Music. Both pedagogues produced instruction manuals for pianists trading on the Virgil brand. According to Kathleen Bayfield, Florence studied with A. M. Virgil, which means Antha (whose second name was Minerva). But Florence wasn't concentrating only on the piano. With singing in mind, she also signed up for enunciation classes at the Henry Gaines Hawn Dramatic School. The school's founder wrote a handbook called *Diction for Singers (To Say Nothing of Composers)*.

And she was not confined to her new home town. In April 1907 Florence was merely an onlooker at a splendid gathering in Washington, DC of the annual continental congress of the D.A.R. The event was dominated by the gift to the tireless president of a silver chalice and a white flag with the stars and stripes at its centre. 'A great many of the Daughters,' it was reported, 'expressed themselves as not caring to see the flag made subservient to a flag of truce.' Florence was among a hundred other bellicose ladies who, after singing 'The Star-Spangled Banner', dressed in gowns, jewels and 'priceless old lace' and convened for dinner round a long flower-decked table in the banqueting hall of the New Willard Hotel. There were plentiful toasts, augmented whenever a rowdy group of international barristers called in from an adjoining room. The British ambassador looked on from the threshold and went no further. Most of the attendees were identified in the *Evening Star* by the Christian name of their husband. A small minority were referred to by their own name, Mrs Florence Foster Jenkins among them.

In December, when her parents visited New York for a banquet at the Waldorf-Astoria, she would have been able to tell them about organising her first ever musicale since moving to New York. It was at a private home in White Plains, a growing suburb just to the north of the city, the programme after luncheon including songs, monologues and piano solos performed to a selection of Euterpe members. By the start of 1908 Florence had a permanent address in New York City – she was living at the St Louis Hotel on 32nd Street. She also completed her journey from the periphery to the official heart of the Euterpe. The club's events were run by a series of officers – a lady in charge of luncheon, for example. There were also various chairmen – chairman of the day, of ways and means, of the reception committee, and of the entertainment committee. In late January Florence was chairman for the day – and chairman of music – at a musical morning at the Waldorf. She exercised a new-found gift for publicity, because for the first time ever the *Times* reported the contents of the Euterpe's musical programme.

The morning's entertainment offers an intriguing insight into Florence's taste, acumen and breadth of knowledge. She laid on an array of duets and solos for male and female voice. A song and an aria by Massenet were in French, but there was an English theme: 'My Mother Bids Me Bind My Hair' was a pleasant canzonetta composed by Haydn during his London sojourn; there were two of Elgar's *Album of Seven Songs* (published only two years earlier) and a recital of Kipling's 'Gunga

Din'. She also chose a song by a female composer, Mary Car-
michael's 'Quaff with Me the Purple Wine'. Significantly she
opened with Verdi – 'Fu la sorte dell'armi a' tuoi funesta', in
which Amneris tricks Aida into confessing her love for Rad-
amès. Members had the chance to perform or recite some of
their own work, and the whole club joined in for a couple of
part-songs. If Florence sang, it was as part of the group. The
guest soloist she booked was Paul Du Fault, a lyric tenor from
Quebec who was a regular performer at such events, suggesting that Florence had familiarised herself with New York's
available talent.

She had an instant impact on the quality of fare at the
Euterpe. In April 1908 she represented the club at a dinner
held by the Women's Democratic Club to mark Thomas Jef-
ferson's birthday. For a wheeze it was decided that each table
in the Hotel Majestic dining room, rather than be numbered,
would be named after a women's club. The clubs would each
nominate a member to be hostess. Florence was chosen to
represent the Euterpe among twenty-eight other clubs. The
diners were treated to no fewer than eleven guest speakers.
In May another musical evening was hailed as 'one of the best
that the club has presented this season'.

As she made her way in New York society, in the summer
of 1908 Florence was given grim cause to doubt the protective
properties of the surname she had chosen to retain. On 15
August the whole city erupted at news of a murder involving
the name of Jenkins. Frank's nephew Captain Peter Hains
shot dead a man he believed to have seduced his young wife,
abetted by his brother Thornton Jenkins Hains. The murder,
which was to become one of America's most sensational
crimes of passion in the first half of the twentieth century,
cast light on Florence's story in two ways. It provoked the only
recorded public utterance by her estranged husband Frank. It

also illustrated the contempt with which dysfunctional males of the Jenkins clan were prepared to treat women who married into the family.

The catalyst of the scandal was Thornton Jenkins Hains, who since his acquittal in 1891 had used his liberty to explore a gift for sensation. He became a successful author of pulp sea stories partly inspired by his grandfather's naval adventures. His tales – with titles like *Bahama Bill*, *The Black Barque* and *The Strife of the Sea* – invited comparisons with Conrad and Melville, even if these were mainly made by himself. Jack London, whose *The Call of the Wild* was published in 1903, was an admirer. Hains grew sufficiently notable to make it onto the front page of the *New York Times* when his yacht sank on the way to the Bahamas ('Author rescued at sea') in 1903. That year his wife, who had endured a brutal marriage, died in childbirth.

But making the life of his own wife a misery was not a big enough field of operation for Thornton J. Hains. He also chose to be an agent provocateur in the marriage of his weak-willed younger brother. Peter Hains had married Claudia Libbey in 1900 when she was sixteen – she threatened to elope if her mother did not consent. They had three children. In 1907 Thornton first suspected that she was conducting an affair with a close friend of his brother, society magazine publisher William Annis. He sent word to Peter, who was serving in the Philippines. Claudia's letters to her husband, which described the riotous time she was having back at home and gently scolded him for his negligence, did nothing to dissuade his imagination from running riot. Captain Hains hastened home to extract a confession from his wife that she had committed adultery. Claudia – described by the *San Francisco Call* as 'a woman of rare beauty' – later claimed she was bullied into signing a confession when under the influence of alcohol and drugs which had been forced upon her. It was even suggested that she signed at the point of a revolver brandished by either her husband, her forbidding father-in-law General Hains, or her vengeful brother-in-law, whose own sexual advances to her she said she had repulsed. She also pronounced her husband a violent pervert (as in homosexual).

Convinced of her guilt, the brothers plotted to eliminate Annis. Apparently without a care whether they were witnessed, Captain Hains confronted his wife's lover as he sailed his victorious sloop into harbour at a yacht club regatta in Queens. He discharged six rounds into Annis's body, in front of a large crowd including the victim's wife and children. His brother kept guard over the dying man with pistol in hand. When Mrs Annis attempted to rush to her husband her way was barred: 'You move and you'll get the same,' the killer's brother scowled.

The New York public was swiftly reminded that Thornton Jenkins Hains had been acquitted of killing a lifelong friend in 1891. The *Washington Herald*, while taking a stern position on adultery and deeming the world 'better off without such a man as Annis', recalled that T. J. Hains had been 'the beneficiary of as gross a miscarriage of justice as ever blotted the criminal annals of the century'. To the same paper his mother – Florence's sister-in-law – made a manipulative appeal for understanding. 'Ask the good people of New York to suspend judgment . . . until the truth is known,' she pleaded. Summoning genealogy to her defence, she added that she had drawn on the same reserves of fortitude 'which, I am told, was always displayed by my father, Admiral Thornton Jenkins, who was Admiral Farragut's chief of staff in the battle of Mobile Bay'. She concluded with a character reference for her son, who doted on his three-year-old daughter. 'This spirit of devotion, so characteristic of him, has prompted Thornton to stand by his brother. So you will see that my boy is not so much of a devil as it has been made to appear since the day of the tragedy.'

Just over a week later Frank Thornton Jenkins, last seen operating as an ear, nose and throat specialist resident in Niagara Falls but now described as 'a doctor of this city', made his own contribution to family honour. He issued a statement that in his view Captain Peter Hains had been driven mad by his wife's conduct, whereas his brother was 'a mental monstrosity' who since early adulthood had been 'wayward, intractable, perverse and stubborn, and he usually managed to set at naught all disciplinary measures aimed at for his good'. He added, for clarification, that the fatal argument in 1891 had been over a woman. This double character assassination was an attempt to exonerate the nephew who had made an unwise marriage to a foolish young woman. To Florence and to any-one who knew of her marriage to Frank, it may have sounded like a coded attack on her. She too was a teenage bride, who had not merely threatened to elope but actually gone through with it.

The unfolding saga must have caused Florence profound relief that she no longer had any direct involvement with such a dysfunctional family of morally degenerate misogynists. It can be easily imagined that the impending trials of her in-laws, who were very close to her in age, was a topic of discussion when she went home to Wilkes-Barre in mid-October to visit her father, who was recovering from a major operation after falling seriously ill (he didn't leave the house until a week into November). It will have been on her mind as Florence spent the autumn conjuring up further triumphs for the Euterpe Club. In November she arranged what the *Times* called 'an unusually attractive program' for another musical morning at the Waldorf. Florence's involvement must have again impressed the committee, because for the Jamisons' annual reception in December she was in charge.

The calendar arranged for Florence's destiny to run parallel with that of Thornton Jenkins Hains in a quite bizarre double coincidence. The Euterpe reception took place on the same day as the trial began. She organised a costume dance and programmed a reading of *Stories from the Orient* by Oliver Bainbridge, an author with a new book out who brought back tales of his recent travels in China. Florence went home for Christmas knowing she had scored her greatest social success yet in New York.

Meanwhile, for the next month, Thornton Hains did his best to measure up to Frank's description. The trial took place in Flushing, which would be connected to Manhattan later the following year with the completion of the Queensboro Bridge. After twenty-two hours of deliberation, the jury was persuaded to acquit him of conspiracy on the so-called 'unwritten law'. Otherwise known as *dementia Americana*, this offered a defendant the option of pleading temporary insanity, incurred when he believes his home and honour to be violated. The husband's brother claimed to have suffered it vicariously. Unprecedented uproar greeted the verdict in court, which was swiftly deplored by leading lawyers. The freed man's parents received the news in the Astor Hotel, where Florence had performed her piano solo two years earlier. In his euphoria Hains pledged to write his masterpiece, a long novel based on the unwritten law.

Having escaped the electric chair, he made an exhibition of himself in his brother's trial three months later, earning an admonition for his theatrical behaviour in the witness box and at one point being thrown out of court. *Dementia Americana* could not save Captain Hains. From the witness box his father the general tried to engineer a positive picture of a war hero who had protected him in the war with Spain in 1897 by throwing his body in the line of fire. To no avail. His son was found guilty of manslaughter and dispatched to Sing Sing, the notorious New York jail. General Hains made strenuous efforts to persuade the jury to appeal to the state governor for a pardon. Two years later his son was released. Claudia Hains did not contest her divorce and lost custody of her three children. She never saw them again.

But that was to come. Soon after Florence returned from Wilkes-Barre at the start of 1909, twelve good men and true retired to ponder the fate of Thornton Jenkins Hains. The very day the jury considered its verdict would be remembered by Florence for the rest of her life.

5: Mrs St Clair Bayfield

On the morning of 14 January 1909 Florence Foster Jenkins was at the Waldorf-Astoria Hotel for a Euterpe Club musicale. From the stage she spotted a face in the audience. Decades later she still had a clear recollection of the moment, down to her own choice of outfit for the occasion. 'I was wearing my violet velvet gown, I saw your smile in the audience from my flowers upon the stage and said to myself, "Why, there is a man with the loveliest smile which I have ever seen in my life." Little did I imagine at that moment, that that smile would bring something into my life for thirty years to come.'

The owner of the smile was tall (six foot three), thin, rangy and English, with strawberry-blond curls and blue eyes set in a long, bony face. His name was St Clair Bayfield. He had a forthright nose but much his most prominent feature – an irony, given the identity of the woman whose life he was about to share – was a sizeable pair of ears. At thirty-three, he was seven years her junior.

Every 14 January for the next thirty-five years, St Clair would send Florence flowers to mark the anniversary of their meeting. There was an immediate connection. St Clair was a professional actor, currently appearing at the Knickerbocker Theater off Broadway in a production of a new operetta called *The Prima Donna* (Florence no doubt hastened to catch it). He was a man of culture with a rich orotund voice, an English accent that was starting to fade, charm, intelligence, education and old-world manners. Also, running through Bayfield's blood was a commodity Florence had been brought up to value: a noble pedigree, even if it did come from the wrong side of the bed.

St Clair Bayfield's great-grandfather was Attorney General then Lord Chief Justice, who took the title of Baron Ellenborough of Ellenborough after a Cumbrian village associated with his forebears. In 1842 his son Edward Law rose even higher. A powerful orator and distinguished administrator, friend of and cabinet minister under the Duke of Wellington, he was appointed governor-general of India and charged with restoring the peace. The task proved beyond him and he was recalled after two years, to be made the first Earl of Ellenborough, a Knight Grand Cross of the Order of the Bath and First Lord of the Admiralty. While these peaks were successively conquered, St Clair's grandfather had an eventful romantic career. His first wife died young of tuberculosis in 1819. His much younger second wife – the intensely beautiful Jane Digby – bore an heir, though Lord Ellenborough was not the father; her cousin was. The boy died before his second birthday and the Baroness embarked on further affairs. One was with the Austrian diplomat Prince Felix of Schwarzenberg; their trysts at his address in Harley Street caught the attention of political cartoonists and in 1830 caused her husband to seek a divorce by Act of Parliament. As witnesses gave evidence to the House of Commons, *The Times* devoted five columns to his public humiliation. The Earl had had enough of matrimony. In 1846, not long back from India, he sired three daughters via his mistress. St Clair Bayfield's mother Ida was the eldest. She was born in Belgravia, and married there too to George Bayfield Roberts, an Oxford-educated curate from Cheltenham.

St Clair's ancestry on his father's side included a bizarre overlap with Florence's English forebears. Like Florence, St Clair had an ancestor who followed William the Conqueror to England, and another who had personal dealings with Richard the Lionheart. There was also a line back to the Saint-Clairs of the Isles, the kings of Orkney; hence his colourful Christian name. More prosaically, his great-grandfather was an eminent metallurgist whose discoveries contributed to advances in the iron industry.

The Reverend George Bayfield Roberts inherited a talent for music-making from his father. Richard D'Oyly Carte, the impresario who built the Savoy Theatre to stage the works of Gilbert and Sullivan, once heard him conduct *HMS Pinafore* in Cheltenham. Roberts would fondly boast that D'Oyly Carte was so impressed he refused him permission to conduct the operettas again for fear of shaming his own touring productions. A committed high churchman, Roberts became an active member of the English Church Union, the body which supported the cause of Anglo-Catholic priests, and wrote its history. In 1902 he was one of the figures interviewed in a book called *Distinguished Churchmen and Phases of Church Work*. St Clair later bragged about his father within earshot of journalists, which is why the Rev. Roberts was once described in a New Zealand newspaper as 'an English divine well-famed for his ritualistic controversies'.

A flavour of Roberts's charismatic kindliness lingers in a wedding gift he and his wife made to a young couple he married in his church in 1900. Two silver vases were accompanied by a sonnet.

> *When, in the glory of a summer day,*
> *A blushing rosebud or a drooping spray*
> *Of honeysuckle charms thy sense;*

Forget not us who live where sewage smells
And immemorially polluted wells
Their aromatic charms dispense.

In 1875 he was working as a curate in Lower Brixham, the Devon fishing village, when John St Clair was born on 2 August, the third of four children. The family moved to Folkestone, where Roberts was required to bury almost all of the 252 German sailors who drowned after their battleship was accidentally rammed by a sister vessel off the English coast. He conducted the services in German, earning the gratitude of Kaiser Wilhelm I. In 1879 they returned to Gloucestershire when he was appointed vicar of Elmstone Hardwicke, just outside Cheltenham. He would preach from its pulpit for more than forty years.

For all the family's aristocratic lineage, not much of the Earl of Ellenborough's fortune of almost £60,000 had trickled down to his eldest daughter when he died in 1871. Unlike their father, there was no question of university for the Roberts children. The oldest boy, Aleth, went to sea with the merchant service at twelve, returned depressed a decade later and did nothing for a year but convert to Catholicism and marry. The young St Clair decided to seek advancement and adventure at the furthest-flung outpost of the empire. In New Zealand he tried his hand at anything going: he worked as a sailor, a dairy farmer, a journalist, a horse trader, got jobs in a gold mine, on a cattle-boat and with the New Zealand government's Survey Department. He also may have volunteered as an infantryman. By 1898, the year he turned twenty-three, he had parlayed his way into a touring variety company led by one Master Chevalier. The *Auckland Star* described Mr St Clair Roberts from England as a 'vocalist of no mean ability, possessing a fine baritone voice of good quality'. He shared the bill with Miss Olive May Stokes, a thirteen-year-old prodigy from Auckland who had been singing, declaiming and playing the piano from the age of ten and had just come from a tour fronting her own comedy drama company.

Rather than stick with his family name, he took the Christian name, Bayfield, by which his father was known, to fashion a more theatrical handle, and embarked on a wonderfully eventful apprenticeship. At some point St Clair seems to have decided that the life of an itinerant performer could be better pursued in Australia, where there were more opportunities. In late 1900 he made his dramatic debut at Her Majesty's Theatre in Sydney. The play was *Henry V*, the role Sir Thomas Grey, who has all of twelve lines. St Clair entered the theatre just as his employer was leaving it: George Rignold had been giving his King Hal off and on for a quarter of a century. He was such a great Shakespearean that Edith Wharton later picked him out as an exemplary artist in *The Age of Innocence*, set in 1870s New York. This was his final tilt at the role before getting on the boat back to England.

St Clair moved on to a roving Irish troupe which called itself the Royal Dramatic Company without necessarily enjoying any sort of endorsement from Her Majesty. For the avoidance of doubt about their style of entertainment, their calling card was a farce helpfully titled *The Irishman*, which the company toured round New South Wales as part of a trio of rambunctious comedies. The management placed an advertisement boasting of bounteous abilities in the company: they had 'carefully selected the best Dramatic Talent that could be procured at great expense . . . The names of the following Lady and Gentlemen Artists will be sufficient guarantee of their good faith.' St Clair's name didn't mean anything at that point, though even in minor roles he was noticed by critics: he was 'undoubtedly good', 'excellent indeed', and performed 'creditably'. In a play called *Vengeance Is Mine* one reviewer said that Mr St Clair Bayfield 'as villain no. 2 . . . performed with power'. That same summer he got his byline into an anthology of writings, illustrations and stories. *Henslowe's Annual* was lauded by the *Sydney Morning Herald* as 'Australian in every respect' even though other contributors included a Harrovian curate and the son of an earl, alongside the grandson of a former governor of India.

At the end of 1900 he joined the Hawtrey Comedy Company. This came about as a result of a family favour. William Hawtrey (as well as his more famous brother Charles) had been a friend of the Reverend Roberts for twenty years. He was now touring Australia, having secured the rights to a big London hit called *A Mission from Mars*, as well as a farce called *Tom, Dick, and Harry* and a sex comedy called *The Lady of Ostend,* plus a couple of one-act curtain raisers. St Clair was given a go in all of them ('Mr St Clair Bayfield had not much to do as an inebriated law clerk, but he did that little well'). He was also assistant stage manager. For the next year Bayfield saw a lot of Australia, from Tasmania to Perth, and Australia saw a lot of him. A photograph of a lean young man in three-quarter profile with a frothing cravat appeared in the Melbourne *Punch*. The company sailed for New Zealand to tour from Auckland all the way down to Invercargill – the last stop before Antarctica, which Robert Falcon Scott and Ernest Shackleton were currently exploring on the Discovery Expedition. St Clair kept a diary for nine months recording his impressions of rehearsals, performances and theatres, and also of the weather and the grandeur of nature. In Wanganui the Hawtrey company took on a local team at cricket. Both XIs were listed by their surnames only, apart from St Clair Bayfield, which was taken by the sub-editor to be a double-barrelled name. At the end of the company's stay in the town

he wrote to the *Wanganui Chronicle* to thank the local physical culture school for use of their facilities, and for courses
in exercise from a kindly instructor. 'From what I have seen,'
he wrote, 'the pupils here have a splendid chance of gaining
striking developments.' St Clair was a scrupulously polite fit-
ness enthusiast – he would be a keen swimmer for the rest of
his life.

By now he was sufficiently worthy of note for newspapers
to report on his movements. In October 1902 the 'Greenroom
Gossip' column in *Punch* told its readers that he was to join
an American company fronted by Janet Waldorf. His departure for Manila was announced, after which he 'intends
proceeding to London via America'. St Clair took a while to
get to London, and indeed didn't join Waldorf for another six
months. In the interim he made his way to New York, where
he joined a large company performing the fifteenth-century
morality play *Everyman*. After the backwaters of Bendigo
and Ballarat, Kalgourlie and Palmerston North, the noise and
mayhem of New York was a violent shock to the system
which evidently appealed. The production, which had started
in England under the aegis of the Elizabethan Society of
London, ran for seventy-five performances in four different
theatres and gave him a solid introduction to the city that
would provide him with employment for the best part of half
a century.

St Clair was lucky in the relationships he formed with that
first American job. The director was Ben Greet, an actor-
manager who toured the classics in England and was now
breaking into America (he was the first producer to take a
professional British cast around US campuses). Greet's
American partner was the powerful producer Charles Frohman, who would shortly have a big hit in London with *Peter Pan*

(a frequent transatlantic traveller, in 1915 he was to be an unlucky passenger on the *Lusitania*).

Before that, St Clair did indeed join up with Janet Waldorf. She was a prodigiously energetic young protégée of her touring partner Mrs Ada Dow-Currier. They had been travelling the world for four years, leaving the US behind for Japan, India, China and Australia. The *Pacific Commercial Advertiser* in Hawaii found St Clair 'highly amusing' in a comedy called *Turned Up*. He also played the lubricious Earl of Lovelace in a play about Nell Gwynn and a general in a Napoleonic melodrama called *The Royal Divorce*. But most of the drama took place offstage as the company's figureheads fell out with each other. With distances so great and travel costs so high, the productions lost money in Honolulu, and Waldorf lost her temper. She told the *Hawaiian Star* that 'four years spent in the orient was time wasted', blaming Mrs Dow-Currier, who replied that Waldorf 'was a financial failure as a "star" attraction in the States'. Although there were reports that some of the actors had not been paid and so were stranded in Honolulu, St Clair slipped out of the country and was shocked to read a couple of months later that Janet Waldorf had died of pneumonia back home in Pittsburgh. Mrs Dow-Currier expressed 'the greatest sorrow at this final severing of so many pleasant associations' while clarifying that when the Janet Waldorf Company disbanded 'all members were paid in full and were provided with funds for their transportation'. A couple of weeks later news percolated through that Waldorf had not died after all and that 'the popular comedienne is enjoying good health in New York'. For St Clair it was not a propitious introduction to female management or star misbehaviour.

Back in New York his Englishness was a calling card, and he could count on alliances he'd made with more reliable

employers. Greet cast him in the eye-catching roles of Shy-
lock's faithless servant Launcelot Gobbo in *The Merchant of
Venice* and the lovelorn shepherd Corin in *As You Like It*. But
England called for real and in the summer of 1904 St Clair
sailed home to see his family for the first time in at least eight
years. There was plenty that he'd missed. His older brother
Aleth had been declared bankrupt after purchasing a church
furnishing business which failed to yield the anticipated
income. The 1901 census found him living outside Derby and
describing himself as a wagon carriage painter. Within a year
he'd died of pneumonia, leaving a pregnant widow and three
children under five.

St Clair stayed for two years and worked sporadically. In
The Era, the theatrical newspaper in which actors placed
news of their movements – before the days of agents – he had
a small weekly ad announcing whether he was either engaged
or disengaged. He was as often the former as the latter. Back
home in Cheltenham over Christmas 1905 he advertised his
availability in the *Gloucestershire Chronicle*. 'Amateur Theatricals. Mr St Clair Bayfield coaches, acts and recites. Late of
Court Theatre, London; Shaftesbury Theatre, London; and
Ben Greet Company. Terms on application.' He gave the
address of the Actors' Association in Covent Garden. The
most prestigious job he secured was at the Savoy Theatre in
a new play about the seventeenth-century courtesan and free-
thinker Ninon de l'Enclos. She was played by Leah Ashwell,
a formidable young actress just embarking on theatrical management. She was halfway through a drawn-out divorce from
her husband triggered by her affair with the American proto-
heart-throb Robert Taber (who promptly died of pleurisy).

St Clair found himself once again under the wing of a
female boss. And yet when she took the production to New
York, he didn't travel with it. Instead he put an announcement

in *The Era* that he had been engaged in a different production in New York. At the Madison Square Theater he resumed his association with his old employer William Hawtrey, who had brought his Australian production of *The Two Mr Wetherbys*, a hit London comedy for which he needed convincing English actors. The play's author was St John Hankin, a minor Edwardian playwright who drowned himself three years later (George Bernard Shaw called his suicide 'a public calamity').

In early 1907 St Clair was back touring with Greet's repertory company, sharing the stage with Sybil Thorndike and Sydney Greenstreet, then both in their twenties. Florence, who was firmly ensconced in New York by now, may well have seen him, whereafter he disappeared from New York yet again, this time to tour *Mrs Warren's Profession*. The advertising made much of its status as 'the most talked of play of the day!' During its first performance in New York in 1905 the theatre was raided by the police, who arrested the cast and crew under the law passed for the suppression of trade in, and circulation of, obscene literature. Shaw's play about the morality of prostitution was closed after one night and only returned two years later once the producers had taken their case to the courts and, for an added precaution, invited the city's clergymen to attend a performance (more than three hundred turned up). In the touring cast St Clair donned a dog collar and went about his father's business. The role took him to the far ends of the US: Omaha, North Dakota, Utah, Washington. 'It is a frank discussion of a serious social condition as it exists in Europe, not America,' sniffed a syndicated review. 'The sanctimonious [sic] of St Clair Bayfield,' it added, 'was well interpreted.'

By the time he met Florence in January 1909, St Clair had been an actor for a decade. He had travelled tens of thousands of miles across the English-speaking world, seen his name on the same bill as some of the giants of the age, and had considerable exposure to the new-fangled theatrical concept of the female employer. The job in *The Prima Donna* was much the most commercial production with which he had ever been associated, and he was hoping for a period of settled employment after his odyssey on the high seas. The auguries were good. Composer Victor Herbert and lyricist Henry Blossom had previously collaborated with the half-Viennese star soprano Fritzi Scheff to create a huge hit at the same theatre three years earlier. In *Mlle Modiste* Scheff played a hat-shop girl yearning to become an opera singer; the show ran for two hundred performances and was revived three times. Scheff stepped into the vacancy left by the waning career of Lillian Russell, the doyenne of New York operetta, whose voice had entered into a decline in her forties. She commanded an astronomical salary of $1,000 a week. She was also one half of a celebrity couple: having divorced her first husband, a baron in the German Army, two weeks into the run she married John Fox Jr, author of the year's big hit novel, *The Trail of the Lonesome Pine*.

When *The Prima Donna* opened on the last day of November 1908 the *New York Times* was full of good cheer. 'An exceptionally pleasurable entertainment,' it purred. 'New York is going to welcome *The Prima Donna* open-handed and keep her for its own for some time to come . . . It will run *Mlle Modiste* a strong race for lasting popularity.' However, Scheff's kittenish allure in long skirts, short skirts and hats aplenty was not enough to rescue a tired libretto about a star of the Paris Opera who is loved by two officers. Having played a French general in Honolulu, here St Clair played a French colonel.

The Prima Donna had only two weeks left on Broadway when St Clair went along to a gathering of the Euterpe Club and met for the first time its chairman of music. He met her again that evening after the performance at a party on Riverside Drive, presumably lured there by her invitation. St Clair was lonely, feeling the pinch and living at a down-at-heel boarding house on West 23rd Street, a few blocks from the theatre.

They were ideally suited. Her vignette of their first encounter encapsulated the dynamic between them. Florence fell for the owner of the admiring smile who validated her sense of herself as a natural stage presence. Her rash escapade with a husband twice her age had been a disaster. At the age of forty, as she established a new identity in a new city, she had no use for such a retrograde prop as a father figure. This younger, gentler Englishman promised uncritical devotion, a craving for her company, and was content to play second fiddle. The subordinate role suited him too. His theatrical experiences as a company member had made St Clair adaptable and accommodating, and knowledgeable in the specialist area of female impresarios. It would be misleading to say that Florence rescued him from penury. The arrangement which lasted for the next thirty-five years was built on a bedrock of affection. And Florence was not yet independently wealthy. It would prove a mutually satisfying union of tastes and temperaments.

It's not certain how quickly the connection deepened into a romance, but some point in 1909 Florence temporarily vacated the St Louis Hotel, St Clair abandoned his boarding house, and they moved to the American Hotel in Union Square. Presumably early on in their new life of domestic proximity, she had to tell him about her hair loss, and about contracting syphilis, the still-unmentionable disease for which there was no certain cure (and wouldn't be until the year before Florence's death). Even though her marriage had ended more than twenty years earlier, she was burdened by the knowledge that syphilis bacteria could lie dormant for decades. The following year an arsenic compound called Salvarsan became available which provided specific chemotherapy against syphilis. But as a powder which had to be dissolved in distilled water then injected, it was difficult to administer and fraught with the potential for unpleasant and even life-threatening side effects. A safer derivative was made available in 1912 and became the standard treatment up until the development of penicillin. As for whether they enjoyed sexual intimacy in the circumstances, posterity has closed the bedroom door.

St Clair was contracted to follow *The Prima Donna* on tour to Washington. Deciding against joining the production the following year, he was spared a farcical merry-go-round in which Scheff suffered from tonsillitis, fainted onstage in Detroit, took off in a huff after her understudy had such a brilliant success, and set fire to her dressing room in Pittsburgh.

Florence meanwhile threw herself back into the life of the Euterpe Club. In early February 1909 she took part in a series of tableaux and dances at the Plaza Hotel, contributing to musical readings of *Love's Regret*. Her precise role – vocal or instrumental – was not recorded. The *Wilkes-Barre Times*, proudly keeping an eye on her activities in its 'Folks You Know' column, described her as a chairman of music of 'the Enterfe Club', a misnomer that wasn't an atypical event from its careless compositors.

Florence could not devote all her time to club activities. In March she was at home for two weeks with her parents, her father being once more unwell. (The local paper got it wrong again when it spotted 'Mrs Jenkins and daughter Florence' paying a social visit.) While in her home town she missed a Euterpe concert which took place that week, another member chairing the musical programme. When her parents went off on a recuperative trip to Florida and Cuba in April, Florence did not join them. Possibly she didn't approve of one of their travelling companions, as would emerge later, or perhaps she was now too absorbed by her obligations in New York. One Sunday that month it was announced that Mrs Agostine Strickland and Miss Lillian George would be giving tea four days hence for Mrs Florence Foster Jenkins at the Don Carlos in Madison Avenue. 'They will receive from 4 until 7.' She had come a long way from the life of Bohème.

While Florence stayed in New York, St Clair had an important journey to make. In late May, not long after Peter Thornton Hains was sentenced, St Clair boarded a steamship for home. He docked in Glasgow on 1 June. Since his last visit there had been two more deaths – his father's sister and his grandmother, the mistress of the Earl of Ellenborough. He paid his respects in Cheltenham. But he also went to Arundel in West Sussex where he had an engagement to break off. The woman who had been waiting for him was quite as impressive a figure as Florence. Rosalind Travers, two years older than St Clair, was the daughter of a retired army major and an artist, with whom she still lived. She was a published poet and play-wright who, while expecting St Clair to return from America, became one of the first English people of either gender to write about their winter travels in Finland. She had come back only a few months earlier.

St Clair hurried home to New York a free man. On 16 August he and Florence entered into a common-law marriage. The private ceremony was almost as clandestine as Florence's first wedding in 1883. It took place in the Hotel Vanderbilt and was witnessed by four people whose identities have not been revealed; they were presumably not young as none was called as a witness in 1945 after Florence's death when St

Clair attempted to support his claim that they had been man and wife. Rings were exchanged: St Clair gave Florence a ring of his grandmother's – presumably his late mother's mother, and perhaps presented to him for this purpose on his recent trip home – while Florence gave him a gold ring with a blue lapis lazuli stone. She called it a ring of intertwining love and he planted it on the fourth finger of his left hand.

There was no legal document to support the marriage. 'My enemy in the whole thing,' he later said, 'was the fact that she had a very unhappy first marriage to Frank Thornton Jenkins. She said that if she ever married again it would be a common-law marriage. She was very superstitious about it.' It seems just as likely that her superstition was a smokescreen designed to cover up the fact that she was not in a position to marry St Clair Bayfield as she was still married to Frank Jenkins.

Soon after their common-law wedding, St Clair Bayfield – described in the *Times* as 'the young English character actor' – was cast in a loose comic adaptation, translated back into English from German, of Dickens's semi-autobiographical *Little Dorrit*. It was called *The Debtors*. St Clair played Mr Chivery, the turnkey at the Marshalsea debtors' prison. In real life he was to be the debtor.

As he went into rehearsals, the *Wilkes-Barre Record* reported good news: 'the friends of C. D. Foster will be pleased to learn that he is improving.' Notwithstanding this cheerful bulletin, the newly wedded Mrs Bayfield hastened home.

6: LEGATEE

'I was with my father that day all morning. Went to the dentist at noon and was with him again during the afternoon.' The woman known above all for the unique character of her voice is, at least in the documentary records, silent for the first forty years of her life. Then on 11 December 1909 Florence Foster Jenkins entered the witness stand in the Orphans' Court in Wilkes-Barre and spoke. Her first words located her selflessly at her father's side, a post she abandoned only to have her teeth checked. But how on earth did Florence fetch up in court just over two months after her father's death?

Charles Dorrance Foster died on Wednesday 29 September, aged seventy-two, having suffered from kidney disease for much of the year. An operation failed to halt his decline, as did the trip to Cuba and Florida, and a final sojourn in the clean air of the Pennsylvania hills. He returned home for the final three weeks of his life, where he was joined for the last two by his daughter. On 30 September an attorney in court suggested a minute be made of the passing of a distinguished member of the Luzerne Bar. The minute might not have been made if the court knew what was to happen next.

The funeral took place in St Stephen's church on 1 October, after which Foster's body was laid to rest in the family mausoleum he had built in the Hollenback cemetery on the outskirts of Wilkes-Barre. His remains joined those of his mother, younger daughter and half-sister. It was a fraught day for the family of the deceased. Mrs Foster was so upset she said she wasn't sure she could attend the funeral. Florence was to be found upstairs, desperately weeping because she believed her father had cut her out of his will. Foster's considerable personal property, real estate and life insurance promised to be a big fortune to miss out on. That night she stayed at the house of a friend of hers called Miss Black.

On 2 October a party of at least ten squeezed into the office next door to the Foster home for the opening of the safe in which the last will and testament had been locked. His widow was among them. So too was his attorney, John McGahren, who was also his partner and friend of many years. Florence was absent, but eight of Foster's Bulford relatives – the descendants of Foster's older half-brother – turned up in hopeful profusion. McGahren opened the outer door of the safe but the key to an inner door which he expected to be there had gone. Two locksmiths were called. Even after the inner door had been drilled open, the shelf on which the will had last been placed was found to be empty. The search continued the next day and again ended in failure.

McGahren's astonishment was soon shared by readers of the *Philadelphia Inquirer*, who were told that charities stood to lose $50,000 unless the will was found. The potential for a swift resolution loomed when McGahren revealed that he had kept a record of the details of Foster's last wishes. These he submitted to the Deputy Register of Wills of Luzerne County, Peter J. McCormick, in the form of an official memorandum. As presented by McGahren, there was a will drawn up by him in 1903, copied from a previous will made in 1898. It made provision for the payment of various debts and small honorary bequests including $1,000 to endow a memorial window in St Stephen's Episcopalian church for Florence's sister Lilly. There was also an annuity for Foster's older half-sister Olive. But it made over the bulk of the testator's fortune to his widow and daughter. Considerable influence was left in their hands. Foster's investments were to remain unchanged except in case of urgent necessity, 'and then only,' he stipulated, 'upon approval of my wife and daughter or the survivor in writing.' Florence and her mother also had to give permission for the sale of any of Foster's real estate or land, of which there was a considerable amount in and around Wilkes-Barre, and there were investments available to provide them with a 'suitable, becoming home' for life, either living together or apart in Wilkes-Barre or elsewhere. The will, being originally written when Florence was thirty, then copied when she was thirty-five, allowed for the possibility that she may yet have children. The only clause that acknowledged the Bulfords, although not by name, stipulated who would benefit if Foster's wife and daughter both died without issue. In that case three-quarters of his property and estate would 'become vested in my next of kin then living, share and share alike those of the half blood taking equally with those of the whole blood when of the same degree'. McGahren was bequeathed Foster's law library and office furniture.

But this was not the only document submitted by McGahren. His memorandum also included a codicil, created on 30 January 1909 by Foster himself, which he asked two members of the Westmoreland Club in South Franklin Street to sign as witnesses. It set aside small sums of money to 'persons having been very kind to me in sickness', including two nurses, and $1,000 to a Miss May Smith. It also introduced for the first time a bequest to William Bulford. Bulford was the eldest grandson of Foster's half-brother and had been farming the family land – quantified here as 321 acres – as a paying tenant. He was now bequeathed ownership of the land for the duration of his lifetime, subject to an annual payment

of $300 each to Foster's widow and his daughter. The farms
– there were two of them – would pass to Bulford's offspring
if he had any. If he died without issue, the farms would go to
the United Charities of Wilkes-Barre. The proviso was that he
– or the United Charities – must continue to pay the $300 a
year each to Florence and her mother for the remainder of
their lives.

These two documents were both missing from the safe. A
few days after Foster's death, the safe was searched again and
another document was found, although not on the shelf
where McGahren originally placed it. It was this single sheet
of paper, containing a second codicil, which would prove most
contentious.

On 16 September, McGahren told the court, Foster gave
him the keys to the box in his office in which the 1903 will
and the codicil of 30 January were kept, with instructions to
examine them and establish that the codicil he had personally
drawn up was legally acceptable. The following day Foster
asked McGahren to add a second codicil. It was executed on
21 September; the only other witness was Foster's male nurse.

In it Foster made substantial provision for three beneficiaries, diverting huge lump sums away from the inheritance
apportioned to his wife and daughter. He gave $5,000 to the
Wyoming Historical and Geological Society, $10,000 to St
Stephen's, and $20,000 to William Bulford in trust to dis-
tribute among the other heirs of Foster's mother by her first
marriage, to be paid five years from the date of Foster's
decease. The size of the sum reflected the abundance of
those heirs. Charles D. Foster's half-sister and half-brother
had both died more than a decade earlier, and the former had
no children, while another half-brother went west and lost
contact with his family. But John Jacob Bulford had three
children who survived into adulthood. Between them the

three proceeded to breed innumerably. It was a vast clan of potential beneficiaries.

This initial hearing exposed the distrust between the widow and the attorney. There had been an atmosphere of tension and suspicion in the household as Foster dwindled towards death. Mrs Foster frequently asked McGahren if she could see the will. As a precaution he took the key to the safe box away with him. Appointed as her attorney, John M. Garman argued in court that Mrs Foster and her daughter were 'the natural and legal heirs of the state', and that the memorandum of the will couldn't be trusted because McGahren was 'personally interested'. McGahren was aggressively questioned for two hours. The two Luzerne attorneys had been sparring in court for years but this new dynamic, in which one cross-examined the other, helped shorten the fuse of both. Garman's plan was to cast doubt over McGahren's memorandum and, in the absence of the stolen will, have the decedent declared intestate. McGahren explained the circumstances of the 1903 will, drawn up when Foster was ill following the family trip to California and copied from a will made in 1898. Garman pointed out the oddity of the provision made for Foster's half-sister, who had been interred in the family mausoleum five years earlier. The district attorney and the county detective duly paid a visit to the mausoleum and reported back to the court that she did indeed die in 1898.

By 9 October the *Wilkes-Barre Times* was referring to 'the now famous Foster will'. Picking up the story as far away as Virginia, the *Freelance* in Fredericksburg added that Foster was survived by his wife and a daughter, 'the wife of Dr. Frank Thornton Jenkins of Philadelphia'. It wildly over-estimated the size of the estate at around $1,500,000. The paper's interest was pricked because the Jenkins family were from Virginia, and one of its scions might be expected to inherit.

It wasn't until the second week of December that all parties were back in court for a hearing to determine whether the contents of the memorandum should stand. After William Bulford petitioned for the will and codicils to be probated, on 10 December Mrs Foster withdrew as a respondent in the will contest, declaring that whatever the outcome she would be of independent means.

On the same day Florence filed an answer to the court that her father was of unsound mind when the second codicil was signed. She also made the sensational claim that there was a conspiracy between McGahren, Bulford and others to procure Foster's signature when, she argued, he was by then too feeble-minded to be aware of the consequences of his actions.

The court proceeded to test the veracity of this claim. First to be questioned was the widow. Mrs Foster painted herself as innocent of all knowledge of an outstanding will, and unable to persuade McGahren to enlighten her of its contents or whereabouts in the days before her husband's death. 'Whenever he got sick he would make wills,' she said, 'but destroyed them when he got better.' When she asked her husband about a will he replied, 'I destroyed all wills, and I don't want to leave any will.' She claimed to have no access to the safe. While he was still alive she conceded that she did try to gain possession of the key from McGahren, but that he was uncooperative and even sent her on a false trail, only to reveal that he would not surrender it without her husband's permission.

After the friendly line of questioning from Garman came a hostile cross-examination from ex-judge Wheaton, representing the Bulfords. Casting around for a motive for stealing the will, Wheaton attempted to extract from her an admission that relations with her husband were 'not pleasant'. He'd heard that she refused to cover him with enough bedding when he was ailing. This she dismissed to 'some misunderstanding with the nurse'.

'Did you persist in reading the Bible to him when he was sick, after him asking you to stop?' asked Wheaton.

'No, sir,' she replied. 'He wanted me to read the Bible to him and took comfort out of it.'

'Did not he protest, and did not your daughter Florence try and get the Bible from you, and was it not torn in the squabble over it?' Mrs Foster's answer was evasive.

When it was Florence's turn to be questioned by Wheaton, she knew even less than her mother about the will or either codicil, had never seen such a document nor known it to be in her father's possession. She was perfectly ignorant of all arrangements to do with the office safe, and denied having taken or destroyed any such document, and she wasn't there when the safe was opened. Wheaton asked Florence if she argued with her mother, if her father had had to 'stand between her and her mother a great many times'. She denied it, though she allowed that her parents had been known to have 'spats' and that, yes, she had tried to prevent her mother reading the Bible to her father and had removed the book.

To counteract this unedifying vignette of the squabbling Fosters defacing a copy of the Bible, Garman now attempted to prove that Foster could not possibly have been of sound mind when he signed the second codicil, and that Bulford and McGahren had conspired to induce him to leave $20,000 to the Bulford clan. As Florence explained, she was there all day apart from her midday trip to the dentist, and testified that her father was drowsy and not roused even when McGahren strode in talking 'in a loud and boisterous manner'. It was 'as if he was addressing a jury', she recalled. She told the court her father had already proved that day that he was of insufficiently sound mind to sign a legal document. He 'wanted a hammock with his name on it,' she said; 'said he wanted it to fly in it'. Florence was asked if she had seen her father signing cheques on 21 September, the day on which he signed the second codicil. 'He tried to that morning,' she replied, 'but was not able.' When confronted with the fact that some cheques signed by him that day had indeed gone through the bank, she replied, 'I don't know about that.' (Her mother confirmed that when a woman visited from the drug-store seeking payment, she had raised him up in bed and held the pencil for him to sign. 'That was all he was able to do.' She added that he had spent the last few days of his life 'dazed, as if under the influence of powerful drugs'.)

Other witnesses were called who corroborated the story told by Florence and her mother. A man who wanted to trans-act some business found Foster's mind unclear. Another was not recognised by him. Miss Black, with whom Florence stayed after the funeral, visited on 17 September and found his mind 'clouded'. There was also disagreement about when the codicil was signed: McGahren claimed it was between ten and eleven in the morning, another witness at midday (when Florence was at the dentist).

In court one last tasty morsel relating to Florence was adduced when Miss May Smith, an extremely devout fifty-year-old spinster, was questioned. As a beneficiary of the first codicil to the tune of $1,000, she was grilled by Garman about the propriety of her relations with Foster on a recent visit to Atlantic City.

'Were you and Mr Foster very good friends?'

'Yes, sir, we were.'

'You went on trips with him?'

'Yes, but I paid my own bills, and Mrs Foster was with us.'

'Didn't you want to go to Atlantic City with Mr Foster and leave Mrs Foster behind?'

Miss Smith hotly denied the imputation.

'Didn't Mrs Jenkins catch you kissing Mr Foster?'

'It's a lie!'

'Mrs Jenkins would not go to Cuba with her parents because you were going along?'

'I don't know about that.'

'She would not sit at the same table with her parents at Atlantic City because you were at the table?'

'I don't know.'

'You are the Miss Smith mentioned in his alleged will for $1,000?'

'I may be.'

Florence seemed to be adept at making enemies in Wilkes-Barre. Garman asked another witness if McGahren 'did not say to Mrs Jenkins that before he was through with her he would make her "crawl on her knees" before him'. An objection was sustained.

Other details which pointed towards a conspiracy were the frequent visits of William Bulford to McGahren's office. McGahren, Bulford and his wife were among those called to the witness stand to testify that there was no conspiracy and that Foster was of sound mind when he signed the second codicil.

The entire case was reported with relish by the Wilkes-Barre newspapers, right up to the explosive final address from Attorney Garman summarising the case. He took the view that the alleged will's beneficiaries were 'malefactors, criminals, thieves, crows, cormorants, turkey buzzards, carrion, eaters, money grabbers, greedy for money, conspirators, knaves, fools, stupid and careless lawyers, crooks and vile schemers'. He talked for the best part of two hours. 'At times,' reported the *Wilkes-Barre Times Leader*, 'he was quite vindictive.'

It took six months for the Deputy Register of Wills McCormick to come to a judgment. A week before he pronounced a verdict, Pennsylvania newspapers were full of news of a major industrial accident which put the case in the shade. An explosion in a quarry in West Coplay killed eight men, only a few miles from the Moravian Seminary Florence had attended in Bethlehem. The foreman left ten children; the rest of the dead were foreigners.

There was a widespread expectation that, all the evidence having been tested, a decision would be made. 'There are perplexing questions of fact confronting us in this great controversy,' McCormick concluded on 10 June 1910, 'in which is involved, among other things, large bequests to charitable institutions and partial disinheriting by a father of his only child.' He could not disguise his bafflement at a situation in which the only living witness for the drafting of a missing will was also both interested as a legatee and its sole custodian. At the end of a long equivocation, McCormick admitted defeat: he could not determine whose claim had greater merit, the proponents who argued for the 1903 will and the two codicils, or the contestants who said Foster died intestate. He could do no more than ask others to decide for him: the case would have to go before a jury. The case of William Bulford v Florence Jenkins was fixed for October.

It was a dreadful mess, all of it the legacy of a prominent barrister. How did it happen? When his widow said that Charles D. Foster didn't want to leave a will, it seems likely that he was giving voice to an anxiety over split loyalties. He felt responsible for his mother's descendants by her first marriage, and perhaps carried a cargo of guilt having inherited his father's farm then rented it out to a relative. And yet he also had a wife and a daughter to provide for. The will, drawn up when he was ill after the jaunt to California, ensured they would always be comfortably off. The first codicil was added just over five years later when he had again been ill. Hence the small bequests to his carers. He no longer expected his now forty-year-old daughter to have children, and therefore he needed to arrange for the disposal of the land after her death. Hence the bequest to William Bulford. In a gesture that suggested he wasn't entirely depriving them of an interest in the farm, he added the proviso that Bulford pay his widow and daughter $300 each per annum.

The speculation centres on the second codicil. Was there a conspiracy? McGahren's contribution can be viewed in either of two ways. On the one hand he made an honest effort to ensure that, after the theft of the will, the wishes of the decedent were honoured. On the other, he and William Bulford drew up the second codicil between them and extracted a signature from a practically comatose man at death's door while his wife and daughter were both out, and got the nurse (who afterwards was nowhere to be found) to sign as a witness.

According to one witness, William Bulford learned from Foster in the spring that he would be given the farm, although Attorney Garman managed to establish that Foster never actually mentioned his will in the conversation. Mrs Foster told the court that Bulford was a frequent visitor to McGahren's office. If they did indeed conspire, Florence's arrival in their midst on 14 September will have underlined that Foster did not have long to live. The opportunity might have suggested itself when McGahren was asked by Foster to ratify the first codicil on 16 September. There he saw that William Bulford had indeed been left the farms but only for the duration of his lifetime. Perhaps McGahren then communicated the good news to Bulford, and they concluded that Foster was disposed to be generous, but might do more for his mother's descendants. Bulford could involve himself in the outcome of the will as an act of altruism. His only child having died at birth, he would be working on behalf of other Bulfords if he laid claim to some of Foster's money now, for distribution among the family, rather than wait for Florence to die without issue. To avert suspicion, and give Florence a theoretical chance to have a child, they would make the bequest available for distribution only after five years. So McGahren drew up a second codicil granting the Bulford clan $20,000, and in order to secure Foster's signature without interference, Bulford asked Mrs Foster to go out for the day with his wife. When Florence visited the dentist in the middle of the day, they pounced. The male nurse in attendance was persuaded to be a witness, perhaps with the help of some sort of inducement to sign and later disappear.

Alternatively, none of this happened. What seems clear is that there was wariness on both sides after Florence's arrival in their midst. She brought with her the airs and scents of another world that to the Bulfords and McGahren will have appeared a profound anathema. Bulford was a horse trader, and the family were farmers – in photographs the various members of the clan wear dowdy dresses and sober suits. Florence had married into a military dynasty from the federal capital, two of whose scions had just been tried for murder. After pursuing a cultural education in Philadelphia, she had penetrated the world of untold American wealth and only recently established herself as a new adornment on the social pages of New York. Finally, she was that ultimate alien, a woman who no longer lived with her husband. When Florence accused McGahren of conspiracy, it was either true, or a devious assault on his reputation from a practically scarlet woman. No wonder if he overreacted and even threatened to make her crawl on her knees.

As for the theft of the will, only three people had access to the safe: Foster, McGahren and his stenographer. As McGahren explained, he kept the keys to the safe in the office, where he placed the will in a locked box, then placed the key to that box in another box, locked an inner steel door, leaving the key in the lock, and then the outer doors using a combination that only he, his stenographer and Foster knew.

The question of how any of the potential culprits could have accessed the safe is beyond the realm of speculation. The fact is that somebody did. Either personally, or acting on behalf of someone else, they stole the will and the first codicil but left the second codicil. So who could it have been? If William Bulford knew the contents of the will and the codicils he had no motive to remove them. If he didn't (as he claimed in court) he might conceivably have seen an advantage in Foster dying intestate so that the Bulfords' claims could be evaluated in court. The other possibility is either Florence or her mother, or a party acting for them. Mrs Foster's attempts to gain access to the safe while her husband was still alive were thwarted by McGahren. Before the safe was opened William Bulford's wife heard her confidently predict that it would contain no will. This would be an odd thing to say if she herself had stolen the will. As for Florence, she seemed to fear that her father had cut her out of the will after her elopement and not reinstated her. In court she claimed to know nothing of any will. If she did know of the second codicil which diverted so much money to William Bulford, she certainly wouldn't have left it behind in the safe. If she didn't, it would explain why it was left behind.

In October there ensued some preliminary jostling over which court would hear the case, while Garman petitioned for the contents of McGahren's safe and desk to be opened. Florence returned to visit her mother but had gone back to New York City by the time the climactic twist in the melodrama was enacted.

On 22 October 1910, before the jury had an opportunity to be sworn in, McGahren received an envelope with a New York postmark on which the address was printed in large letters. Inside was the will and the first codicil. The names of the witnesses to the will had been cut off. There was nothing else in the envelope. A similar envelope containing an earlier version of the will was posted to the People's Bank of Wilkes-Barre. The case of Bulford v Jenkins was immediately withdrawn. The documents were admitted to probate on 26 October and the will was recorded. Florence and her mother were given no notice. Florence made a last intervention to forestall the enacting of her father's dying wishes and the bequest of so much of his fortune to the Bulfords, sending an attorney to request a conference before the will could be probated. He was told he had arrived too late. With the court case no longer needed, eight attorneys, four on each side, missed out on the fees that would have come their way. More than two years later some were still attempting to extract from the estate fees owed for the original hearing.

The motive for mutilating the stolen will, then returning it, seems as unfathomable as the original theft. Whoever returned it may have calculated that snipping off the names of the witnesses would invalidate the document. Or perhaps the prospect of a decision being placed in the hands of twelve good men and true seemed too precarious. A jury might decide that the second codicil was signed by Foster when not of sound mind. Or the opposite.

The value placed on the Foster estate was $237,000, of which $100,000 was real estate. The *Wilkes-Barre Times*, hungry for more drama, reported a possibility of further legal proceedings. The Fosters' attorney expressed surprise at the speed of events, and said that Mrs Foster would make a public explanation as 'a cloud has been cast over her'. No record has survived of a challenge to the will, nor of the widow's statement.

Even after the Bulfords collected their money, mother and daughter were very comfortably provided for. But Florence's experience in a Wilkes-Barre courtroom would mark her for life. She would never again put her trust in a member of her father's profession. Nor did she have much faith in dentists.

7: CLUB WOMAN

How good was the ear of Florence Foster Jenkins? History knows the answer to the question, and remembers her for that reason only. But there is countervailing evidence that she had extremely good musical antennae. She awaited the outcome of the case in 1910 in the welcoming bosom of the Euterpe Club. For a morning concert in January at the East Room of the Waldorf-Astoria, one of the performers Florence booked was Edna Showalter. When Showalter sang again two months later, it was in Carnegie Hall with the New York Philharmonic under the baton of Gustav Mahler.

The programme for the musicale, Florence's most ambitious yet, offers an insight into her eclectic taste. She mixed works from the European canon (Schumann, Debussy) with the more recherché (Caracciolo, Kaun) and new songs by living composers too. One was by Kurt Schindler, an assistant conductor at the Metropolitan Opera. A song called 'Roguish Cupid' was by German immigrant conductor Franz X. Arens, who had brought affordable music to the students and workers of New York by introducing seasons of People's Symphony concerts in 1900. Another was by popular young songwriter Harriet Ware, who three years later would triumphantly perform her own songs at Carnegie Hall.

The impressive young soloists booked to perform also included the pianist Harry M. Gilbert, then thirty, who would go on to play for Presidents Hoover, Roosevelt and Truman in the White House. But it was Miss Showalter who stole the show. Her aria from *La traviata* was sung 'with brilliancy of execution and ease', and she was praised for 'showering upon her audience high Cs and cadenzas'. Among the soloists for an evening programme in March were Vivian Holt, who would later make several pleasant recordings of folksy tunes as part of a female duet, and Carl Schlegel, a baritone who would perform nearly four hundred times with the Metropolitan Opera. These events were mentioned in the *Musical Courier*, a trade outlet begun in 1880 which would provide friendly coverage of Florence's projects almost to the very last. Coverage could be bought, with the result that Florence turned up in its pages never less than monthly and sometimes weekly during the season, out of all proportion to her musical relevance. Here it reported the enthusiastic applause of an audience consisting of 'handsomely gowned women'.

The world of handsome gowns was where Florence now spent her time. After her father's will was probated towards the end of the year, she went to an evening dance in which the main feature was a series of tableaux for a large cast of young people, including the children of the members – the president's daughter among them. Florence was one of a number of older women, described as matrons, who joined in. The tableau vivant would become an essential feature of a Euterpe extravaganza. Somewhere between amateur dramatics and staged painting, it took a famous scene from myth or history and allowed club members and their younger relatives to pose as gods and icons. The officers threw themselves towards the front. The most elaborate that evening was entitled 'The Rose Queen and Her Court at the Fete of Flowers'. It offered a starring role to Mrs Alcinous B. Jamison, the eminent proctologist's wife, as its central figure flanked by other lustrously adorned matriarchs of the Euterpe. All money raised by such extravaganzas was donated to the club's philanthropic fund for later distribution.

Florence didn't programme every one of the Euterpe's musical mornings, but when someone else was in charge the performers tended to be less eminent. Increasingly she had commitments which lured her elsewhere. She joined the Mozart Society of New York, newly formed in 1909 by Dr Adelaide Wallenstein with the object of the advancement and enjoyment of good music. It met for the standard diet of afternoon musicales and private evening concerts. In the Prussian-born conductor Arthur Claassen it had a figurehead of some pedigree. As a student composer in Weimar he was noticed and encouraged by Liszt. Lured to New York by Leopold Damrosch, another Liszt protégé, he set up in Brooklyn as the conductor of the Arion male chorus, which performed for Kaiser Wilhelm II in 1900 and with whom he made several recordings. He will have cost the Mozart ladies quite a bit to hire, as would the orchestra and professional soloists such as Carl Schlegel. A typical programme that Florence had to learn comprised several songs across a range of styles. In December 1910 they sang Grieg's stirring 'Land Sighting', a Victorian part-song by English composer Eaton Faning, and 'Love's Dream After the Ball', a dreamy waltz by Austro-Hungarian Alphons Czibulka. Florence remained a member of the club for another decade.

In May 1911 the Mozart Society of New York sent a formidable choir of 132 women to Washington, DC to perform for the wife of President Taft in the White House garden. Claassen had previously performed with other societies for the President and First Lady and had asked if they'd like to hear his Mozartian ladies. The entire choir stayed at the Arlington Hotel and enjoyed a day trip down the Potomac to George Washington's home at Mount Vernon. As they chugged downriver, perhaps Florence told her fellow choristers about the plans to stop the tidal floods designed by her brother-in-law, the military engineer General Hains.

A few days after the performance at the White House, no doubt inspired by her participation, a photograph of Florence was published in the *New York Times*. It was taken by the Campbell Studio, a leading firm of society portraitists which opened its New York branch on Fifth Avenue in 1900. Its first manager, William A. Morand, used his high-society connections to build a portfolio of influential clients. After his death in 1909 the studio branched out into theatrical photography, which explains Florence's wide-brimmed hat and the bouquet of flowers clutched dramatically to her bosom like a favoured lapdog. Unlike other portraits of her, her face is calm and free from affectation.

Aside from music, the Euterpe gathered for luncheons where the same names were always in attendance: Mrs T. W. G. Cook, Mrs William H. Corbin, Mrs Frank Parsons Lant, Mrs Eduardo Marzo, Mrs Thomas Byrne, Mrs Addison J. Rothermel, Mrs J. Alphonso Stearns, Miss Ida Judson, Mrs George Hattler. As ever Florence, being sundered from her husband, was the only one regularly identified by her own Christian name. Sometimes one or another of them was off to California for the winter or just back from a world tour. (The typesetters, crushed by the sheer weight of names listed in the social columns every week, often varied initials or spellings or marital status.) They subscribed for tables at card parties at the Waldorf-Astoria where 'handsome prizes' were promised, or 'silver prizes for each table'. Card parties were a respectable and enjoyable means of gathering women together without the business of arranging musical or theatrical performance. And they knew the rules to sundry card games: pivot bridge and euchre were the staples – in the accepted shorthand, such and such a host would be said to 'give a bridge' – but they were supplemented by audition, five hundred, pinochle. Some card clubs were open to all; others guarded their exclusivity. A pivot bridge club Florence joined which met twice a month over the winter at the Hotel Marseilles was 'strictly social, and in no way a public card club, members being admitted only when known to [its founder] Mrs Wood and two of the members or patronesses'. The bridge club also held a *thé dansant* twice a season, plus assembly dances on New Year's Eve and Lincoln's birthday.

Membership of one women's club by no means precluded joining others. Early in 1912 Florence arranged a musical and literary programme at the Hotel Astor for a club founded in 1907 called the New Yorkers. Music was much less central to a society whose function was to 'facilitate social intercourse, broaden intellectuality, encourage congeniality and harmony, and promote the general progress of New York women'. Membership was open to women born in the state or those who had been resident for five years. Florence could have joined no earlier than six months previously.

A compendious guide entitled *Club Women of New York* listed two hundred such clubs and patriotic societies, incorporating their manifestos plus the names and addresses of presidents and other officers. There were well-meaning clubs devoted to economics, education, women's suffrage, hygienic reform, relief of the needy. Some helped women maintain their ancestral or geographical identity: the Society of the Daughters of the Seventeenth Century or of 1812, the United Daughters of the Confederacy, of Ohio, Indiana and so on. Many were formed for cultural appreciation. The object of Gotham Club (est. 1907) was 'social enjoyment and the consideration of philanthropy, art, literature, hygiene, music, drama, dancing and patriotism'. At the Minerva Club

(1898) 'book discussions take place and papers on current topics are read for analysis and comment'. The Société des Beaux Arts (1908) was 'purely educational' in its study of fine arts, literature and science (membership limited to one hundred). The Club for the Study of Life as a Fine Art considered 'the dignity and worth of the body and soul and the relation of one to the other'. The goal of the International Sunshine Society (1896) was 'to incite its members to a performance of kind and helpful deeds and thus to bring the shine of happiness into the greatest possible number of hearts and homes'. It claimed more than three hundred thousand members. The mother of them all was Sorosis, formed in 1868 to 'render women helpful to one another; actively benevolent to the world; and to aid in promoting useful and agreeable relations between women of literary, artistic and scientific tastes'. The club's paragraph in *Club Women of New York* added that as with all pioneers their history was one of 'hardships encountered, prejudices conquered, and difficulties overcome'. The Waldorf-Astoria did very well out of all these clubs. The biggest hotel in the world had room for them all.

There was even a City Federation of Women's Clubs which had elected officers for everything from suffrage to anti-suffrage via household economics, the milk committee, probation, taxation and temperance. The activities of all these organisations were scrupulously detailed in the pages of the city's newspapers. They didn't always meet in hotels. 'Small luncheons, teas, and card parties by the dozen have been the popular entertainment this week,' reported the *Times*'s 'Activities in Clubland' column. 'Not in months has there been such a number of cozy affairs given in people's homes rather than in hotel parlors.'

Florence spent the decade accumulating memberships and positions. In the 1910–11 edition of *Club Women of New*

York she listed memberships of not only the Euterpe and the New Yorkers but also the New York branch of the Dickens Fellowship (est. London 1902) and the Pocahontas Members Association. She spent the decade expanding that portfolio to become vice-president and chairman of music of the National Round Table, historian of the National Opera Club ('educational work in music'), plus a member of the Rubinstein Club ('musicales and social meetings . . . membership limited to five hundred'), and the quasi-masonic Eastern Club. For the Twilight Club in 1912 she was on a committee in charge of organising a dinner where the topic under discussion would be 'The Task of the Dramatist'. Among the eight speakers booked were writers, critics, an actor, a rabbi and Hans von Kaltenborn, later destined for distinction as a broadcaster. They were all men. Brought up to vaunt her antecedents, Florence also had life membership of the New York Genealogical and Biographical Society. It wasn't all about culture: she joined the Knickerbocker Relief, founded in 1906, to help the needy, especially those in danger of eviction for non-payment of rent, offering clothing, money and access to medical care. They met twice a month at the home of its president to raise money through 'euchres, musicales, teas and other social functions'. Perhaps even more than other society women in New York, Florence was prodigiously busy. An exceptionally attentive reader of the society pages might sometimes find her name cropping up twice or even three times in relation to quite separate gatherings: an Italian *conversazione* with speakers and singers at the National Opera Club, say, alongside a regular event in the Euterpe calendar.

The rise of the women's club was a result of unprecedented historical circumstances. Growing wealth concentrated in the largest cosmopolis of a society which felt it was creating the world anew meant that a lot of wives had time on their hands, an increasing desire to be active outside the domestic environment, plus disposable income and a collective will for improving society and themselves. 'Women who are not obliged to work for a living should work in one way or another, either politically, artistically, or philanthropically,' argued an essayist in a 1909 issue of the *North American Review*. 'Domestic requirements no longer sufficiently employ either the modern woman's time or her intellect.' The potential for influence was felt to be limitless as New York women filled their days with debates and lectures, clubs and leagues. 'The only danger,' the essay added, 'is that she may take up too many interests, so that with multiplied and divergent claims she may be unable to further any one in particular . . . the interests most adapted to her position or individual capacity should be the ones to command her attention. In these days of specialised effort, one cannot be a Jill of all trades nor a finished performer on more than one instrument.'

Club Women of New York listed Florence's official address as 34 E 32nd Street, which was the St Louis Hotel just off the thrumming thoroughfare of Park Avenue. In fact her living arrangements were a little more complicated. After Florence's death St Clair's list of lodgings where he and Florence cohabited included, in 1910, an establishment called Mrs McGill in Rockaway Beach – a summer retreat on the far side of Long Island which had lost the battle with Newport as the society's most exclusive seaside haunt. From 1911 they boarded on West 109th Street and Amsterdam Avenue. It was a noisy place to live as on their doorstep was the Cathedral of St John the Divine, the world's biggest Anglican building site. The green oasis of Morningside Park was a couple of blocks away, but prey like other parks to petty crime.

Meanwhile Mary Hoagland Foster had moved to New York and settled at the Waldorf-Astoria Hotel. Without having any idea that she was his mother-in-law, she quickly developed a fondness for the tall Englishman who happily escorted her around the city. She called him Mr Roberts, and often urged him to make her daughter into Mrs Roberts. 'You must make Florence marry you!' she'd say.

Having schlepped energetically around the globe, St Clair found that work in New York was growing sporadic. Early in 1910 he was in a musical comedy called *King of Cadonia* about a royal suitor disguised as a peasant. Despite music by the young Jerome Kern, the *New York Tribune* thought it 'rose in no particular above mediocrity' and constituted 'uphill work' for the cast. Later in the year St Clair was part of an emotional production at the Manhattan Opera House which brought carriages thronging to the premiere. Impresario Oscar Hammerstein I had built the theatre on 34th Street and Eighth Avenue in 1906 in order to house a rival to the Metropolitan Opera Company. The venture proved so popular that the Met privately offered Hammerstein a $1.2 million inducement to cease trading. This he accepted, it is thought, to forestall bankruptcy. None of this was known to the public in September 1910 when St Clair joined the cast in *Hans, The Flute Player*, a piece of comic froth from Monte Carlo about a town in the grip of moral torpor. The composer was Louis Ganne. 'To say that he has a good memory,' quipped the *Times* critic, detecting plagiarised tracts of *Parsifal* and *Butterfly*, 'would not detract from one's enjoyment.' During one of the intermissions Hammerstein addressed an audience in tumult. 'The keen and poignant grief which I felt at having been compelled to abandon the field of grand opera is somewhat softened by this reception tonight.' Roses rained down on the lavishly ornamented stage. No one knew about the bung from the Met.

St Clair didn't work in New York for another seven years,

apart from performing pro bono in one-offs. He did a benefit for the Anti-Vivisection Society in 1911. The next year the Shakespeare Club marked the Bard's birthday with a performance of *Hamlet*. Playing Polonius at the Wallack's Theater was the closest St Clair would come to a featured role in America's theatrical capital. The following week the cast repeated their performance as a contribution to the relief fund for bereaved relatives of the *Titanic* dead. The ship had sunk earlier that month, and the inquiry was held at the Waldorf-Astoria. The following year, notwithstanding the threat of icebergs, St Clair sailed home to England again. On his return he toured in a new play about Benjamin Disraeli starring English actor George Arliss, who would return to the role for the next twenty years, filming it as a silent movie then as a talkie, and winning an Oscar for the latter. St Clair's performance as Disraeli's gardener was, alongside that of the rest of the cast, 'entitled to commendation', said the *Herald* in Washington. He saw a lot of America between 1913 and 1915: the train took him to Eau Claire, Wisconsin, Fort Wayne, Indiana, Louisville, Kentucky, Wichita, Kansas, as well as the odd metropolis – Chicago, Pittsburgh, San Francisco, New Orleans. As he travelled up and down the continent from Winnipeg to Louisiana to Oregon, syndicated newspaper reports listing the actors on the undercard would almost invariably conclude with the words 'and St Clair Bayfield'. Despite that smile which seduced Florence, he rarely saw his name clamber towards the north end of the credits. And so it would remain. Later in life he was tormented by the memory of turning down a role in a play which went on to be a big success and made a star of the actor who accepted the part instead.

If the tour was within hailing distance, Florence joined him. She came to Philadelphia, Baltimore, Washington, Atlantic City and Boston. When St Clair was further away, they wrote. A total of five hundred letters passed between them over thirty-five years. Samples of them proved useful when, after her death, St Clair was attempting to prove that they indeed were married. Very few of the letters have survived, but the ones he submitted to the court betray genuine affection and do indeed suggest that Florence thought of herself as St Clair's wife. This letter found him in Portland, Oregon, in late 1914, written in her forthright sloping hand:

Dearest Brownie:

Your two little letters one containing that pretty Xmas card and one the two parcel orders reached me safely this morning. Thank you so much for them both, darling. I will buy something pretty with the money which I trust you will like, dear. I sent from Reed and Bartons a ring, a set of studs and a pair of cuff buttons to you. That ring is your Xmas gift the buttons your birthday gift and the studs your anniversary present on January 24. By the way it's an iron wedding this year, did you know? That's a difficulty then, isn't it? I think I shall send you a horse shoe. With the ring sets. I sent the patch.

I hope you will have the jolliest times you have ever had in your life on Xmas. I am giving a dinner of four people in my mother's honor that day . . . and on New Year's Day I shall be at the Astor. I am a very gloomy rabbit when I think you will not be with me.

Best and wish you all joy and happiness and trust that the very best luck will follow you always. The rooms you describe must be awful . . . The new conductor of the Mozart Society led the Chorus with a knitting needle! Isn't that the limit?

I have been so busy I've scarcely had a chance to breathe and am writing this at speed for yours is about the only Xmas gift I've had time to buy. Do let me know at once if you get all these things and with love and best wishes.

I am always yours dearest Brownie
PS I will look for the pudding.

The letter offers an insight into the lightness of her personality, but also illuminates the imbalance in the relationship. Florence had the financial power to be more bounteous in her giving. St Clair's generosity was as a listener, an enabler. His attempts to supply her with actual presents were sometimes simply rejected. 'She was superstitious about everything,' he said. 'For instance, I was never allowed to put a hat on the bed. She never would give or accept a present with a point. Thought it would break friendship. She wouldn't let me give her a beautiful paperknife once for that reason.' Another undated letter, in reply to one sent by St Clair from Kansas City, again alluded to the gloominess of his lodgings. 'I hate to think of the poor little stuffy rooms you have had and your sitting there in your pink pajamas and blue woolly coat.' St Clair was on tour a lot in these years, so much so that Florence complained of hardly ever seeing him. 'Oh, believe me! The way we have lived for the past four years, I could be married to anybody else, at all, and see as much of you as I do, for after the honeymoon and the first few months are over, nearly any wife can get away for a month or two during the year.'

Despite her wide array of commitments to other clubs and societies, back in New York the Euterpe Club was never far from Florence's thoughts. Hammerstein's experience with the Metropolitan Opera is instructive. The Met, founded in 1880, had in recent years been graced by visits from Enrico Caruso. In 1908 it poached its director Giulio Gatti-Casazza from La

Scala in Milan, who in a tenure of vast creative innovation engaged Mahler and later Arturo Toscanini. The Met's first ever world premiere took place in 1910 when Puccini's *La Fanciulla del West* opened in the country where its story is set. The Metropolitan Opera House at 1411 Broadway, with capacity for nearly four thousand, was the dominant force in the art form. When the Met could shut down a rival with a furtive bribe, it was more or less unthinkable that a women's club might mount an operatic production without any sort of institutional support. And yet that is what Florence planned next.

One evening in March 1912 the Euterpe booked the lavish, stuccoed ballroom at the Plaza Hotel, the recently built palace on Fifth Avenue. The room was lined with pilasters topped by gilt Corinthian capitals. Florence filled it with an orchestra, scenic designs, and a considerable audience, whom it entertained with excerpts from *Carmen*. The opera, like others which followed, was intended to resemble in every particular a production audiences might see at the Metropolitan or other great opera houses.

They may have looked like grand opera productions, but they didn't necessarily sound like them. *Carmen* was sung in English translation (as were all subsequent Euterpe operas) and the performance confined itself to the highlights rather than slog through the whole thing. As for the soloists, there is no record of the singers booked for *Carmen* which suggests that they weren't worth boasting about in any of the women's clubs columns.

According to the (questionable) testimony of her pianist Cosme McMoon, it was in this period that Florence resumed singing in public. She had not sung in front of an audience of any size since she was a young woman. Why she stopped is open to speculation. 'During the whole lifetime of her father,' said McMoon, 'she did not sing but she had this terrific repression. Finally, when he died, he left her very well provided for and her mother was a little more lenient than her father had been, so she was allowed to take singing lessons again, but not to sing in public.' This wasn't exactly how it happened: Florence was getting good notices for her singing in the 1890s. When she started again, her performances were discreet and below the radar, because they went unreported, but in 1915 her mini-résumé in *The Musical Blue Book of America* (subtitle: 'recording in concise form the activities of leading musicians and those actively and prominently identified with music in its various departments') described her as a singer and a pianist. Kathleen Bayfield refers to an injury to Florence's arm which meant she had to give up playing the piano. It seems likely that one means of musical self-expression replaced the other.

The same letter in which Florence replies to St Clair's dispatch from Kansas City refers to her singing in opera programmes and taking part in several concerts. The letter is undated but also alludes to St Clair touring to Philadelphia and Omaha. After he met Florence his only tours of that scale took place in the 1910s, suggesting that Florence was an active, ambitious and – above all – perfectly competent singer in her mid-forties. 'Have had three concerts in a week – one last Wednesday at the Waldorf, one at the Astor on Sunday night and a musical at the Biltmore on Tuesday where I sang the whole programme myself. I am to sing in a concert given by Polaccos, Second Conductor at the Italian Club, which is a critical place to sing.' The same letter referred to both of them writing articles – him for the *Stage*, her for *Expression*, which she fondly upbraided him for failing to mention.

A year on from *Carmen*, in 1913, Florence scheduled another opera, this time *Cavalleria Rusticana*. She may well have attended the American premiere in Philadelphia's Grand Opera House in 1891. Its modest proportions – the competition its composer Pietro Mascagni won in Rome the year before was for one-act operas – meant that it could be performed in its entirety. There was room on the programme for other splendours: a carnival ball tableau with a Spanish ballet, and other tableaux featuring 150 young people. Rehearsals lasted all of March.

Although she had no children of her own, Florence had a good deal of contact with other people's. A matron at a Euterpe evening of tableaux, she was a chaperone to young revellers at a dance to raise money for Stony Wold, a sanatorium in upstate New York for underprivileged women with tuberculosis. The cult of wealth had yet to be subordinated to the cult of youth but, as young people pursued increasing opportunities for pleasure, the chaperone was a figure of growing significance in a city where, in the age of Mrs Astor, rigid etiquette and pitiless snobbery continued to instil a fear of moral ruin. A gossip columnist such as 'The Saunterer' in the society rag *Town Topics* ticked off fast girls for breaches of etiquette. So did *The Bazaar Book of Decorum*. From a slightly earlier era, Mrs Annie White in *Polite Society at Home and Abroad* explained etiquette as 'the frame which is placed around a valuable picture to prevent it being marred or defaced'. The Euterpe and other clubs that arranged social events played host to hundreds of young women at a time, which acted as a honeypot to young men not all of whose motives could be trusted. Where etiquette was a self-policing code of conduct, the chaperone was there to enforce it, often on behalf of the girl's mother. Having eloped at fourteen with such unhappy consequences, Florence was well acquainted with the dangers of male charm and female naivety.

Florence's musical entertainments were only the most

spectacular manifestations of an ever-growing interest in music-making in New York society. 'Club women are more interested in musical affairs this winter than they have been in some seasons,' reported the *New York Times* before Christmas in 1913. 'Besides the morning musicales and afternoon musicales with tea, there is music in the evening, sometimes followed by dancing, sometimes not. The afternoon tea dance has somewhat superseded the afternoon bridge party, and it is no unusual thing for the young girls to dance together after a program of music, such a hold has the tango taken on the young set.' Meanwhile, on the same day, Florence was a bit-part singer as the Mozart Society sang at the Astor before an audience of two and a half thousand. The star of the evening was Frances Alda, a doyenne of the Met (and wife to its Italian director), who regularly duetted with Caruso. It was 'one of the most brilliant evenings in the history of the club'.

Having mounted *Cavalleria Rusticana* in March 1913, a year later the Euterpe moved on to *Pagliacci*, the Leoncavallo opera with which it was joined at the hip almost from its inception. For its third operatic production Florence felt emboldened to publicise the singers she'd booked to sing the main roles. They were by no means of the same calibre as the soloists she'd booked for musicales – none would go on to have any sort of operatic career. Marta Kranich advertised her services as an opera and concert soprano in the *Musical Courier*, and was perhaps related to the founder of the hugely successful New York piano manufacturers Kranich and Bach. A jobbing tenor called Horatio Rench was also in a barbershop outfit called the Criterion Quartet which for several years recorded spirituals and folk songs. Both did well enough to be invited back for a morning musicale in the autumn, alongside other Euterpe favourites. As a taster for the main event there were no fewer than nine tableaux. Afterwards came dancing. Florence knew how to lay on an entertainment, though even she accepted the limits of possibility. The Euterpe was not to mount another complete opera, although the excerpts chosen were from operas created on a grander scale. In 1915 the Euterpe staged the garden scene from Gounod's *Faust*, giving extensive rein to Florence's developing mania for cluttering the stage with botanical ornament.

By now the war in Europe was filling the papers, the news from the western front reaching America ever more swiftly (the first trans-continental phone call was made in 1915). A whiff of turmoil on the old continent even found its way into the refined feminine oasis of club gatherings. Florentine tenor Umberto Sorrentino, working out the conflict by touring America, seduced the ladies with lush romantic tunes including 'O Sole Mio', though his choice of encore, the popular English ballad 'I Hear You Calling Me', was thought unwise by the *Musical Courier*. Nine months before she played for the Euterpe, Lucile Collette, a violin prodigy from Oregon, had been in France on the fateful evening of 28 July 1914. She was about to perform at the casino in Le Havre when news that war was declared reached the orchestra, who swiftly abandoned the stage to don military uniform. 'Mother and I were obliged to leave all our earthly belongings behind us when we returned to this country,' she told the *Oregonian* and no doubt the Euterpe. 'Upon leaving France I never expected again to see the shores of America, as the mines and submarines were plentiful. I never was so thankful in my life as when I saw once more the Statue of Liberty.' Her performances with, among others, Sir Henry Wood's orchestra in London had to be abandoned.

The doings of high society continued. Almost a year to the day after the outbreak of war, Florence joined the throng of well-dressed ladies at a fashionable horse show in Long

Branch, New Jersey. Among the many gowns attentively item-ised by the *Washington Post* was Florence's white embroidered lace robe, with a white-and-black-striped sport coat banded with white fur. The war impinged more on the conscience of St Clair, being a British national. Despite having turned forty in August 1915, he tried to enlist three times with the British Army, which had a recruiting office in New York. On each occasion he was turned down owing to an injury sustained falling from a horse, presumably as a young rancher in New Zealand in the 1890s.

His contributions to the war effort had to be restricted to the stage. In October 1915 he went up to the Canadian cap-ital to join the cast of a new play called *Under Orders* designed to stimulate volunteering by dramatising actual incidents from the conflict. The play, which was set in Tipperary, climaxed with a German submarine failing to torpedo a Canadian transport ship carrying two thousand troops. 'Probably the best acting of the evening,' said the *Ottawa Journal*, 'was that of St Clair Bayfield as the Englishman, Percival Fitzgibbens Fauntleroy.' In professional theatre there was less of that kind of employment to be had. His longest job in the war years was in a musical comedy called *Nobody Home* which toured widely in 1916. Its promotional material referred to it as 'That Fox-Trotty Combination of Fast Fun, Joy and Elite Zip'.

A tour later in the year found him in Buffalo where a letter from Florence alludes to him meeting up with his older sister Ida, who had at some point emigrated to America. The letter refers to another singing engagement and the next Euterpe opera. Tantalisingly it mentions a $25,000 lawsuit, the details of which do not survive.

Dearest Brownie

I wonder if you got my little letter sent to Buffalo. My

cold is all well now I am glad to say. And I am to sing a week from Sunday again. It has been very wet and stormy here and I am busy getting the things ready for the Opera on March 30th. Have a $25,000 damage suit in [illegible] and have been down at the City Hall with a big [illegible] and [illegible]. I am glad you are getting a chance to visit your sister anyway.

Find this is all at present, from a very lonely, and homesick Rabbit.

The opera was her most lavish triumph yet. A week before America entered the war, the Euterpe Club presented the fourth act of *Rigoletto* in a soirée that also presented guest instrumentalists and an array of tableaux vivants, including Mrs Alcinous B. Jamison as the Queen of Harmony in *The Bal Masqué*. While by no means able to summon world-class talent, Florence secured the best cast yet in the Euterpe's brief history as a private producer of grand opera. The title role was taken by Alan Turner, a British baritone who had made popular recordings and sung with the Chicago Opera Company (and would eventually set up his own touring company). Miriam Ardini had already sung the role of Gilda with the Boston Opera Company. A Señor Jimenez, with a Havana Opera Company credit to his name, was the Duke. Annie Laurie Leonard, who made her living as a vaudeville crooner, sang Maddalena. Ten years earlier the bass Francis Motley, who sang Sparafucile, had appeared with the Met.

None of the theatrical effects could have been achieved without the experience and commitment of St Clair. He was an essential resource in the vast technical complexities of competent staging, lighting and set design. But the public credit was Florence's. The Euterpe evening was 'another great success for its popular directress,' explained *Town Topics*:

'artistically and socially, and a distinct triumph for the clever and distinguished lady who is devoting all of her time and energies to the club's aims and ideals, which, mainly, are the fostering of a love and patronage of grand opera in English.'

As ever at the end of a Euterpe event, a vote of thanks was extended to the chairman of music by the president 'in recognition of her valuable services to the club'. If thanks were never more merited, they were also a sort of farewell. The energetic club woman had already announced an expansion of her activities, and yet more glory was to come for someone who, *Town Topics* concluded, 'it goes without saying, ranks high among America's Representative Women.' The clue to Florence's next venture was in the name of the composer who supplied the evening's entertainment.

8: THE SINGING PRESIDENT

Mrs Eugene Sieffert has been lost to history but for her walk-on role in the life of Florence Foster Jenkins. She was a guest at a private musical benefit for the Red Cross. At the completion of the entertainment she put to the event's chairman of music that she should start her own club. Florence, she argued, would then be able to create her own musical programmes and donate the proceeds to the Red Cross. Florence was sceptical, and for all her commitment to clubland, shrank from the idea of becoming a president. 'How many present would join such a club if I should decide to form it?' she asked. It wasn't long before she was handed the names of twenty-five potential members. While she remained non-committal, the notion loitered at the back of her mind. She was at a dinner soon afterwards where, with professional musicians present, she repeated the suggestion made by Mrs Sieffert. They all urged her to do it. 'You could do so much for music in New York City,' they trilled in unison, 'and we would all like to become members of such a club.' The list of potential members swelled. Still Florence gave it no real consideration.

Then one morning she was having a lesson with her singing coach Carlo Edwards. They were working on 'Pace, mio Dio', the aria from *La forza del destino* in which Leonora prays for peace in death, opening and closing with high held notes of piercing intensity. Edwards was also a part-time journalist and photographer, not yet an assistant conductor of the Metropolitan Opera – he didn't conduct his first opera there for another decade. The article he was just writing for *Pearson's Magazine* happened to be about Florence's musical work. As he dashed off at the end of a lesson, he asked Florence, 'Of what club are you president?' The answer emerged as if from the soup of Florence's unconscious: 'The Verdi Club,' she said.

So the story was told, doubtless finessed and with corrugations removed, in the club programme explaining its own origins. Florence later recounted a different version in which it was Edwards who suggested the name. In either telling, this is the moment the public legend was germinated – of Florence Foster Jenkins, the self-appointed diva, the so-called 'singing president' who attracted a devoted following.

Mrs Sieffert takes some of the credit, but there were other tectonic forces at work. Early in 1917 Florence was immobilised by a broken leg. St Clair Bayfield, who was on tour, made frequent trips to visit her in hospital whenever he was within striking distance of New York. The enforced pause in her frenetic activities gave her the opportunity for reflection. On 6 April the United States of America declared war on Germany. Then, just shy of her forty-ninth birthday, a change of status was thrust upon Florence.

Frank Thornton Jenkins lived out his final years knowing of a substantial hoick in the fortunes of the woman whose elopement with him had caused a rift with her parents. Apart from his one statement about his nephews in 1908, Florence's estranged husband remained incognito in the gloaming of history, to resurface in the record books only on the date of his death: 13 June 1917. He was sixty-five. The end was sudden. His wanderings ceased a long way from the East Coast in Milwaukee County, Wisconsin. A short entry in the

Evening Star in Washington, which was presumably alerted by his sister Alice, concluded with a request in brackets: '(New York papers please copy.)' In death the midshipman expelled from the US Navy was restored to the heart of his family, relatives of the military dead having the right to be buried in Arlington Cemetery. Florence's response was to start owning up to the source of her surname. In a *Town Topics* profile the following year she styled herself as 'the widow of Dr Frank Thornton Jenkins, son of Rear Admiral Jenkins'. The marriage may have been functionally dead for thirty years, but there was nothing now to stop her making belated capital from her in-laws.

Around this time there was a significant shift in her relations with St Clair, who may have been bruised by such a public reclamation of Florence's first and official husband. After eight years, their cohabitation came to an end. On 22 October a small announcement appeared in the *New York Sun* under the heading West Side Suites Rented: 'to Florence Foster Jenkins at 66 West Thirty-seventh Street'. At the street level a black nameplate was affixed with their names hyphenated and alphabetised: Bayfield-Jenkins. But Florence had no intention of living there herself. It was not remotely an apartment in the style to which she had once more become accustomed since her inheritance. If Florence's Bohème years were over, St Clair's were to continue. The rent on the apartment was paid by Florence in lieu of the salary St Clair might otherwise have earned for the work he performed on her behalf, from now on more than ever.

The apartment was on the fourth floor. On the door was a silver star, a heart-shaped wooden plaque and a small horseshoe, perhaps the present from Florence to mark their iron wedding anniversary. The hall was minuscule. The rest of the apartment's ascetic accoutrements included an iron bedstead covered with a faded maroon silk spread, a couch with a matching bedspread cloth, a blue wicker chair and table, a wooden desk heaped high with St Clair's papers, a round piano stool at a dressing table on which he ranged photographs and his military hairbrushes, and a half-moon table. Over the years the walls filled with photographs of Florence. In due course a cloth was hung on the wall featuring the masks of tragedy and comedy and bearing the legend, Verdi Club.

The Verdi Club announced itself at the start of the season on 18 November 1917.

> The Verdi Club, Mrs Florence Foster Jenkins president, will have its first morning musicale on November 28 at the Waldorf-Astoria. The new club's aim is to honor the genius of Verdi. Its war fund, the proceeds from club entertainments, will be given to the Red Cross. During the season there will be three musical mornings, two musical and dramatic afternoons and a song recital at the Waldorf-Astoria. A musicale and reception will be given at the Hotel Astor, a piano recital will take place at Aeolian Hall and the club's events of the winter will wind up with a dance in April. Among the members are . . .

And here the *New York Sun* reeled off twenty-three names of subscribers whose commitment was calculated to attract more members. The list betrayed the key influence of St Clair. Rather than assign precedence to the society dames of the Euterpe (Mrs Jamison and Mrs Marzo enrolled), at the top were Mr and Mrs George Arliss. Arliss was the acclaimed English star of *Disraeli* whose actress wife toured everywhere with him. St Clair rejoined the Arlisses in 1916 to tour in a play about Paganini. There were other lesser-known actresses. One of them, Edyth Totten, was president of the Drama

Comedy Club, which Florence promptly joined. Florentine soprano Olga Carrara Pescia also signed up. Even Enrico Caruso was soon a member, along with the American socialite Dorothy Park Benjamin, twenty years his junior, with whom he eloped in 1918.

The printed programme of the first musicale crossed the Atlantic in the possession of Mrs Sieffert's husband, who carried it as a mascot around the battlefields of Europe. When he returned he gave it back to Florence to be inserted in the club's scrapbook.

The commitment to raise money for the Red Cross was central. In 1915 the American Red Cross Society had announced its plan to raise $100 million for war relief, and the women's clubs threw themselves into the effort. They did not share the view of gossip columnist and hostess Elsa Maxwell that society women regarded the war as 'simply a beastly inconvenience that interfered with their annual trips abroad'. A year before the United States entered the conflict, New York society women were praised for working 'like beavers' to meet an urgent request cabled from the front for surgical dressings. 'Scores of rich and fashionable women gave up all social engagements and worked ten and twelve hours a day to prepare bandages,' reported the *Evening World*. A shipment of 150,000 gauze bandages was dispatched to hospitals in France.

Through the season of 1917–18, Florence entered a period of intense activity as she helped to raise money on several fronts. Her commitments to the Euterpe Club continued unabated. She laid on such curiosities as a wandering Danish lutenist and a young American pianist called Jacques Jolas (who would go on to enjoy a more conventional career than his brother Eugène; he was a poet and translator whose literary magazine *transition* had a profound influence on James

Joyce as he wrote *Finnegans Wake*). For its next operatic spectacle the Euterpe tacked away from the core repertoire to stage a scene from Friedrich von Flotow's 1844 opera *Martha*, a French-flavoured bauble which had enjoyed a great fillip a dozen years earlier when Caruso reintroduced it at the Met. One of the singers engaged for the performance was a coup for the club. Ernest Davis, a promising young American tenor of Welsh descent, spent the season with the Boston Grand Opera Company burnishing his reputation. His voice was 'of large volume and beautiful quality,' said the *Chicago Journal*. 'The range is exceptional, giving high C and D with entire ease and thrilling effect. In addition,' it noted with approval, 'he has enthusiasm.' Davis's enthusiasm would later be severely tested by the Verdi Club president.

Meanwhile the Verdi Club's early gatherings found Florence pinching some of the artists she'd already booked for the Euterpe – a Spanish dancer called Little Dolores was one such – but the way in which she deployed them revealed a more ambitious strategy for her own club. The major guest at one Euterpe musicale was Hungarian violinist Jan Munkacsy, already some way into a long, fruitful career. In January 1918 Munkacsy was booked again by Florence, this time to participate in what was grandly known as the 'Verdi Club's string quartette'. Florence was learning the science of branding. The programme also had Euterpe favourite Carl Schlegel alongside more singers with Metropolitan Opera House credits to their names.

In the same month she chaired the annual musicale of the New Yorkers Club at the Astor. While the clubs all had armies of officers and chairmen who ran the luncheons and notified the members, on an artistic level these commitments could not have been met without St Clair, even though he was busy elsewhere. That month he was rehearsing and opening as

Launcelot Gobbo in *The Merchant of Venice* at the Cort Theater ('a capital, diverting wittol': *New York Tribune*). He then went straight on to take part in the New York premiere of Ibsen's *The Wild Duck*. But he was also moonlighting as Florence's amanuensis and acted as creative consultant when the ballroom of the Waldorf-Astoria was decorated for the Verdi Club's so-called Ball of the Silver Skylarks.

Florence took the name from the ode by Percy Bysshe Shelley. The cover design of the ball programme was 'originated' by Florence herself although executed by an artist. The caption elucidated thus: 'Shelley, the poet, with the Muses in the background, Literature, Art and Music, with the Spirit of the Dance, springing from Music's brain, receives an inspiration from a flight of skylarks soaring toward the sun, which is immortalized in Shelley's poem . . .' (The least of Florence's syntactical quirks was a Teutonic preference for aggrandising nouns in upper case.)

The inauguration of an annual ball was a statement of her limitless ambition for the club. Organised by a committee of officers, it offered an operatic performance with full orchestra, a concert which featured an unfolding series of tableaux vivants and afterwards dancing into the small hours. The boxes around the ballroom were decorated with images of the great operatic composers, Verdi taking pride of place. During the course of the evening Florence was presented with a golden laurel wreath surrounding a golden lyre with an enamelled shield of red and grey – the club's colours. The gift to the president came from the officers of the Verdi's inaugural season (and it was presented by a real officer: Lieutenant William L. Sayers). This was Florence's reward for raising enough money to enable the Red Cross to buy and equip an ambulance for France. She gave an interview about this personal triumph to Carlo Edwards in *Pearson's Magazine*, in which she explained that the Verdi Club had become god-mother to an entire ambulance unit which could count directly on the support of the club for its various needs.

'Here is aid of the most practicable and available sort,' she enthused:

> I know of no way by which we can half so readily translate our impulses into actual help. The tragedy has been that so many of us have passionately wanted to do a little something toward alleviating the frightful suffering in Europe, but either we did not know of anything really helpful to do, or at any rate we could never have the satis-fied feeling that our efforts were really doing anything. We could never feel our own hands giving aid. Now, we of the club are in personal touch with the front. The doctors will send immediately to us for supplies, often so desperately needed, and we are going to meet our duty as duty has never been met. What an incitement to us in our musical work! All the funds derived from the club performances are at the disposal of the men at the battle front. It is as it should be: art the handmaid of humanity.

The magazine printed a picture of Florence with a short dark cropped wig and a single string of pearls, looking rather younger than fifty.

Florence's name was now ubiquitous in the society pages. In the same week she hosted a luncheon at Delmonico's and dashed off to Washington to fulfil her duties as a delegate for the Daughters of the American Revolution. These events were covered in the same edition of the *New York Sun*'s report on activities in women's clubs. (On the same day, Manfred von Richthofen, better known as the Red Baron, was shot down and killed.) Later that month a self-styled 'gushing Texan' wrote home to San Antonio to report on the success in New

York of a locally born pianist. Her list of the VIPs at the recital included several professional musicians but the first name was Florence Foster Jenkins, president of the Verdi Club.

Meanwhile St Clair dashed south. That month he was turned down by the British Army for the third time. He had to find another way of contributing to the war effort, so he devised a production to entertain troops awaiting shipment to the theatre of war. He put together a company to perform a light comedy called *It Pays to Advertise* to trainee soldiers stationed at Camp McClellan in Alabama. The winter drama season now being over and leading actors out of contract, the cast he managed was full of Broadway players. In case anyone might suspect them of shirking their duty, the *Anniston Star* reassured readers that 'all the members of this company subject to draft have fulfilled all requirements exacted by the government'. The company went back south in July and were 'liberally entertained' at a reunion dinner with officers.

Florence's visit to Washington for the Daughters of the Revolution was her first since she was widowed. The *Washington Herald* described her as well known in the city 'not only as the daughter-in-law of the late Admiral Thornton A. Jenkins and wife of the late Dr Francis Thornton Jenkins, but as a singer.' It mentioned her appearance at the White House before the First Lady. It didn't mention that she shared the stage with 131 other members of the Mozart Society of New York. (The sense that these news items arrived at the newspaper's office as more or less pre-written press releases is sometimes overpowering.) Frank's death brought about a rapprochement with Florence's sister-in-law Alice, who, it was announced in early May, had been invited to stay with Florence in New York in November.

In the intervening years Alice Thornton Jenkins had become a person of note herself, not in the sphere of music in which she had excelled as a young woman, but as a leading figure in the struggle for American women's suffrage. In February 1912 she wrote stirringly to the *Evening Star* in Washington to oppose the casuistical arguments against giving women the vote which were deployed even by men who supported their right to it. 'The moment a man admits that woman is entitled to the franchise,' she reasoned, 'that moment it becomes his duty to make no argument against her obtaining it.' Her letter concluded with a derogatory allusion to 'the pampered rich, well cared for women, who think they enjoy life better without whatever responsibility the ballot might impose'. The next month she wrote to the same paper to upbraid it for its misinterpretation of the battle for women's suffrage in the United Kingdom. Soon she was in New York as the leader of the Washington delegation in a suffrage parade of fifteen thousand women. Another of the marchers was an octogenarian who had worked as a nurse in the Civil War.

Militant striving for a new world existed side by side with her support for militancy in its more traditional form. The previous week she was up in Maine to represent another veteran of that conflict – her own father – when a torpedo boat destroyer was 'christened' in the rear admiral's name. The *Washington Times* included a photograph of a powerful-looking woman with a direct gaze and angry eyebrows, ill suited to the cinched waist and pearl necklace of her evening gown. She was accompanied to Maine by her younger sister Carrie, but lived in downtown Washington, DC with her youngest sister Nettie, another committed suffragist now divorced from her heroic, facially disfigured husband George, who had remarried and climbed to the rank of rear admiral. Florence is not known to have had any thoughts about her right to vote, for which not every society lady hankered. 'When in the company of suffragettes, a perverse desire to condone all men's errors possessed me,' recalled Consuelo Vanderbilt in her autobiography, 'for I found female self-sufficiency somewhat ridiculous.'

Alice duly arrived in New York for the opening of the Verdi Club's second season on 6 November 1918 at the Waldorf-Astoria. Other guests of honour were seven brides, including the newly wedded Mrs Caruso. Alice stayed for a week and was there for the Armistice. She found Florence installed in an apartment in the Seymour Hotel in West 45th Street off Fifth Avenue. The twelve-storey residential hotel was in considerable contrast to the apartment she rented for St Clair. The drawing room was a decorous riot of elegant furniture and silk cushions. A chandelier hovered over the room; signed photographs covered every surface. On the grand piano, which dominated one end of the room, was a snap of Florence and above it looking down from the wall hung the two oil portraits of Florence as a child and in early middle age, probably painted by her mother. Other mementos of her youth included her dance cards from the 1880s. Edwin McArthur, who would later become Florence's accompanist, remembered a suite 'filled with an assortment of bric-a-brac such as you've never seen. Pictures of herself in various poses, statuettes, lamps of all descriptions, photographs of artists she knew. And she knew everybody.' There she had use of a daily maid to dress her, lay on breakfast and serve when guests came round for regular private musicales at which promising young soloists were invited to perform.

That week St Clair was busy rehearsing an English war spy drama, *Pigeon Post*, about the winged messengers of Verdun (with real pigeons which 'fluttered and hopped about, cooed and preened their feathers'). The play was a first effort at serious drama by Florenz Ziegfeld, better known for titillating New Yorkers with the fashionable tableaux of the Ziegfeld

Follies. Ziegfeld had spied a commercial opportunity in dramas from the front, which now abounded in theatres on both sides of the Atlantic. St Clair was soon in the cast of another London import, this time a musical comedy called *The Better 'Ole* based on a popular wartime cartoon Tommy called Old Bill. It was 'as artless and unsophisticated as the original drawings,' said the *Times*, but 'of the utmost freshness and delight'.

In early 1919 Florence's connections with the great and good of the opera world were strengthened when the Verdi Club celebrated what it branded Caruso Day, which didn't quite fall on the great tenor's birthday in February. He did not deign to sing in (or indeed attend) an all-Verdi programme, but the credentials of the guest soloists were trumpeted: club member Olga Carara-Pessia was a soprano 'from the Royal Theatre, Madrid'; alto Cecil Arden had made her debut with the Met the previous year. This was merely a foretaste of the second Silver Skylarks ball, which was widely advertised. The campus newspaper *Columbia Daily Spectator* advised its readers that tickets costing $2.00 were available from the Columbia University Press bookstore. There was a performance with full orchestra of *Il Trovatore* (another booking for Ernest Davis, one of the professional members, supported by an amateur chorus), plus Spanish dancing, Lucile Collette sawing on the violin, and yet more arias and songs. After the entertainment, members enjoyed the chance to become characters from the world of Verdi themselves in a pageant: society dames came dressed as Verdian heroines Amneris, Violetta, Gilda, Desdemona and Mistress Quickly. A male member played the part of Verdi. Others filled out the scene as gypsies and Egyptians. Florence herself was at the head of a group costumed in the Verdi period in a dress festooned with skylarks. The artistic director was none other than

President Woodrow Wilson's niece. The ballroom of the Waldorf-Astoria was hung with the flags of the Allies while the consulates of France, Italy and Greece sent representatives to witness this gesture of international solidarity. Guests were also welcomed from the Red Cross and the Tank Corps.

Florence's holidays were a continuum of the social whirl in New York with added ocean breezes. In August 1919 she took the sea air in Rhode Island as an attendee at the amusingly named Snow Ball at Narragansett Pier. St Clair travelled in the opposite direction, heading to the Midwest to do good. He put together a company to present a play as part of Chautauqua, an adult education movement which former president Theodore Roosevelt was once moved to describe as 'the most American thing in America'. It had evolved into a touring entity (known as the Redpath-Vawter system) which was starting to branch away from an unrelieved diet of improving lectures. St Clair assembled a cast of Broadway actors to stage the play, which had also been approved by Roosevelt: 'That's a great play, Mr. Zangwill, that's a great play,' shouted the president from his box in 1909 when he saw Israel Zangwill's drama about idealistic refugees from Russian pogroms hoping for a life free of rancour in America. Zangwill, who was British and described as 'the Dickens of the ghetto', later received a letter from Roosevelt acknowledging the play as 'among the very strong and real influences upon my thought and my life'. St Clair's company toured Missouri with their own lighting and set. The *Macon Republican* reported that it would surpass 'anything of its nature ever attempted by the Redpath folks'. In three months St Clair returned to the Midwest to perform a Shakespearean double bill of *Hamlet* and *Romeo and Juliet* in Cincinnati.

Back in New York the interests of the common-law couple reconverged. Florence, the former student of elocution, was a fan of theatre who attended all of St Clair's first nights. In February 1920 she was appointed chairman of music for the Dramatic Art Society, a new club devoted to 'the pursuit and promotion of the best type of American drama, a closer relation between dramatists and theatregoers, and the exchange of opinions on all things concerning theatre'. The first subject for discussion was 'the modern quiet method of handling dramatic situations', a stylistic development to which the new society gave its stamp of approval. There was a reading from J. M. Barrie's 1918 war play *A Well-Remembered Voice*. In April St Clair was enlisted as a performer at the Silver Skylarks ball on the theme of the Arabian Nights. A thousand guests mustered at the Waldorf-Astoria to see him dressed as an Arabian prince while Florence, costumed as Scheherazade, gleamed in a turban with a conical coronet and a sweeping train, and dangling globular earrings.

Their philanthropic interests coalesced too when the Verdi Club expanded its field of operation and began staging Shakespeare. They started with *King John* and followed it up with *Twelfth Night*, which St Clair directed as well as taking the part of Malvolio. His recreation of the play's earliest known performance in Middle Temple Hall in 1602 was deemed an artistic triumph. All money raised from tickets of $2.50 went to the Italian Red Cross (which in due course presented Florence with a diploma and a gold medal). Later that season he contributed a talk on the play he had been appearing in at the Belasco Theater. The club took inspiration from these performances and in its 1921 ball there were tableaux vivants on the theme of Shakespeare and/or Verdi, concluding with the shrine of the Sun Goddess, embodied by the club's president and founder. There was also a full performance of *Aida* with a chorus of 150 voices: Florence's zest for laying on epic soirées was growing exponentially each year. And at the end of the entertainment she had her annual apotheosis as one or other great feminine icon. The cheers and applause, it seems sensible to assume, had an addictive quality, and went straight to her head.

While the calendar of the Verdi Club set the pattern of Florence's year, she still dashed off to Washington as a Daughter of the American Revolution, attended gatherings of the Euterpe and other clubs, often as guest of honour and sometimes programming their musicales. Singing with the Mozart Society involved rehearsals for three evening concerts and monthly musicales at the Hotel Astor; these would take up a whole Saturday afternoon starting with music, then luncheon, then dancing. The season ended with the choir's annual May breakfast where 1,200 women would turn up in floral hats; Florence was one of the guests of honour escorted to her place by twenty women of the reception committee carrying bowers of roses.

By the start of the 1920–21 winter season Florence had established herself sufficiently to take an audacious step: she decided to perform to the members of the Verdi Club. She put herself on an evening programme at the MacDowell Club on West 55th Street. The choice of venue said much about her perception of herself as a contributor to the city's musical life. The club was part of a network of what grew to four hundred clubs spread all over the country, set up to honour the memory of composer Edward MacDowell. The New York branch was established in 1905 and supported an artists' retreat in New Hampshire. Its aim was 'to discuss and demonstrate the principles of the arts of music, literature, drama, painting, sculpture, and architecture, and to aid in the extension of knowledge of works especially fitted to exemplify the finer purposes of these arts'. Florence surrounded herself with competent amateurs rather than professionals likely to

show her up: a violinist, a pianist playing Chopin and an elocutionist reading poems by Oscar Wilde. The applause from
loyal acolytes resounded all the way up to the MacDowell
Club's vaulted ceiling. It may have been sincere, but it was
also an extension of the gratitude shown by the members who
at the end of each season showered Florence with gifts: a gold
bracelet studded with diamonds and sapphires one year, plus
a dinner in her honour, a heart-shaped pearl pendant with a
large ruby another year. The club was also presented with a
bust of Verdi by sculptress Lily C. Mayer (née Gidlio). Florence ensured gifts – a pearl necklace, an ostrich-feather fan
– were presented to other officers.

Thus the cycle began: in return for her vast social and cultural largesse, Florence received uncritical approbation for her
singing. Emboldened, in early 1921 she was invited to sing to
the women of the National Society of Patriotic Women of
America at the Hotel McAlpin (also a holder of the record for
world's largest hotel). This was another society into which she
threw herself, its aim being 'Americanisation', its educational
fund paying for ten teachers spread across New York. Her gift
to the cause was a duet from *Aida* with the tenor Ernest
Davis. Davis knew which side his bread was buttered and
sang along, after many rehearsals at Florence's Seymour Hotel
grand piano. He also sang 'Celeste Aida' on his own.

By 1920 there were a million members of women's clubs
in America. Their widespread and profound influence on the
culture of New York was most manifest on presidents' day,
when club leaderenes annually gathered for a celebration
involving talks and performances. Florence was one of the
twenty-eight presidents gracing the event with their presence
at the Waldorf-Astoria as the season drew to a close in April
1921. The newspapers obligingly alluded to all such attendees
as 'prominent persons'. The ballroom was packed. Many of

their activities involved music. The clubs' cultural contribution was acknowledged by Walter Damrosch, the conductor of the New York Symphony Society, a couple of years later: 'I do not think there has ever been a country whose musical development has been fostered so almost exclusively by women as America.'

The Verdi Club's sphere of influence enlarged: at the start of the next season a hundred new members were ready to enrol. The less cheering news was that the club's honorary member Enrico Caruso had died of pneumonia, prompting a memorial musicale in tribute with a speech from, among others, the gnarled old Oregonian poet Edwin Markham. With infirmity on Florence's mind, the club formed a committee to arrange visits to members who were unwell. Perhaps they managed to bring succour to Mrs Alcinous B. Jamison, the president of the Euterpe, before she died at the start of 1922.

Florence rallied to stand before the Verdi Club at an afternoon musicale and deliver a selection of Italian arias and English songs, in gratitude for which she was presented with a set of ruby hairpins. (No matter that she wore a wig.) 'Mrs Florence Jenkins and Mozelle Bennett Are Artists at Waldorf,' announced a *New York Tribune* headline. (Bennett was a violinist well known enough to have a short article that month on the craft of good bowing in the *Violinist* magazine; she was also dragooned into the newly formed Verdi Club Trio.) The task of chairing the event was taken by another of the club's officers because Florence could not be seen to programme herself. As it happened the day's chairman, Miss Edna Moreland, was also a soprano who for three years had been given the opportunity to sing for the Verdi Club. She now returned the compliment. The difference was that Moreland had enough talent to set sail for France later in the year and try

Florence's father, Charles Dorrance Foster, was a wealthy Wilkes-Barre lawyer who spent much time in politics and property.

Florence's mother, Mary Hoagland Foster, was a keen painter and genealogist who gave several different birth dates to the US census.

The so-called Diamond City on the banks of the Susquehanna owed its surging population to the discovery of anthracite coal.

Rear Admiral Thornton Alexander Jenkins, a hero of the Civil War and father to many daughters, plus Florence's underwhelming husband Frank Thornton Jenkins.

Frank's nephew, Thornton Jenkins Hains, was a successful author of adventure yarns who twice in his life was acquitted of murder.

A studio portrait of Florence taken after the age of forty, soon after her arrival in New York, betrays a flair for self-dramatization.

The serious actor St Clair Bayfield aged around thirty, not long before he met Florence.

The Waldorf Astoria on Fifth Avenue, built in the German Renaissance style, was the largest hotel on the planet. Women's societies, including the Euterpe Club and the Verdi Club, often met here for their musicales.

Florence had a special weakness for eye-catching hats and headdresses, which she often wore in her Ritz-Carlton recitals.

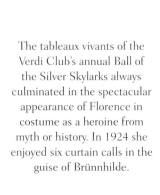

The tableaux vivants of the Verdi Club's annual Ball of the Silver Skylarks always culminated in the spectacular appearance of Florence in costume as a heroine from myth or history. In 1924 she enjoyed six curtain calls in the guise of Brünnhilde.

Age did not wither Florence's taste for fancy dress, but some of her folkloric outfits gave audiences ever more reason to laugh at her.

At the Ball of the Silver Skylarks in 1940, Florence cast herself as the winged inspiration of a great American composer when re-enacting Howard Chandler Christy's painting 'Stephen Foster and the Angel of Inspiration'. Newspapers had much fun with this image.

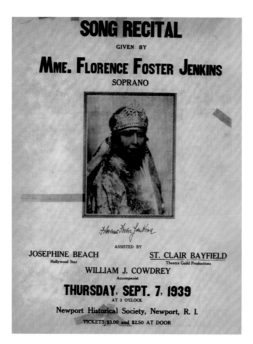

SONG RECITAL

GIVEN BY

MME. FLORENCE FOSTER JENKINS
SOPRANO

Florence Foster Jenkins

ASSISTED BY

JOSEPHINE BEACH
Hollywood Star

ST. CLAIR BAYFIELD
Theatre Guild Productions

WILLIAM J. COWDREY
Accompanist

THURSDAY, SEPT. 7, 1939
AT 3 O'CLOCK

Newport Historical Society, Newport, R. I.

TICKETS, $3.00 and $2.50 AT DOOR

From 1930, Florence gave an annual recital in Newport, Rhode Island, the society watering hole she first visited in 1902. St Clair Bayfield sometimes participated, too. This performance took place the same week war broke out in Europe.

In 1937, *Life* magazine sent the photographer Margaret Bourke-White to capture one of Florence's private gatherings in her Seymour Hotel apartment for its series 'Life Goes to a Party'. Here, Florence sings for her guests. The photographs were never published.

Cosme McMoon was an Irish–Mexican composer who set Florence's lyrics to music and was her loyal accompanist on stage at Carnegie Hall.

Carnegie Hall in the 1930s, capacity 3,000. The night before Florence's performance, Frank Sinatra had appeared there at a Democrat rally.

FLORENCE FOSTER
JENKINS
COLORATURA SOPRANO
Assisted by
THE PASCARELLA CHAMBER MUSIC SOCIETY

CARNEGIE HALL
Wednesday Evening, October 25th
At 8:30 o'clock

PROGRAM OVERLEAF

The cover of the programme for Florence's Carnegie Hall recital. Florence is wearing a coronet and a thumb ring.

The full programme for Florence's Carnegie Hall recital. 'Do not try to beat your neighbor to the street', advises the fire notice.

CARNEGIE HALL PROGRAM
SEASON 1944-1945
FIRE NOTICE — Look around *now* and choose the nearest exit to your seat. In case of fire walk (not run) to *that* Exit. Do not try to beat your neighbor to the street.
PATRICK WALSH, *Fire Commissioner.*

Wednesday Evening, October 25th, at 8:30 o'clock

Florence Foster Jenkins
Coloratura Soprano
Assisted by
The PASCARELLA CHAMBER MUSIC SOCIETY
COSME McMOON, *Pianist*
•
Programme
I.
ENGLISH SONGS
Phyllis ....*Young*
Love Has Eyes....................*Bishop*
Lo, Here the Gentle Lark ....*Bishop*
(Flute obbligato by Oreste De Sevo)
MME. JENKINS
II.
Quartet, Allegro con brio, Op. 54, No. 19.......*Haydn*
PASCARELLA CHAMBER MUSIC SOCIETY

Program Continued on Second Page Following

PROGRAM CONTINUED
III.
ARIAS
Divinites du Styx (Alceste) ....*Gluck*
The Queen of the Night (Magic Flute) ......*Mozart*
MME. JENKINS
INTERMISSION
IV.
RUSSIAN NUMBERS
(Sung in Russian. In costume)
Biassy (words by) ....*Pushkin*
Melodie (song by) ....*Count Alexis Pavlovitch*
Prelude XVI (Accompaniment),
Johann Sebastian Bach
FANTASY STORY
A Baron rides through the sky where snow is falling fast. The moon as a coquette smiles fitfully between the clouds. The horses are lost in a trackless waste lured by an evanescent devil, who is also a friend of the House Devil and many other imps who join in a carnival. The question is—"Is this the funeral of a great King, or the marriage of a beautiful witch?"
In the Silence of Night.............*Rachmaninoff*
Floods of Spring...............*Rachmaninoff*
MME. JENKINS

PROGRAM CONTINUED
•
V.
Quartet, Op. 11. Andante cantabile........*Tschaikowsky*
The Mill. Allegro from Quartet, Op. 102, No. 2,
Raff-Pochon
PASCARELLA CHAMBER MUSIC SOCIETY
VI.
ITALIAN AND SPANISH SONGS
Aria. In Quelle Trine Morbide,
(Manon Lescaut) ....*Puccini*
Interlude ....*Kostelanetz*
Clavelitos ....*Valverde*
Serenata Mexicana ....*McMoon*
(Quartet Accompaniment)
Las Hijas del Zebedeo...................*Chapi*
MME. JENKINS
Steinway Piano
•
Recital Management
GEORGE LEYDEN COLLEDGE
RKO Building, Radio City, New York Tel. CIrcle 7-1962

her luck in Paris; she was seen off with a reception in Florence's apartment. Miss Moreland made sure to keep Florence separate from professional singers, but not by much. Only the morning before, the club had been entertained by Austrian baritone Robert Leonhardt, since 1914 a star of the Met where he had sung Papageno and Amfortas (although his career there had been suspended in 1918 because he was deemed an enemy alien).

For that year's fifth Silver Skylarks ball a programme was printed which detailed the names of twenty-six people who had taken boxes, seventy-eight patrons and patronesses, and seven ushers. There was a strong presence among the guests of military top brass, including two admirals and a general who, having sat through *La traviata* and a variety of tableaux, were invited – or possibly obliged – to take part in a grand march to initiate the ball.

Every summer Florence now disappeared, to rest on her laurels for four months in Larchmont on the north shore of Long Island Sound. She entertained the many members of the Verdi Club who passed through at the Horseshoe harbour club, one of the oldest yacht clubs in America. In August of 1922 the lazy summer bacchanal was enlivened by a performance of *A Midsummer Night's Dream* by an amateur cast driven to heights, according to local paper the *Evening World*, that rivalled Broadway. 'And why? There is but one answer and that is St Clair Bayfield.'

St Clair was indefatigable. He had spent six months up until May in *Bulldog Drummond*, a transfer from London based on H. C. McNeile's popular stories about a gentleman adventurer back from the trenches, but still he found time to direct and take part in a one-act play for the Verdi Club. Florence had expressed her appreciation for him on Valentine's Day by throwing a reception in the MacDowell Club for his fellow Cheltonians resident in New York (one of whom was in the *Bulldog Drummond* cast with him). The expatriates of Cheltenham were treated to a programme of English songs by their hostess. Thus did Florence Foster Jenkins find her name trumpeted as a 'well-known society leader' in the *Gloucestershire Echo*.

Grateful to escape the broiling heat of his New York apartment, St Clair, as ever, devoted his summer to a worthy cause, in this case the Larchmont Library, to be built on land donated by a prominent resident and theatre owner. He sifted through aspiring amateur thespians among the local lotus-eaters for a cast, then drilled them in rehearsals. For an auditorium he used a leafy alfresco setting by the yacht club which enchanted the audience, who were 'unable to believe that centuries had not melted away leaving them seated on the side of Mount Olympus to watch the gods at play'. Those gods included Larchmont children as fairies in wispy white. The library received $1,500. St Clair gave his Bottom, out of whose mouth came the words that encapsulated the *Weltanschauung* of his common-law wife, who was a patroness in the audience: 'Let me do it. I can do it best.'

The Verdi Club was five years old and, to celebrate, Florence opened the season by singing to its members. Her selection included an aria from Gounod's *Roméo et Juliette* and a suite of French songs for which she hired as her accompanist an Italian violinist from the Metropolitan Opera. The applause was ecstatic. After the encores she was presented with a tall silver vase lined with gold and fifteen large floral pieces by a small regiment of ushers. Her roses and chrysanthemums had to be sent home in a separate taxi. 'Many friends wired her,' reported the *Musical Courier*, 'sent her letters and called her the next day on the telephone, one of these poetic admirers wiring: "Heaven gave you a silver throat, and blessed you with golden tones.'" The *Courier* was certainly paid to reproduce these blandishments verbatim.

One of the guests of honour was the pioneering Welsh choir mistress Clara Novello Davies, who brought a five-piece ladies' vocal group with her to perform. (Her more famous brother was Ivor Novello, composer of the wartime anthem 'Keep the Home Fires Burning'; he had conquered the London stage as a composer and actor and was about to become a movie star.) Another eminence who now appeared on the Verdi Club's list of vice-presidents was Rosa Ponselle, the young star of the Met who started out in vaudeville.

The annual ball of 1923 heaped further praise on Florence's head. After acts four and five of *Otello* she featured in the pageant as the Snow Queen, following which club member Bruce Adams paid gushing homage in a speech which told 'of the love all bore her, of their devotion to the Verdi Club and its fine president'. He had already published two poems in praise of Florence in the programme, a paean which cannot have happened without her blessing. To conclude the ceremonies, she was presented with a platinum wristwatch set with fifty diamonds. She had the decency to blush.

Armed with these assurances of devotion, and having now established herself as a soloist in New York, Florence made her first foray outside the city. After the summer she travelled down to Washington, DC where the Washington Hotel held a benefit for the Japanese relief committee. For the first recorded time in her life, she did not share the bill with any other musician. For her accompanist she equipped herself with the best. Malton Boyce was an English-born organist and choirmaster in charge of music at St Matthew the Apostle's church in Washington. The church (which became a cathedral in 1939) went to some lengths to employ him: he was

working in the University of Regensburg when the rector
scouted him in 1906. Boyce's speciality was Gregorian plain-
song, so Florence's repertoire called for quite a step change,
while he was also given the floor to perform bits and pieces
of Chopin and Debussy. He doubtless welcomed the exposure
to high society and the money: he had five children to support, two of them his wife's from a previous marriage, and
already supplemented his income by running a boarding
house. Florence's eminent church musician was still accompanying her twenty years later. The *Sunday Star* wasn't invited
to that first recital, but received 'word . . . from those in
charge' that it was 'a pronounced success'.

The series of permissions which Florence gave herself to
perform came in incremental stages. The next arrived just
over a year later when, for the first time, she put her own
name down on a programme she herself had devised. This
was not for the Verdi Club but the New Yorkers meeting at
the Astor. The newspaper announcement conjured up an
image of butter not melting in her mouth: 'The chairman of
music, Mrs Florence Foster Jenkins, will present the program,
including piano solos by Gladys Barnett; songs by Florence
Foster Jenkins; harp solos by Arthur Jones.'

The aura of brazen indomitability was worn as an actual
costume by Florence at the Verdi Club's seventh annual ball
in 1924. *La forza del destino* was presented, but the climax
of the evening, even after all the singers had drawn gales of
applause, came in the last of a series of tableaux on the theme
of 'A Dream of Fair Women'. Raised on a base of rocks, brandishing a silver spear and golden shield and wearing a white
cloak and a mighty horned helmet was the imposing figure of
President Florence Foster Jenkins in the guise of a breast-
plated, flaxen-maned Brünnhilde in flowing robes. Such was
the ovation from the audience that the curtain was drawn

back half a dozen times so that the Wagnerian apparition could be marvelled at again and again. The printed programme for the evening had promised as much: its cover featured a portrait of Florence thus bedecked. Her choice of character was redemptive. As a young music graduate Florence chose to sing from *Die Walküre* at the Sängerfest in Philadelphia, a performance she almost certainly recalled now, omitting to mention her near-paralysing attack of nerves. Thirty-five years later she incarnated herself as a Valkyrie to the thunder of approbation.

A typical Verdi Club season featured events for all times of day and dotted around the hotels of the city. The composer's birthday on 9 October was celebrated at a musical luncheon, whereafter the winter passed in a series of morning musicales, supper dances, *thés dansants* and celebrity breakfasts before the season reached its climax in the annual grand opera, pageant and ball and, finally, the Rose Breakfast at the Westchester Club, an opulent affair in which guests came in costume. Florence always wore pink and carried a shepherdess's crook. 'Important Note,' advised a club leaflet one April as the season closed: 'Verdi Club dues for next Season are due on April 5th. It will lighten the labors of your Treasurer if you will pay them promptly.' For one day only in late April the joining fee was waived to encourage new members to step forward.

As Florence choreographed her rise up the ranks of New York society, St Clair's career soldiered on. To supplement his income he taught drama at the Institute of United Arts in Riverside Drive. The special classes in drama he advertised incorporated theatre decoration and stage design, and offered lectures by an impressive roster of guest speakers that showed just how well connected St Clair was. Norman Bel Geddes was a stage designer who had worked with Max Reinhardt and Cecil B. DeMille (and was the father of Barbara Bel Geddes, later JR's wife in *Dallas*). Russian immigrant Josiah Zuro was a busy New York conductor who spent much of the 1920s in Hollywood composing film scores. Stark Young was the influential drama critic of the *New Republic*.

In early 1925 St Clair had a relatively rare streak of three consecutive jobs. The plays were typical of the sort of fare that New York audiences craved and producers supplied: comedies, and moralising melodramas with a British accent. *Lass O'Laughter* told of a young Scottish woman who rises into the peerage. John Galsworthy's *A Bit o' Love* dramatised the hounding by his congregation of a clergyman who allows his wife to leave him for the man she loves.

St Clair was frequently called upon to play British characters but he hadn't seen England since 1913. His steady income in 1925 may have helped him decide to spend that summer visiting relatives in Cheltenham. There was no question of Florence accompanying him. Her experience of sea travel in the juddering colossus SS *Deutschland* had put her off sailing for life. She was content to observe the ocean from the comfort of the Larchmont yacht club terrace. Nor did she have any feel for the natural world she sang about. The child who was once taken to her father's farm, and went camping in the Adirondacks, 'had no longing for the beauties of nature, trees, green fields, fresh air, the sea, the sun and the moon', St Clair later told his wife Kathleen. The bustle of the city was less appealing to St Clair as the motor car conquered New York. Before he sailed for England he voiced his concern in a letter to the *Times*. His theme was the rights of pedestrians given insufficient time to get across the road by the whistling cops who marshalled traffic coming from six directions, and the difficulty of catching a car without stepping into the road, thus risking injury and arrest for jaywalking.

Does the motorist ever consider that he sits in a firm seat
and moves by well-regulated machinery, while the pedestrian moves on 'shank's pony' [sic], a very uncertain carrier
for a body which has to be kept well balanced? He may
twist his ankle, have a sudden pain, trip, get a crick in the
back, become nervous, be distracted by the fearful noises
all round him, but the motorist as a rule does not leave
an inch of space for any such possibilities. The motorist
sits where he is protected from sun-glare, dust, rain,
wind. The pedestrian often moves from deep shadow to
glaring sunshine, sometimes cannot avoid having the sun
in his face; wind distracts him, rain and dust temporarily
blind him; does the motorist allow for such possibilities?
Not a bit of it.

St Clair had a Luddite's anxiety about the modern age. A
month in the sixteenth-century Plough Inn in Temple Guiting,
near Cheltenham, provided respite. His aunt and widowed
sister-in-law both lived in the same village. It was a long way
from the Seymour Hotel, the Ball of the Silver Skylarks and
the singing president. He sailed back to New York in late
August. (The trip was evidently to his taste, because he
returned two years later and again in 1928. Each time he
went there were fewer family members to greet him: two
aunts were dead by 1927 and in June 1928 he sailed to England on the day his mother died.)

The *Musical Courier* had the stiffest test yet of its journal-
istic integrity when invited to witness a recital given over
almost entirely to Florence's singing. The programme consisted of no fewer than a dozen arias and songs in an array of
languages calculated to display Florence's range of taste if not
ability. Spanish songs were the most natural fit, it was courte-
ously suggested: 'her high tones and animated way of singing

made effect'. Less effective, by implication, were her attempts at Mendelssohn and Handel or her flirtatious foray into the operatic stratosphere in Musetta's waltz from *La Bohème*. Being an intimate of the composer's sister, she even had a crack at a Novello tune. The list was 'sung with due appreciation of their musical contents, accompanied by facial expression of appropriate nature'. The report was accompanied by an out-of-date photograph of Florence in a low-cut satin evening dress, a long string of pearls hanging from her plump neck and a widely feathered hat atop a dark wig.

Florence was evidently thrilled by the results, because that evening she formed two associations that would last her for the rest of her singing career. The venue was a new one for her: the magnificent ballroom of the Ritz-Carlton. Her recitals there were to become an annual event. Meanwhile the only other soloist on the programme was a young pianist called Cosme McMoon, who performed his own compositions. He would be with her to the end. Among his unreliable recollections of the singing president was a suggestion that Florence's first solos with the Verdi Club were at the Silver Skylarks ball, when she would sing an aria during the intermission. No eyewitnesses mention such an event. And there is a hint of hyperbole in his explanation for the growing frequency of her performances. 'So great was the enthusiasm and the mirth that people clamoured for more,' he said. 'She was encouraged to sing more and more, both by professionals and laymen. There were a great many singers from the Metropolitan in this club and all these people, to kid her along, told her that she was the most wonderful singer that ever lived, and encouraged her that way.'

There is no independent account of Florence's singing in the 1920s. It can only be guessed that she never rose above the mediocre, and steadily deteriorated with age. But it is

difficult to credit that in her fifties she sang quite as catastrophically as she would later on. It was very difficult for
anyone to tell her the unvarnished truth: not Verdi Club
membership, not the many opera singers launched upon New
York thanks to Florence's patronage, not charities who profited from her fundraising, not journalists (real critics being
uninvited), certainly not St Clair. In whatever spirit they were
offered, Florence chose to believe every compliment and
accept every invitation. Some of these occasions were both
solemn and prestigious. In February 1927 she sang at the
195th anniversary of George Washington's birth.

As the Verdi Club approached its tenth anniversary Florence had cemented for herself an unassailable position at the
top table of New York society. Her tools were charm, taste,
money and influence. In May 1927 an interviewer from the
Morning Telegraph's Realm of Women page was admitted to
her apartment for an audience, to be confronted by the 'large
blue eyes that beamed with amiability'. Florence talked
about the Verdi Club's fundraising efforts for the Italian Red
Cross, the Veterans' Mountain Camp for soldiers wounded in
the war and, a recent addition, the charity for indigent theatre
professionals, the Actors' Fund of America (presumably
included at St Clair's suggestion). The interview was quietly
riddled with misinformation in which Florence disavowed her
past: she said she had been a New Yorker nearly all her life,
and recalled performing to audiences of ten thousand as a
child pianist, in the light of which her claim to have sung
twenty times that season invites caution. The paper printed a
stern photograph of Florence in a black mantilla. The caption
referred to her as a 'renowned musician'. In the circular world
of New York's society coverage, the *Musical Courier* reported
on this report with its 'most conspicuous picture'.

The interview was certainly on the members' lips as the

Verdi Club gathered later that month at the annual Rose Breakfast. The guests of honour included a countess and a princess from Italy, while the committee contained a baroness. But European blue blood allowed Florence precedence, who in the opening promenade – dubbed the March of the Roses – made her entrance flanked by four young girls carrying wands and rose baskets. Luncheon with a side order of musical performances cost $3.50 and bus tickets from the city centre a dollar. 'No covers laid until paid for,' advised the invitation.

These sums were paid in high numbers by the members of the Verdi Club even as the Wall Street Crash arrived in 1929. The society seemed to exist within a bubble, immune alike to the vulgarities of vaudeville, the blasts and parps of the jazz band and even thirteen years of Prohibition from 1920. The club's membership fed itself on other intoxicants: arias and flowers and usefulness. The Silver Skylarks Ball in March 1930, the first since the Crash, was as lavish as ever. There were guests from the army and navy, the French consul attended, and a souvenir programme contained a photograph of the president in a shimmering evening gown and an Egyptian headdress as well as portraits of the soloists and the ball committee. Two conductors were engaged, one to oversee a performance of Ermanno Wolf-Ferrari's one-act intermezzo *Il segreto di Susanna*, another to steer the orchestra and choir of women's voices performing Neapolitan songs. They were trained by Martha Attwood, who had sung Liù in *Turandot* at the Met two years previously. There were scenes from the life of Byron, and a staging of *Disraeli*, the hit play St Clair had performed professionally in 1913. First in the long list of participating members' names was that of the Verdi Club president, who the *Musical Courier*, ever ready to buff the image, had taken to calling Madame Jenkins. Last was 'St Clar

Bayfield', whose name the *Courier* had less compunction about spelling correctly. For her evening's work the president and founder got a diamond bracelet; her tireless helpmeet got a typo. That May, St Clair sailed home to England and didn't come back for four months.

9: LADY FLORENCE

On 7 November 1930 the death of Mary J. Hoagland Foster, 'widow of Hon. Charles Dorrance Foster, beloved mother of Florence Foster Jenkins', was announced in the *New York Times*. The funeral took place at Campbell's Funeral Church, a burial and cremation company on 66th Street and Broadway. On 10 November her body was interred in the family mausoleum in Wilkes-Barre. She had spent the last twenty years of her life in New York, living like Florence in a hotel apartment; first at the Waldorf-Astoria, later the Plaza.

Mrs Foster had used her widowhood to pursue her enthusiasms. Her paintings were exhibited in New York and beyond, and according to her obituary 'won many awards'. Her other hobby was accumulating memberships. She died a member of forty-two clubs and societies, many of them reflecting the stress laid by a young nation upon genealogical pedigree. The Eastern Star, the Huguenot Society, the Society of Virginia Antiquities, the National Society of Patriotic Women and the Society of Daughters of Holland Dames of New York could all count on her support. But the primary focus of her interest was always the Daughters of the American Revolution, meetings of which she continued to attend as a delegate to Washington. One of her last acts of philanthropy was to restore Fleming's Castle, the small tavern in her native New Jersey whose historic significance derived from a mention in George Washington's journal. In 1928 she donated it to a chapter of the D.A.R. which took its name from Colonel Lowrey, a non-combatant in 1776 from Mrs Foster's home town. The year before her death the Colonel Lowrey Chapter was invited en masse to a Verdi Club musicale at the Waldorf by Mrs Foster as she edged towards her eightieth or alternatively her ninetieth birthday, depending on which birth date is to be believed from what she told the US censuses between 1860 and 1910.

But her most personal gesture was inspired by her late daughter. To the Wyoming Historical and Genealogical Society, which tasked itself with preserving the records of local history in the valley, she made a donation of $5,000 in Lillian's name. She could of course afford it, but this was a far greater gesture in her daughter's memory than the $1,000 with which her husband endowed a church window in Wilkes-Barre. On Mrs Foster's death the society's trustees publicly resolved to send condolences to her surviving daughter.

Earlier in the year Mary Foster had been preceded to the grave by William Bulford, who inherited the family lands in 1909. He did well by the bequest. To his widow he left $150,000. To his brother George Bulford he left the farm, and the responsibility to continue paying Florence and her mother $300 each a year. Other Bulford relatives benefitted too from an estate which was valued in its entirety at $400,000, more than $150,000 in excess of Charles D. Foster's estate when he died.

Meanwhile, in the week of her mother's passing, Wilkes-Barreans were informed of the Verdi Club president's most recent recital, and a photograph which had appeared in the New York society columns. 'Mrs Jenkins's costumes,' the *Wilkes-Barre Times Leader* reported, 'were extraordinarily rich and costly, and the one in which she was pictured was Oriental, with pearl-seeded turban, earrings of cabochon stones, and a white silk brocade robe.' Even if the recital took place before Florence's bereavement, her old home town did not approve of this mode of display.

The death of Florence's mother brought the other half of her father's fortune into her possession. She therefore became twice as comfortable just as America plunged into the Great Depression. The jobless started to queue at Salvation Army soup kitchens and camp in Central Park shanty towns, while in 1931 nearly a hundred people starved to death in New York. Not all privileged New Yorkers noticed. 'I don't think I was aware of the poverty of the Thirties,' said writer and editor Claudia Stearns. Those who did have their eyes open saw that musicians were not immune. 'You'd be walking down the street,' recalled one eyewitness, 'and somebody would say, "See that guy there? He used to be with the New York Symphony . . ." They'd just be sittin' there dejected with a wine bottle in their hands.'

The immensely rich simply became a little less rich. 'We just don't have money the way people used to have it,' moaned Laurence Rockefeller. Various Vanderbilts and their ilk upped sticks from their burdensomely staffed palaces and moved into the big hotels. Further down the scale, people stopped employing maids. But the charity balls continued; the Metropolitan Opera remained a haven of conspicuous display. By one reckoning, the box holders on opening night had a collective wealth of nearly a billion dollars. Florence had a pair of tickets for the Met every Saturday evening in the season, but her finances did not qualify her for membership of this stratosphere. According to the calculation of an article on 'society and near-society' published in *America* in 1932, entrance into the New York *Social Register*, the elite directory of prominent families, was open to pretty much anyone who had an annual income of $20,000. Even in the 1940s Florence's income from her invested wealth was $12,000.

The 1930s was a period of great popularity for opera, even for those who couldn't afford the tickets. The first entire production was broadcast on American radio in 1931. Three years later *Four Saints in Three Acts*, written for an all-black cast by Virgil Thompson from a libretto by Gertrude Stein, became the longest-running opera in Broadway history. In the new age of celebrity, soprano superstars such as Geraldine Farrar and Lily Pons took opera towards the mainstream. And in 1940 an opera was telecast in the US for the first time.

Florence was sixty-one when her mother died, and her appetite to perform only sharpened. There was the discreetest hint of this when, six months later, the annual Rose Breakfast closed the Verdi Club's season at the Westchester Biltmore Country Club. After the Silver Skylarks Ball this was the most splendid event in the club's calendar, for which the committee solicited hostesses to help run things six months in advance. The club laid on coaches to ferry members and their guests to the gathering, which always opened with the floral pageant known as the March of the Roses. There was a prize for the best-dressed woman in this promenade which in 1931 was awarded to Henriette Wakefield of the Metropolitan Opera Company. Perhaps the prize was a gift for services secretly rendered.

Wakefield made her Met debut all the way back in 1907 and would go on to appear with the company nearly eight hundred times over just short of thirty years. She was by no means a name to sell tickets or take major roles. Among her many Wagnerian performances in 1912, for example, was Grimgerde, one of the nine Valkyries. Ten years later she had graduated to Waltraute, another of them. Another decade on she was still singing the role. But she had another clandestine occupation: Wakefield was Florence's vocal instructor.

How good or bad a musician was her pupil? Aside from the hired pianist seated at the Steinway in Florence's Seymour Hotel apartment, only St Clair Bayfield knew the identity of Florence's teacher. That Wakefield wished for no publicity implies that, long before the end, Florence's singing abilities were no more than modest. The comportment of those who came to see her perform suggested as much. The 1930s found the cult of the singing president develop from an intimate cabal of devoted Verdi Club ladies to something larger and unrulier. But not all audiences were the same.

By 1931 the principal building blocks of Florence's recital calendar for the rest of the decade were all in place. Each spring she went down to Washington, DC to entertain the members of the League of American Pen Women, set up in 1897 to support female writers and artists. (Florence would eventually be anointed president.) The year after its foundation in 1936, she sang for the Order of the Three Crusades, open to those who, like Florence, could trace their ancestry back to the early crusaders; a senator and a major-general were among the audience. With the eminent organist Malton Boyce supplying discreet accompaniment, in St Clair Bayfield's estimation these were the most successful of her annual engagements. The audience consisted of hand-picked insiders from the upper echelons of Washington society – including family members. These visits to the capital gave Florence a chance to resume relations with her sisters-in-law. In 1931 she gave a luncheon for fourteen guests, among them not only Alice Thornton Jenkins but also Frank's youngest sisters whom she first knew in the 1880s as Nettie and Carrie. Nettie turned seventy that year. Florence was still keen to brag about a family connection which resonated in the capital: the *Star* reminded readers who her father-in-law was.

Another annual tradition was inaugurated in Newport, Rhode Island. At the end of the summer holiday in 1931, Florence performed in the rooms of the Newport Historical Society. For several years she shared the bill with Leila Hearne Cannes, a pianist who was good enough to have her own featured hour on the radio in the late 1920s. She was also a fellow president, in her case of the Women's Philharmonic Society, founded at the turn of the century to make musical performance accessible to the poorer parts of New York. 'Both are artists of ability, quite at home with the best music,' cooed the *Newport Mercury and Weekly News* reporter who 'much enjoyed' their concert in 1932. Florence brought along her own accompanist in the shape of Edwin McArthur.

McArthur was a young Juilliard-trained pianist from Denver who in 1928 was barely twenty-one when Florence heard him performing at the Barbizon Hotel, a recently opened residence for professional women. She invited him for an interview at her apartment; it presumably took the form of an audition in which he had to accompany her. In 1930 he married and, like many who drifted into her orbit, was grateful for the work. 'I got many engagements through our association,' he said in an interview nearly twenty years after her death. He also attested that Florence was 'intelligent and well-informed'.

Florence gave two or three concerts a year at Sherry's Hotel on Park Avenue, one showcasing living American composers, another in honour of Poetry Week, one for the Society of New York State Women (when 'many encores were demanded'). But the summit of her annual round remained her Verdi Club recital. A club pamphlet which previewed forthcoming offerings ended with the promise – upper case as ever to the fore – that 'features of the season will include a Song Recital given by the President in the Grand Ball Room of the Ritz-Carlton'. At the event itself, the *Musical Courier* was always on hand to serve up a pen portrait that showed Florence in the best possible light. The wording would deftly steer a diplomatic course between trading in outright false-hood and keeping a toehold in truth. A 'brilliant' audience 'heard and applauded' and 'paid homage to president-soprano-hostess Jenkins, for in this triangular role she regally filled each part. It was the consensus of opinion that she never sang better.' That was in 1930. 'The musico-social affair invariably finds a large audience,' it advised a year later, when the applause was 'cordial'. 'Doubtless the Blue Danube waltz, with its trills and staccato, and "Clavelitos" provided the most enjoyment.' A reader in the know might pick up encrypted signals that the writer was tipping them the wink. 'The pres-ence of various presidents of women's clubs, of prominent musical and society folk, all combined to make the recital highly successful.' The write-ups could be taken at face value, or understood to mean something more subversive.

Florence's repertoire was an eclectic grab-bag that dis-played great knowledge, ranging from baroque via grand opera to folksy modern tunes. As embodied in the two masks on the Verdi Club emblem, she commuted between tragedy and comedy. Technical difficulties held no fear for Florence. If anything they spurred her on. In 1930 she launched an undaunted assault on 'Elsa's Dream' from *Lohengrin*. Having already introduced songs by Strauss into her programmes, in due course she became only the second soprano in New York to sing Zerbinetta's aria from *Ariadne auf Naxos*. Her rendition was 'flowing and melodious,' said one reviewer, 'broken by an elaborate, coloratura cadenza climaxing in a high D'.

Florence's pursuit of altitude was a matter of personal pride. A singer who hit the high notes attracted notice. In 1930, starring in Gershwin's *Girl Crazy* on Broadway, Ethel Merman sensationally held a high C for sixteen bars. While New Yorkers watched successive skyscrapers climb ever further away from the gathering poverty in the streets below, Florence practised in the hope of surpassing her own personal peaks. Her high B flats, high Cs and high Ds had something in common with King Kong scrambling to the spire of the just finished Empire State Building.

The repertoire's expansion over the years shows the volume of work she undertook to learn and practise new songs and arias. Indeed she was often complimented for her taste and for her industry. At her Newport recital in 1932 she presented songs 'of the sort to be appreciated by those who know music when they hear it, for only those who are talented and have been carefully and skilfully instructed, and have done much conscientious work themselves, could present such a program as this'. Florence was nonchalant about scaling the perilous summits of Italian opera: she warbled her way through 'Una voce poco fa' from *Il barbiere di Seviglia* and 'Vissi d'arte' from *Tosca*; she even roused the ghost of Verdi with her lovestruck version of Violetta's 'Ah, fors'è lui' from *La traviata*. As the decade continued she started inserting little commentaries into her programmes – lavish productions in red ink printed on expensive silvered paper – which blithely solicited comparison with those who had gone before. When she took on Chapi's 'Las hijas del Zebedeo' she advised that 'its sparkling words, its fiery rhythm, and withal its authentic Spanish grace, have made this song a favorite parade ground of the great sopranos since the inimitable Garcia and Louisa [sic: her name was Luisa] Tetrazzini.'

Florence was a singer for all moods and occasions: she

attempted the stately (Gounod's 'Ave Maria') and the numinous (Gluck's 'Divinités du Styx'), lauded the almighty in Mozart's 'Alleluia' and Bach's 'Jubilate', and threw caution to the wind at the frenetic end of the repertoire, most audaciously of all in 'Clavelitos', a Spanish *zarzuela* sung at breakneck pace. Her rendition of Carl Gilberté's 'Laughing Song' was replete with high hoots and coloratura cackles. And in her late sixties she could also unblushingly play the fragrant innocent in 'The Virgin's Slumber Song'.

She was particularly attracted to songs which invoked a congruence between the soprano voice and the airborne twitterings of the bird kingdom: she sang of canaries and doves, larks and nightingales. The unintended irony was not lost on the audience when she sang a song called 'Charmant Oiseau' which was 'interrupted by applause, for antiphonal and piquant singing stirred the hearers'. She even sang of wild geese, which was 'especiall [sic] to those who are thrilled by the wild, free notes of these birds,' said a reviewer perhaps reminded all too clearly of a goose's squawks. And if a song floated free into the realm of the wordless, Florence would gamely give chase. A staple of hers was 'Song Without Words' by contemporary Dutch-American composer Richard Hageman (who would have a big hit composing the soundtrack to *Stagecoach* in 1939). It fetched up on a high D. Above all, her assault on Delibes's 'Indian Bell Song' from *Lakmé* was destined to be preserved for the appreciation of posterity.

But then Florence always accelerated with purblind enthusiasm towards a challenge. She explained with relish that Mozart's 'No, no, che non sei capace' was composed for his sister-in-law 'with whom at one time he had been in love but now detested, so as House-Composer compelled to write for her, he tried to make the aria impossibly difficult to sing'. She was hardly likely to duck that one. Languages did not present any obstacle either: she sang suites of songs in French, German, Italian, Russian, and even ventured fearlessly into the polysyllabic minefield that is Hungarian, accompanied by a Hungarian pianist who coached her linguistically. She had a special weakness for the drama and sexual heat of Hispanic music. Her programmes frequently offered Spanish and Mexican songs that found her flirting and swooning and sort of strutting.

The dramatic comedy of Madame Jenkins in performance had a visual element too. Many years of dressing up for the Verdi Club tableaux vivants had given her a taste for fancy dress. In each recital the stage was ceded to the pianist or to an ensemble of Italian-American brothers who called themselves the Pascarella Chamber Music Society. While they played, Florence had time to pull on a new costume backstage – a sultry Mexican temptress in a sombrero, or a Russian peasant, or Hungarian national dress with flowers in her hairpiece. And she was a great believer in the power of props: a fan, a parasol, a spinning wheel for the garden scene from *Faust* (which was stored at St Clair's apartment), a basket of carnations for 'Clavelitos' whose contents she would fling into the audience. The effect was topped off by her slapdash misapplication of make-up – lipstick smeared, rouge overdone.

In each song she drew on her Philadelphia training to sell the story, but her style of delivery learned in youth was not necessarily suited to a woman advancing into old age. 'Her gestures and expressions were just as funny as her singing,' recalled Adolf Pollitz, a German immigrant who joined the Verdi Club as a young pianist. 'She added histrionics to every number,' recalled Cosme McMoon, 'generally acting the action, if it were an aria, or other appropriate action if it were a descriptive song, or else she would go into different dances during these numbers, which were extremely hilarious.'

Quite how unpromising a clotheshorse an elderly Florence must have seemed onstage is suggested by a set of photographs commissioned for *Life* magazine's regular 'Life Goes to a Party' feature. They were taken by Margaret Bourke-White in 1937 at one of Florence's Seymour Hotel soirées (though never published). A dozen guests in conventional evening dress mustered in her drawing room, including the caricaturist Al Hirschfield. It was an abstemious gathering: no one had a drink in their hand. Florence changed halfway through the evening from a floral print dress accessorised with scarves, jewels and a headdress to a carpet-sweeping gown which all too faithfully hugged her contours. Both were silk. In some of the images Florence is standing among her politely rapt guests singing, her eyes sometimes closing, her hands clasped in an attitude of prayer. In one photograph two middle-aged women were captured in the act of helping Florence out of a chair.

It was on a night such as this that one witness peered into the bathroom off the long dark corridor leading to the drawing room, and saw the bathtub filled with a vast quantity of potato salad. When Florence catered, she catered in bulk. (For herself, she was a devotee of sandwiches and Manhattans.) A more permanent quirk of her apartment was a collection of upright dining chairs in which eminent Americans had supposedly breathed their last. People tending to die in their beds rather than at dinner, this has the look of another tall story. But through her various genealogical memberships, Florence would have had privileged access to the furniture of deceased generals, senators and judges and thus been able to pursue this arcane interest. Perhaps the collection included the chair of her father-in-law, the rear admiral.

Verdi Club concerts were free to the members but tickets could be bought by the public, which meant that audiences soon started to swell with non-loyalists who had never been to a Silver Skylark ball or a Rose Breakfast. Word spread in the early 1930s about the unique phenomenon of the singing president. In 1934 the audience contained a rogue element who paid $2 for a guest ticket, made their way to the back of the auditorium and laughed their heads off. New York critics were not invited to the concerts but a journalist (from an unidentified publication) snuck in to witness the event and broke cover in a short satirical sketch. It briefly outlined the history of the recitals and explained the source of Florence's inherited wealth.

'Mrs Jenkins,' it calculated, 'is well able to pay for the hall. Last week she hired the ballroom of the Ritz-Carlton Hotel and smartly dressed New Yorkers fairly fought for tickets to get in and see Florence Foster Jenkins perform.' There was a description of her appearance in flaming velvet, her wig a pile of blonde ringlets, before the report moved on to the music. Florence began with two Brahms lieder. For 'Die Mainacht', the programme printed the composer's admonition to the soloist: 'O singer, if thou canst not dream, leave this song unsung.' This was tempting fate. 'Mrs Jenkins could dream if she could not sing,' snarked the reviewer. The next song was titled no more propitiously: 'With her hands clasped to her heart she passed on to "Vergebliches Standchen", which she had labeled "The Serenade in Vain".' The audience, 'as Mrs Jenkins's audiences invariably do, behaved very badly. In the back of the hall men and women in full evening dress made no attempt to control their laughter.' For the first time in print, someone had said it: Florence Foster Jenkins was a joke.

As a result, Florence in her own quaintly naive way attempted to gag the press. 'Are you a . . . a newspaperman?' she once asked a suspect gentleman who personally applied for tickets at her apartment. 'No, Madame Jenkins,' he replied. 'A music-lover.' 'Very well,' she said. 'Two-fifty each, please. Now would you like some sherry?'

The recitals acquired a cult popularity. In St Clair's estimation this was down to what he called her 'star quality'. This was something he knew about, having observed it at close quarters in the theatre – he certainly didn't have it himself. 'On the stage a person will draw the attention of the whole audience,' he explained. 'There is something about her personality that makes everyone look at her with relish. That is what my wife had.'

In 1930 there were three hundred in the audience, but when word spread the number swelled to eight hundred. In 1935 there was standing room only as the *Musical Courier's* account of the evening became a little less coded. 'Outbursts of applause punctuated the items presented' was another way of saying that the clapping interrupted the singing. This increasingly happened at Florence's recitals: applause was deployed as a way of shrouding guffaws which could not be stifled. McArthur once saw a man stuff his handkerchief into his mouth and roll out of his chair onto the floor.

'Don't go away,' she would say at the end of a set of songs. 'I'll be right back.' Nobody was going anywhere. The cheers were appreciative and even sincere. Madame Jenkins needed no encouragement, but she got it anyway. 'A frequently wildly applauding audience left no doubt of the enjoyment derived by the throng.' In 1936 the 'eagerly awaited' concert was watched by the *New York World-Telegram* and 'a large and highly responsive audience'. Next year the paper was back to hear Florence.

> Of course, with due respect to the other artists, the audience had really come to hear the stylistic and inimitable song-readings of Mme Jenkins. And, to tell the truth,

there was more than gratification for all the listeners present. Mme Jenkins's art is many-faceted. It makes no specialty of any one composition or, for that matter, of any one composer. Witness the exacting – not to say exhausting – list of offerings the soprano had chosen for herself. Needless to state, Mme Jenkins gave her interpretative abilities full and untrammeled sway . . . and that it was so was attested to by the cataract of audible sounds from the hearers that greeted her at practically every one of her nonchalantly tossed off phrases and again by the torrent of applause that followed every selection.

So her Ritz-Carlton concerts were rowdy affairs, but rarely did the behaviour of her spectators take on a malicious flavour. According to McMoon, 'the audience nearly always tried not to hurt her feelings by outright laughing, so they developed a convention that whenever she came to a particularly excruciating discord or something like that, where they had to laugh, they burst into these salvos of applause and whistles and the noise was so great that they could laugh at liberty.'

St Clair's memory was different, that the misbehaviour stemmed from the enmity of aspiring singers whom she had not booked for the Verdi Club. 'Many artists had it in for her,' he said. 'She couldn't hire everyone, so those she didn't hire for the concerts she sponsored became jealous. They formed a little claque that went to her concerts to laugh.' Increasingly St Clair made it his business to police the auditorium. 'I tried to keep them out. At one concert I ordered that no one be allowed in the gallery except those to whom we had given free tickets. We gave many tickets away. When the concert began, the guying started. It came from the gallery. I went up and told those people they had no right to guy when they were guests of the artists. People are so ignorant.' It was perhaps to discourage misconduct that in the late 1930s the recitals started to omit the intermission.

But the ignorance was more a question of behaviour than of judgement; even St Clair could not defend Florence to the hilt. 'She had perfect rhythm,' he said. 'Her interpretation was good and her languages wonderful. She had the star quality. You could feel that in the applause. People may have laughed at her singing, but the applause was real. She was a natural-born musician. But instrument, there was very little instrument.' His euphemistic appraisal was not open to misinterpretation: even St Clair knew Florence could not sing.

However absurd she may have seemed as a singer, or as the costumed chatelaine of the Silver Skylark tableaux vivants making her climactic appearance, Florence knew how to charm and persuade. Principally through her tireless leadership, the Verdi Club had jostled a position for itself as a significant presence in New York. In 1933 Florence's annual recital at the Ritz-Carlton with the Pascarella Chamber Music Society was sandwiched in the *New York Times*'s concert listings between two performances by the New York Philharmonic conducted by Bruno Walter in Carnegie Hall. The following year her concert was announced in the same column as others involving Jascha Heifetz, Paul Robeson and Otto Klemperer. Another year a Verdi Club recital was listed in the same column inches as news of Prokofiev and Enescu conducting in New York.

Meanwhile leading sopranos beat a path to the club's door. In March 1932 the Swedish dramatic soprano Göta Ljungberg inspired an ecstatic review from the *Times* singing Isolde in her debut season at the Met (whose audience 'applauded and recalled her . . . with a fervor that had not attended any Metropolitan performance of this work in years'). In November

Ljungberg opened the new season at the Verdi Club. She signed her photograph in the programme 'to Mme Florence Foster Jenkins: with love and sincere admiration'. Then there was Elda Vettori, an Italian-born former hatshop girl from St Louis who made her Met debut in 1926 (to 'deafening and insistent applause'). She went on to sing Aida and, opposite Antonio Scotti, Tosca. She hailed Madame Jenkins as an 'incomparable woman and artiste' and 'an inestimable friend to all worthy musicians', and offered her 'warmest appreciation of your extraordinary accomplishments'. 'To the lovely and gifted Lady Florence Foster Jenkins,' said Texan soprano Leonora Corona, another Met Aida. This stream of bouquets cannot have failed to add another ring of steel to Florence's adamantine self-belief.

To such a generous patron of the arts, the acquisition of what sounded like an aristocratic English title will have felt like a comfortable fit. She had the decency to deploy inverted commas, as if aware of the transgression. 'Happy Easter! To Charlie and Betty with love from "Lady Florence".' To her accompanist she wrote, 'To the very best accompanist Edwin McArthur and his charming wife Blanche. With my love from "Lady Florence" July 19th, 32.'

The exchange and mart system of patronage and flattery by which Florence profited extended from soloists to composers. New compositions came her way from the likes of Charles Haubiel ('Song'), Elmer Russ ('The Ant and the Grasshopper') and Luigi Dell'Orefice ('Notte'). A programme note would clarify that they were 'dedicated to Mme Jenkins'. Sometimes her accompanist would be unseated so that the composer could leap onstage and play along with the soloist. One such was Grace Bush, whose 'Spring Gladness' offered 'opportunity for the exuberant style of Mme Jenkins' according to the *Musical Courier*. Most egregiously, Louis Drakeford wrote a piece called 'Your Slave Am I'. At a certain point Florence turned to writing lyrics herself, the first of which McMoon either offered or consented to set to music. Premiered in Newport in 1933, the piece took the name of 'Trysting Time'.

> Beneath a rare June moon,
> In the fragrant leafy cove
> Of a bower of honeysuckle,
> I'm waiting for my love.
>
> And mem'ries, Ah, so tender,
> That crowd my reverie,
> Seem softly to be whisper'd
> By the murmur of the sea.
>
> Oh, hours of weary waiting
> By the cliffs that gauntly tower,
> So lonely and so beauteous
> Stilled by the rock's majestic power.
>
> And then, and then,
> At last, your arms around me
> The rain of kisses on my lips,
> Your dark eyes burning into mine,
> The world forgot, my soul complete.

Hearing these sentiments people had no choice but to clap. Later, Adolf Pollitz brought Florence a bunch of trailing arbutuses from his home in Oyster Bay, and she was inspired to write a song in memory of a wintry equestrian outing with her now dead and buried father to find the rare flower. 'The scent of Arbutus fills the air,' she concluded. 'To my aching heart, it brings a message, Of hope and joy, to the love that is there.' Elmer Russ, who was a very successful composer, set it to music.

Florence migrated between pianists, all of whom were

tasked with keeping a straight face and supplying sympathetic accompaniment. None of them was exposed to her over a longer period than McMoon. At some point after his death a rumour bloomed that McMoon was actually an exotic pseudonym behind which Edwin McArthur protected his identity and his dignity as he played for Florence. It's true that McMoon was an invented surname. He was born Cosme McMunn in 1901 in a small town in the Mexican state of Durango. His father, whose parents emigrated during the great potato famine, was of Irish descent. The McMunns were uprooted again in 1911: to escape the revolution in Mexico, they moved to San Antonio in Texas. Unlike the rest of the family, the young Cosme gave his name a charismatic tweak, perhaps to encourage the pronunciation he'd grown up with in Mexico. As an eighteen-year-old with a new surname he started appearing in local recitals in the summer of 1919; he had the chutzpah to unveil a composition of his own in a recital also offering Chopin, Brahms, Grieg and Liszt. He soon made for New York where in 1922 the *Musical Courier* caught him in performance and predicted 'a bright future . . . He has real talent and, in addition, a pleasing stage appearance.'

In his recollection, McMoon met Florence socially about a year before the death of Mrs Foster. In fact he performed as a guest soloist at her first Ritz-Carlton recital several years earlier in 1925. His contribution drew on his origins: he performed a Mexican tune called 'Jarabe' and a waltz of his own creation which he titled 'Dolores'. In 1931 he played the song again when Florence was invited to give a recital at the home of friends in Fayetteville in upstate New York. By now McMoon was one of her regular accompanists and he had written a Spanish song of which she was, naturally, the dedicatee. (Consistent with the unspoken arrangement by which invitations were reciprocated, their hostess that evening was Claire Alcee, a singer who would open the season for the Verdi Club a month later.)

It wasn't easy for any of Florence's accompanists but some kept their dignity better than others. When she was performing the Jewel Song from *Faust* at her recital in 1934, at a certain point the lighting fell on McArthur in such a way that the audience laughed. Whatever he'd done by accident to stimulate the laugh he did again by design. Florence was furious. 'I suppose you won't have anything to do with me now,' he said. 'I certainly will not!' she replied.

Almost instantly McArthur traded up. In February 1935 the Norwegian dramatic soprano Kirsten Flagstad made her debut at the Met as Sieglinde in *Die Walküre*. It was broadcast all over America, as were other performances which established her as the world's leading Wagnerian soprano. Her popularity was such that she could rake in huge sums for the indigent Met when appealing for donations during broadcast intermissions. McArthur applied for the post as her accompanist and was promptly hired to tour with her, later becoming her conductor too, with whom she insisted upon working all the way through to her retirement. From Jenkins to Flagstad – no sopranos' accompanist has ever made a more antipodean transition from the ridiculous to the sublime.

McMoon also struggled. 'It wasn't only trying to keep a straight face, but she would leave out whole parts of a song unexpectedly. You were always hard put to follow her.' Others found that McMoon milked the concerts for comedy. 'I thought it was terrible,' remembered Verdi Club member Florence Malcolm Darnault. 'He was paid as an accompanist and then laughed while he played the accompaniment and winked at the audience. He lived on her, she gave him everything.'

Darnault had a pivotal role to play in what was both the

greatest and the most revealing moment in the Verdi Club's history. Since the death of Caruso, much the grandest figure to drift into the orbit of the club was the Italian conductor Arturo Toscanini, whose latest sojourn in America coincided with his disenchantment with Fascism in his native Italy. The conductor's political sympathies were not necessarily shared by the predominantly Republican world of women's clubs. One *New Yorker* cartoon by Helen Hokinson, whose speciality was twitting the activities of the clubs, depicted a president addressing the members thus: 'The vote is now fifteen to one that we deplore Mussolini's attitude. I think it would be nice if we could go on record as *unanimously* deploring Mussolini's attitude.' Among those not deploring his attitude would have been Florence. When the National Fascist Militia Band arrived from Rome for a long tour in 1934, touting themselves as 'ambassadors of goodwill uniting the musical hearts of America and Italy', she was one of the sixteen honorary patrons for their Carnegie Hall concert in August.

That year Toscanini attended the grand unveiling of a new bronze portrait of Verdi by Darnault. He was joined in the ballroom of the Plaza by the Italian consul general and Baroness Katharine Evans von Klenner, an elderly doyenne of music education who picked up the title when she married an Austrian diplomat. Darnault was not yet thirty, and it should have been a career high to have her work shown in such company, but it was marred by what she later called 'the worst thing that ever happened'.

I was excited. It was going to be a very nice unveiling and a lot of people were there who were friends of mine. They came and told me to come onstage right away because they were going to have the unveiling and I said, 'Well, where is Mrs. Jenkins?' 'She's in that room there.' I went off the stage and there's the room where people get ready. I opened the door and looked in and there she was. Half naked. Sitting there without a thing and her wig was sitting there alongside on the table. She was completely bald. Completely shiny. I just couldn't believe it. But completely shiny. She was polished. I was so embarrassed because I'd seen it and now she knew it. She saw me in the mirror. She gave a yell [. . .] I never said a word about it to her.

Darnault's bronze showed the composer in the Grecian style, with bare shoulders. The bust was mounted on a modernist base with a thickly whorled surface. A fan hailed the new work in the *Times*: 'Since seeing it I have felt that there is hope for American art . . . that America was really coming into an art of its own, for the sculptor appeared young and represented today. If that is the art of today, then we are having a great day.' Darnault duly picked up other commissions. At the end of the same year her portrait of the Broadway producer Daniel Frohman, brother of the late Charles, was gifted to the Actors Fund of America. In a speech at the unveiling St Clair was one of the actors paying tribute to Frohman, who was sufficiently moved to commission a bust of his brother from Darnault. Florence, having recovered from Darnault's visit to her dressing room, attended a reception Frohman held for the sculptress before its completion. And yet according to Kathleen Bayfield, Darnault was never paid the $2,000 due to her for her bust of Verdi.

Among those who knew her, Florence's stinginess was by now an accepted fact. By the 1940s her investments gave her an income of $12,000 a year, from which she paid $2,000 to run the Verdi Club; the rent on her apartment in the Seymour cost her $330 a month, and St Clair's apartment was a further

$1,050 a year. These, claimed St Clair, were her only extrav-
agances. 'Instead of sitting back with a French maid and a
chauffeur and going to swell restaurants,' he said, 'she econo-
mised all the time so she would have enough money for her
clubs.' Others with a less rose-tinted perspective took a
harsher line. 'As far as money was concerned Mrs Jenkins was
tricky,' Darnault recalled. 'She was very careful about money.'
Darnault remembered once buying a coat for $12 which Flor-
ence admired. 'She called me up, and she said to me, "Have
you heard about those coats?" I said, "Yes, I have one." I had
bought one and I fooled everybody, so I said, "Well, I'll show
it to you," and she said, "Oh, that's stunning, a beautiful coat."
And she went and bought one and she wore it everywhere,
and everybody thought it was fur.' Florence didn't disabuse
them. (According to Darnault, Florence was a dowdy dresser
who 'just didn't know how to put things together. She never
looked smart.')

In Darnault's experience Madame Jenkins was evasive
when it came to picking up bills too. 'She'd say, "Let's get a
cab," and she'd always get me or anybody else to pay the bill,
always, always. And I got so that I'd never, never go out. She'd
ask me to come to lunch, but she never paid, never. She had
asked me to lunch one day, and we had lunch in a very nice
restaurant in a very good hotel. And then she got a phone call,
and she went to answer the phone. She sent the bellboy back
saying she just had to rush.'

For all her personal charm – Darnault 'never heard her say
a mean thing about a human being' – Florence was deeply
untrusting, particularly of those in professions where trust
was an essential element of the relationship. Her suspicion
of lawyers was rooted in the trauma of her father's will case
but also perhaps in a deeper ambivalence about her father
himself, who for a long time she feared had disinherited her.

It found expression in the sheer number of law firms she instructed between 1913 and 1944. Although she was nominally Episcopalian, and came of devout stock, ministers of the church earned her disapproval too. As for dentists, 'They're the biggest frauds of all,' she once said. And perhaps thanks to her experience of marriage, she had very low esteem for the medical profession.

Once, she noticed Adolf Pollitz talking to her about something to do with club business with his eyes closed. 'You closed your eyes!' she exclaimed in disbelief. Florence kept her searching blue eyes open all the time. 'She didn't trust,' said Pollitz. 'She watched all the time.' Both he and Darnault suspected that she didn't even trust St Clair.

In fact she had some reason. Until the end of her life Florence was able to count on St Clair's devotion. She held him utterly in her sway. He was expected to dine with her at six o'clock sharp, and he often accompanied her to the Met on Saturday nights. He ran errands for her and acted as her manager, wrote press releases, booked venues and even engaged the ushers for her Ritz-Carlton recitals. Most importantly, he was the creative director of her empire. It was St Clair's long experience in the field, and his ability to recruit volunteers from professional theatre, which gave the Verdi Club's operatic evenings and endless parade of tableaux vivants a patina of artistic credibility.

In 1932 St Clair met and fell in love with an Englishwoman called Kathleen Weatherley. Nearly a quarter of a century his junior, Kathleen was born in St Pancras in 1899 and brought up in Surrey by her widowed mother; her father, an insurance underwriter, died when she was six. She worked as a music teacher until, needing a change in her early thirties, she volunteered for an organisation which sent missionaries around

Canada. The Caravan Mission was the creation of a formidable spinster from the north of England called Eva Hasell. With only a lifelong companion for support, Miss Hasell marshalled a fleet of Ford vans which took Christian succour into the furthest rural reaches of the vast Canadian landmass. She spent the winter recruiting in England and beyond – two women per truck, one of them required to be strong enough to handle the vehicle over off-road terrain. Kathleen was one of a large group of ladies whose passage was paid for by Miss Hasell in May 1931.

The same month, nearly three decades on from his first appearance in *Everyman*, St Clair joined an eighteen-strong reunion of the Ben Greet Players for a charity performance of *A Midsummer Night's Dream*. It went so well at the American Women's Association, with a string quartet supplying snippets of Mendelssohn's music for the *Dream*, that the whole thing was done again twice in July at the George Washington Stadium with the New York Orchestra. St Clair spent the rest of that summer in England. At a certain point after her summer duties were done, Kathleen gravitated towards New York. There she had Australian friends who gave a tea party to which St Clair was also invited.

By the time St Clair met Kathleen, what passed for ardour in his relationship with Florence had eased and the separate living quarters at West 37th Street which she paid for and he lived in now became a convenient hideaway in which to conduct this new liaison. After Florence's death St Clair explained away the oddity of two separate apartments for an allegedly married couple as an escape for both of them. 'It was our retiring place where we got away from the telephone and railroad tactics of the Seymour,' he said. 'The phone was always ringing there. My wife had connections with more than three thousand people.' But he overstated the frequency of Florence's visits, and her absence now worked to his advantage.

He called her Kay and she called him Bay. Kathleen was tall and thin but otherwise her attraction for St Clair was not dissimilar to Florence's: she too had a domineering personality. It wasn't quite domineering enough to persuade St Clair to break with Florence. He simply didn't have the strength of character to cut himself off from the privileged access to high society that Florence provided, while Florence in turn insisted he continue in his role as her escort and artistic director. If anything, his commitment to the Verdi Club's annual jamboree increased after he met Kathleen. In 1933 he wrote, directed and acted in a play called *The Dream of King Henry VIII*, in which six matrons of the Verdi Club played the king's wives. It was adjudged 'imaginative and poetic to a high degree' by the *Musical Courier*. In 1934 he wrote a paean to the American revolution called *A Romance of '76*. In 1935 he adapted Schiller's *Mary Queen of Scots*. The spectacular tableaux vivants were as ever his artistic dominion and responsibility. He also popped up elsewhere. In 1937 at Florence's Newport recital he read from *As You Like It*, shared stories of the great actors with whom he had been associated and recited verses he'd written as a disenchanted young man eager to run off and join the circus.

And his personal commitment to Florence did not waver throughout the decade. His 1939 diary reveals a routine that was built principally around Florence, interspersed with a supporting role for Kathleen alongside fleeting references to Chamberlain and Hitler. Florence is referred to in the diary as B (for Brownie). 'January 20th. Wrote Kay. B & self dined City Club. A very delightful quiet evening. January 21st. With B to *Cavalleria* and *Pagliacci* at Metropolitan which we enjoyed very much. January 22nd. Lunch with B. B at dinner.

January 23rd. Quiet evening with B.' Kathleen was occasionally out of town but whenever she was in New York the diary looks like the journal of an affair narrated in code. 'K arrived . . . Lunch K . . . K called late . . . Walked in park with K . . . Tea with K.' One night Kathleen went 'as substitute for B to Carnegie Hall'. But the abbreviations and gnomic annotations cannot hide the bias of his loyalty. Next to 'B looking well and so glad of that' on 19 March, St Clair drew a heart. There is only one sign of discord: a few days before Germany invaded Poland, when he was performing in Provincetown, he received an 'angry letter from B'. He was always on hand for the big events. 'March 9th. Verdi Club "Ball of the Silver Skylark" went off very well . . . July 19th. Took B's Birthday presents.' And most loyally of all, whatever he later said in interviews after Florence's death, in the privacy of his diary he revealed an unshakeable conviction that her singing more than passed muster. 'B sang well last night . . . B sang extremely well . . . Heard B singing – very good . . . B sang delightfully at night. B sang better than ever in public. Floral tributes. A triumph for B.' And then at the end of the year, 'B sang at night but became very exhausted and alarmed me.'

St Clair's concern for Florence's health seems not to have been reciprocated. He was often ill in 1939, either generally off colour or with a swollen left side of his face, but made no note of her concern for him. The discrepancy in their status was at its starkest in the heat of summer. As she got older she rented an air-conditioned apartment at the Shelton Hotel in Lexington Avenue, while still maintaining her Seymour Hotel apartment and allowing St Clair to roast on West 37th Street. Previously when the season ended, and before the Wall Street Crash, he had the funds to escape to England to stroll around the Cotswolds and recharge. But St Clair didn't go home again after 1931, not even when his father died in a London hospital in April 1937. It was just as well that he was keen on exercise, because as often as not he would follow Florence to the ocean where she'd stay in the Westchester Club while he rented a modest room as close by as he could afford. One entry in his diary during the Depression offered a grim vignette of the distribution of power between them: 'It was a long, hot walk up to the Westchester Club, two miles.' A similar situation would arise when she moved to Newport for her annual concert. Florence would stay with wealthy friends in hotels or the resort's well-appointed cottages, while St Clair would languish in a rooming house. At least the ocean enabled him to swim great distances.

And so St Clair lived a second secret life. While his own common-law wife denied him in public, he had to ensure she did not discover his new relationship with a woman more than three decades her junior. They were safest away on furtive trips out of town. A photograph of them together taken beside the ocean shows the couple in their bathing costumes – a two-tone belted singlet for him, a floral one-piece for her. Kathleen is perched on St Clair's shoulders, her feet and calves tucked behind his back. They smile brightly for the camera. St Clair is a lean, scraggy figure with pipe-cleaner legs, a high forehead with light hair and always those protruding ears. Kathleen is svelte with narrow shoulders, slender legs and an oval face with short brown hair. She is wearing a thick necklace of beads or shells. They look physically intimate.

Florence paid rare visits to St Clair's flat and on one near-disastrous occasion Kathleen was there. 'He had risked much to have me to his apartment,' she recalled. 'It was July 4th weekend and hot as hell. Suddenly the doorbell rang at his apartment at 7am. He knew instinctively what it was; quickly he told me to get into the closet leading out of the north room. It was all jumbled up with Verdi Club theatricals. As she came in he suddenly spied my very pretty green leather mules under the bed, but he stood in front of them. She only visited for about five minutes. It was the worst I've ever experienced. For him it would have been agony if she had found out, though he always said she was psychic . . . I knew that if anything happened he would desert me at once. He was absolutely tied to her by an umbilical cord.'

After five years Kathleen's inability to prise St Clair away from Florence's clutches drove her back to England – it's not clear for how long – but she returned to the US in the summer of 1937. If Florence knew about her rival, those in her circle in the Verdi Club were never vouchsafed a hint from her. Adolf Pollitz was convinced that she knew all about St Clair and Kathleen but was content to turn a blind eye so long as there was no public scandal. No matter the double standard this position entailed. After the outbreak of the Second World War, when Kathleen was heading back to Britain to enlist, Florence told a member of the Verdi Club that St Clair had an English friend who was joining up. The member replied that he expected every loyal Englishman would follow suit. 'It isn't a man, it's a woman,' came the tart reply. 'And I hope the boat sinks!'

Kathleen once went to a Verdi Club ball and took along some British merchant seamen in uniform. 'He [St Clair] said I should be lost amongst the crowd and not observed and he could have a dance with me. I had on a lovely white ball gown with a peculiar velvet sash and he looked ravishing in his tails. I was sitting on a side table and beckoned him as he came round. Somehow or other we missed, and he didn't hear me call out "St Clair!" as he passed and he didn't notice me. He had so much on his mind, naturally anxious that the ball should go well. I was so timid and also scared of anything going wrong that I should have been noticed. I would have loved to dance with St Clair at the Plaza ballroom. He often talked of it after and he felt the sadness of it really acutely.'

As the 1930s drew to a close the cult of Lady Florence acquired an unstoppable momentum, and she did everything to encourage it. In the annual tableaux vivants she trans-mogrified variously into Louis XV's mistress the Comtesse du Barry (in a golden wig and gown) in a Three Musketeers tab-leau, and then Catherine the Great (in which guise she was 'the cynosure of interest'). In every one of her triumphant apotheoses, she was blissfully unaware of the judgement of younger onlookers. Florence Darnault remembers her appear-ing as Aida, this time to sing. 'She came out in costume, she had all these harem women, she had all the other faces dark-ened, but she didn't darken hers. These women were all dark, none of them sang, they couldn't sing a tone, they were from the Verdi Club, they were all big women and they all had these chiffon trousers . . . I think that was the worst I ever saw, I think that was really the end of everything.'

And yet Lady Florence was increasingly sought after and celebrated. In 1938 she gave a private recital to two hundred guests at a house in Queens, and embarked on her first ever concert tour of New England. In McMoon's memory these were dismally attended; in Provincetown she sang to an audi-ence of fifteen. When she returned to embark on the Verdi Club's twenty-first season, she was presented with a portrait bust of herself. The sculptress was Baroness Liane de Gidro, whose previous subjects had included Caruso, Liszt and Mus-solini. A jowly and resolutely unflattering bronze portrait was unveiled in a ceremony directed by St Clair and attended by, among others, the Italian consul general and a retired rear admiral who spoke of the great contribution made by women as society's champions of culture. To add to the jollity of the occasion, a motion picture of one of Madame Jenkins's recent concerts was shown to the 250 guests. Florence's Ritz-Carlton recital was now filmed as a matter of course, and then shown at subsequent musicales. Verdi Club members were encouraged to 'come and see yourselves as you appear in a moving picture'.

As Florence's career as a society soprano continued to levitate, the career of her vocal coach Henriette Wakefield ran aground. She made her last appearance with the Met in 1935, and became the chairman of the Verdi Club. Under Wakefield's aegis, on 9 October 1939, the club celebrated Verdi's birthday with a morning musicale at the Regis Hotel, as it did every year. A soprano sang, a violinist fresh off the boat from Czechoslovakia played. And the address was given by Edward Page Gaston, a temperance activist and vocal supporter of returning the remains of Pocahontas from England to her native America. The title of his lecture took the form of a question: 'What Would Verdi Do If He Lived Today?' Some in the audience perhaps considered the possibility that if Verdi were indeed alive in the 1930s, he would have been relieved of the task of spinning in his grave.

10: QUEEN OF THE NIGHT

On 15 April 1940 an enumerator for the US census visited the Seymour Hotel. There were thirty-three inhabitants, listed as 'guests'. The majority came from all over the country, while another three were English, one German and one Irish. Florence's name was last but one. She described herself as a widow. In the box where her age was entered, the number sixty-six has been circled, perhaps on grounds of implausibility. While even St Clair Bayfield was unsure of her true age, in reality she was a few months shy of her seventy-second birthday. Even more questionably, in the column marked 'Occupation. Trade, profession, or particular kind of work, as – frame spinner, salesman, laborer, rivet heater, music teacher', Florence described herself as a 'concert singer'. Three days later she did indeed sing in a concert in Washington where she performed, among others, works by Handel, Gluck, Rimsky-Korsakov, Rachmaninov and McMoon.

While the audiences at the Ritz-Carlton paid to take part in an uproarious celebration of her uniqueness, in the capital Florence could still count on a respectful reception. Although her Washington-based sister-in-law Alice had died in 1935, the audience continued to consist of a handpicked gathering from the worlds of politics, the military and high society. From the evidence of her next trip, in April 1941, she seemed to be able to hand-pick her own critic too. Someone called Bartlett B. James (PhD) wrote a gushing encomium containing artful arabesques of approval. Florence's programme was 'of such excellence that it will stand out among the notable performances of this New York musical celebrity. The hall was filled and the audience select, critical and appreciative.' Dr James chose to contextualise her recital as cultural balm available to sensitive Americans while Europe girded itself for the next phase of self-immolation. A snippet of Haydn, her rendition of 'Ah, fors'è lui', plus bits and pieces by minor composers including McMoon – all moved Dr James to see her work as a contribution on a larger plain.

> In her great musical achievements in New York, in Newport, and in the nation's capital, Florence Foster Jenkins is vindicating the as yet but faintly realised type of society. That in which, even as God is symbolically represented as walking in the gardens of Eden, the spirit of man will move triumphantly amid the ruins of economic and mechanistic force – or the shadows of its unloveliness. By thus weaving the singer's performances into basic significance it is possible to see in them the continuity, amid chaos, of the things which endure and enlarge. Thus, was it interpreting, her program – uplifting!

If this hyperbole was tongue-in-cheek, it wore a straight-faced disguise.

The war was soon to leave its stamp on New York. Rationing, shortages and blackouts became commonplace. There were meat shortages at the Astor and Waldorf-Astoria, which did not dissuade officers from heading for the roof to dance under the stars. Brooklyn Navy Yard became the busiest shipyard in the world. Women, personified as 'Rosie the Riveter', took men's places on the production line, while there was a growing presence in the streets of young men in uniform, all of whom wanted entertaining. One or two managed to scalp a ticket to Florence's recitals. Concerts to support 'Bundles for Britain' were hosted at Carnegie Hall, where on the day the Japanese Air Force attacked Pearl Harbor in Hawaii, audiences were not told until the New York Philharmonic had finished.

The war seemed to pass Florence by. The First World War had galvanised her; her compulsion to do good fundraising work for the Red Cross had greatly contributed to establishing the reputation of the Verdi Club. Now the Verdi Club simply marched on. The season just ended included a Ball of the Silver Skylarks in which Florence outgunned herself as an apparition of majestic absurdity. The occasion featured a grand pageant in which members were given the opportunity to dress up not only as iconic figures from literature, the arts, history and legend, but also as the performers who brought them to life on stage and screen. Thus Mrs Ross Raymond Sigsbee became Geraldine Farrar as Musetta in *La Bohème*, Mrs Oliver Pittman Cooke became the Milanese soprano Amelita Galli-Curci as Gilda from *Rigoletto*; from the silver screen Mrs Louis Dana Knowlton impersonated Norma Shearer as Marie Antoinette, Feodor Nikanov dressed up as Valentino in *The Sheik*, perhaps hoping that women would faint as they had at the original in the film. Theatrical doyennes included Lillian Russell in *Wildfire* and Julia Marlow as Mary Tudor. There was a Schubert, a D'Oyly Carte, a Nell Gwynne, a Salome, a Carmen and a Violetta. Someone came as the Swedish Nightingale Jenny Lind, another as Anna Pavlova doing the Blue Danube Waltz. Exhuming the memory of a former club member, Mr Franklin Schalk even dressed up as the great Caruso as Don Alvaro. And of course there was a Verdi.

Around forty people paraded around the ballroom of the Waldorf-Astoria before the grand finale. The theme of this last tableau vivant was 'Stephen Foster Inspired by the Angel of Genius', in which a painting by Howard Chandler Christy was reproduced with living figures. This was a double celebration of great Americans. Foster was universally acknowledged as the father of American music, whose songs from the middle of the nineteenth century included 'Camptown Races', 'My Old Kentucky Home' and 'Hard Times Come Again No More'. Christy was the great popular painter of the age. He made his name with stirring images of military combat and appeals to patriotic duty on recruitment posters before spending the interwar years obsessively documenting every contour of the naked female form; he married one of his models, then, after a bitter and public divorce, married another (who was a Verdi Club member). He had a child with a third.

The great artist himself, only a few years younger than Florence, was on hand to make suggestions to St Clair Bayfield about how to bring the Stephen Foster characters from his canvas to life. The painting showed the angel with a sizeable wingspan, dressed in a plunging bodice and clutching a golden lyre. She floats down from above to touch with a single index finger the forehead of the young composer as he sits at the piano. Behind are bonneted maidens and smiling young African-American musicians, all waiting for inspiration to strike so that they can be released by Foster's imagination. Verdi Club members came as Drake from 'Swanee River' (a song also known as 'Old Folks at Home'), and Jeannie with the Light Brown Hair. Ol' Black Joe was interpreted by Randolph Symonette, a young Bahamian bass destined for greater things. Adolf Pollitz incarnated Foster himself. Florence unabashedly assumed the guise of the Angel of Genius, draped in jewels over a floor-length figure-hugging gown, a feathered headdress and a vast pair of golden wings.

Florence's apotheosis as the inspiration for American music drew vastly on her reserves of self-aggrandisement. A couple of years later a Washington gossip columnist would blithely report that Florence was Foster's direct descendant – in short, a daughter of the father of American music – though quite how the journalist came by this misinformation is lost to history. And yet a winged Florence was merely a foretaste of her next project. With the 1940–41 season rounded off by the Rose Breakfast in Westchester, in May Florence decided to augment the job description she'd provided to the census. She took a short cab ride to 25 Central Park West with the intention of turning herself into a recording artist.

In fact Florence had been recorded before. In 1934 at Ithaca College in upstate New York she was invited to make electrical recordings of her voice by Professor Vladimir Karapetoff, an electrical engineer from St Petersburg who was also an accomplished cellist – that year he was awarded an honorary doctorate by the New York College of Music. After Karapetoff's death a fire in Ithaca College's record room destroyed his archive of recordings, depriving the curious of a chance to measure the deterioration (if any) in Florence's singing.

The studio Florence chose was a private operation whose advertised services included studio and off-the-air recordings, transcriptions and processing. Its two female proprietors were Mera and Lola Weinstock. They called the place Melotone Recording Studio although it had no relation to the budget record label of the same name, discontinued in 1938, which released music by popular dance bands and the likes of singing cowboy Gene Autry and the Delta bluesman Lead Belly. These were not Florence's label mates. And yet, although frequented by amateurs, Melotone also attracted substantial clients. It recorded the Metropolitan Opera's broadcasts as well as those of the New York Philharmonic, whose guest conductor John Barbirolli visited the studio.

Florence took along Cosme McMoon, who had been presented with a medal for his services at her most recent Verdi Club recital. For her first recording she breezed into the studio and plucked from her repertoire the Queen of the Night's aria from *The Magic Flute*. She had been singing 'Der Hölle Rache' for two years so felt confident that she knew her way around the peaks and pitfalls of the vengeful queen's furious challenge to her daughter to murder Sarastro. But Florence had a different sort of murder bubbling up in her larynx. Without anything so precautionary as a warm-up or rehearsal, she filled her lungs and Mozart's most instantly recognisable aria proceeded to deliquesce into a sequence of hesitant pauses and hopeful yelps. The queen's thrilling fusillade of coloratura high notes found her occupying a lower harmonic line as if dangling by her fingertips from a jagged cliff edge. She didn't seem to sing in German, though nor did her hoots and howls have the veneer of English. McMoon at the piano did his loyal best to supply a guide rail for Madame Jenkins's faulty tuning and stodgy time-keeping, delivering a drastic *rallentando* as the soloist macheted a path through dense thickets of Mozartian quavers. If she stabbed at a note correctly it was more by accident than design. She concluded on a piercing shriek and the studio fell silent. The face of the engineer can only be imagined as Florence, offered the chance of a second take, declared herself satisfied.

A single-sided shellac 78 rpm disc was printed and Florence took it home. It was only the next day after she had listened again to the result that she was visited by a rare moment of doubt. She telephoned Mera Weinstock to report her worry about 'a note' towards the end of the aria. Weinstock seized gratefully on a semantic loophole. 'My dear Madame

Jenkins,' she replied, 'you need feel no anxiety concerning any single note.' And so she didn't.

After her mugging of Mozart came her demolition of Delibes. 'The Indian Bell Song' from the opera *Lakmé* had been in her recital repertoire since 1935. In the correct rendition by, say, superstar diva Lily Pons, it opened with a wordless, unaccompanied stream of sound before the soloist narrates the legend of a pariah's daughter who saved Vishnu, the son of Brahma. Florence clattered and caterwauled through the opening, deploying a random parade of notes with only the vaguest relationship to the written music. As McMoon came in, her version of the lyrical tale emerged in a hideous tangle of squeaks and squawks. She also recorded a number especially written for her by McMoon called 'Serenata Mexicana', a colourless legato dirge she premiered at the Ritz-Carlton in 1939. It was calculated by the composer to fall at least theoretically within the dedicatee's limited abilities, but still missed by a distance.

Florence's original intention was to distribute her recordings privately among Verdi Club members. The first one she made available was 'The Bell Song'. Onto Melotone's sky-blue label, with the words 'Your Portrait in Sound' italicised at the top, were typed the credits. Florence's name was in upper case and red ink. It sold out swiftly, and customers clamoured for more. So Mozart and McMoon were pressed onto either side of a second disc. As demand increased the labels had to be pre-printed rather than typed.

Weinstock's recollection of Madame Jenkins's visits to the Melotone studio made their way into the liner notes of a long-playing compilation on 33 rpm released swiftly after Florence's death. 'Rehearsals, the niceties of volume and pitch, considerations of acoustics – all were thrust aside by her with ease and authority. The technicians never ceased to

Three times Academy-
Award-winning actress
Meryl Streep between takes
as she plays Florence
Foster Jenkins.

Debonair St Clair Bayfield,
played by Hugh Grant.
For the film's dance sequence,
Grant practised for several
hours each day for six weeks.

Bayfield and Florence return from Carnegie Hall after hearing Lily Pons sing. Inspired, Florence decides to take more singing lessons. And so her journey to Carnegie Hall and infamy begins . . .

Florence and Bayfield listen to a recording of 'The Bell Song' sung by Lily Pons, one of the great sopranos of the age. The part in the film was performed by Russian star Aida Garifullina.

Above. Florence performs the 'Laughing Song' from *Die Fledermaus* at the Ritz-Carlton Hotel before a carefully selected audience. 'My waistline so slim and charming!' she sings.

Opposite, top. Pianist Cosme McMoon, played by Simon Helberg, attends a party thrown by Bayfield and his girlfriend Kathleen after Florence's concert at the Ritz-Carlton Hotel.

Opposite, bottom. Florence and Bayfield enjoy the reviews of her Ritz-Carlton concert. 'By the end of her performance, the stage was a bower of blooms, and Madam Jenkins retired to thunderous applause,' reads Bayfield.

Florence records 'The Bell Song' at the Melotone studio. 'You wanna try
another take?' asks the sound engineer. 'I don't see why, that seemed
perfect to me,' replies Florence.

Bayfield learns that Florence has booked Carnegie Hall, where she intends
to sing. 'You're not strong enough, Bunny,' he worries. 'What if it kills you?'
'Then I shall die happy!' replies Florence.

The moment of truth: Florence, with trusted Bayfield at her side, prepares to make her entrance onto the Carnegie Hall stage where she opens her show with 'Valse Caressante', a song written by Cosme McMoon.

Meryl Streep, playing Florence, prepares to sing the second Queen of the Night aria on the set of Carnegie Hall. The set was built within the Apollo Theatre, Hammersmith, where Streep sang live to over 600 actors and supporting artists.

be amazed by her capacity for circumventing the numerous problems and difficulties peculiar to recording. She simply sang; the disc was recorded.' She also told a story which illustrated the artiste's unshakeable self-belief. It featured cameos for two of the great sopranos from the golden age of opera – Frieda Hempel, the diva of Leipzig who was a favourite of the Kaiser, and Luisa Tetrazzini, the Florentine prima donna renowned as 'the queen of staccato'. 'Lady Florence reported to the studio that, at a recent soiree of one of her friends, all of them music lovers, [they] listened attentively to recordings of the *Magic Flute* aria by Tetrazzini, Hempel and the redoubtable Jenkins. Unanimity of opinion, Mme Jenkins informed us with modest hesitancy, was that the latter recording was without a doubt the most outstanding of the three.'

McMoon told a similar story of Florence putting records on the Victrola when she hosted in the Seymour Hotel. Her guests were asked to compare her with the great coloratura soprano Amelita Galli-Curci, who was a hugely popular recording artist. 'She would put on "The Bell Song" by herself and by Galli-Curci, and then she would hand little ballots out and you were supposed to vote which one was the best. Of course they all voted for her, and one woman once voted for Galli-Curci so Madame said, "How could you mistake that? My tones are much fuller than that!" So she really didn't hear the atrocious pitches in these things. She used to sit delightedly and listen for hours to her recordings.'

These vignettes are corroborated by another account of her technique for manipulating compliments out of her circle. Adolf Pollitz, who was Stephen Foster to her Angel of Inspiration, was once giving Florence and St Clair a lift to the meeting of one of her clubs. 'She used to love to put people on the spot,' he recalled. 'At that affair there was one woman who came up to us and spoke and said, "You were a singer, weren't you?" "I *am* a singer!" And then she said to me, "Now, describe the concerts." So I had to launch into a description of her concerts and tell about the smart audiences, wonderfully dressed, and her wonderful tone and the most difficult coloratura and the highest notes ever written and go through all that. I don't think I did it to her satisfaction either.' And if others could not be relied upon to sing her praises, Florence sang them herself. In one Verdi Club programme she wrote, 'Tetrazzini took three breaths to sing this phrase, I do it in one.' A woman at a recital begged to differ: 'She did it in twenty-four.'

After the success of 'The Bell Song', the Mozart/McMoon disc was released onto the market in what Florence called a 'souvenir recording'. Customers were required to mail cheques written out to 'Recordings: Mme Jenkins' to a PO Box in Times Square station. It was also available at Melotone, which is how someone at *Time* magazine came to hear about it. In an edition with a cover image of Chen Cheng, a leading figure in the Sino-Japanese war, on 16 June 1941 *Time* published a small item about Mozart's 'immensely difficult coloratura soprano aria, even for markswomanly singers'. It went on:

> Last week a recording of this air [sic], advertised entirely by rumour, enjoyed a lively little sale at Manhattan's Melotone Recording Studio. It was recorded – to sell to her friends at $2.50 a copy – by Mrs Florence Foster Jenkins, rich, elderly amateur soprano and musical club-woman. Mrs Jenkins' night-queenly swoops and hoots, her wild wallowings in descending trill, her repeated staccato notes like a cuckoo in its cups, are innocently uproarious to hear, almost as much so as the annual song recital which she gives in Manhattan. For that event, a minor phenomenon in US music, knowing Manhattanites

fight for tickets. Mrs Jenkins is well pleased with the success of her Queen of the Night record and hopes to make others. Her fans hope so too.

There was a picture of Florence taken on the day Liane de Gidro's portrait bust of her was unveiled, wearing a tall Austrian hat with various flowers and medals pinned to her tweed jacket.

The Gramophone Shop on East 48th Street listed her first release under 'Historical' and described it as 'a most unusual record which must be heard to be believed'. Readers of the October issue of *Esquire* were encouraged to write to Melotone and order a copy. The magazine's record reviewer, Carleton Sprague Smith, who also happened to run the New York Public Library's music division, usually concentrated on more refined releases. Elsewhere in the same column another soprano's release elicited comparisons with Tetrazzini and Flagstad. Florence was relegated to the bottom of the column. The shock to Smith's ears resulted in a misnomer. 'To add spice to your collection,' he said, 'write to Melotone Recording Studios . . . for Florence Foster Jones's singing of the dramatic aria of the Queen of the Night from Mozart's *Magic Flute*. What I might say about it would be libellous, so I won't. You buy it and, if it isn't worth the price of admission, I'll refund your money.'

Did St Clair Bayfield attempt to stop Florence's craving for publicity? His affair with Kathleen Weatherley may have been a distraction for him, as well as a spur for Florence. Florence had other companions, young acolytes like Pollitz and well-bred hangers-on such as Prince Michael Galitzen, a White Russian refugee and minor member of the noble Russian house who found a home in the Verdi Club. Once, a gossip columnist got the wrong end of the stick and suggested an autumnal romance between the prince and 'the veteran cantatrice, whose annual concerts at the Ritz have been the musical sensation of every season for two or three decades'.

Meanwhile St Clair's career had entered a slump. Just before Christmas in 1940, for three performances only, he appeared in an Irish play set in County Down by tub-thumping anti-Catholic playwright Paul Vincent Carroll. It was called *The Old Foolishness*. In the month before Florence embarked on her recording career, he was in the large cast for a family entertainment, set in a Sixth Avenue luggage shop, by the giant of comedy S. J. Perelman and his wife Laura called *The Night Before Christmas*. After it closed he had no stage work again in New York for another three years.

Even if he'd wanted to, he couldn't stop Florence from singing. But he viewed her performing as a harmless indulgence for which she had earned the right. 'Why did she go on singing?' he said. 'Because she loved it. After all, she spent all of her time and money promoting other musicians . . . Singing was her only form of self-expression. She was entitled to give her personal recitals. She was so engrossed in her singing, she didn't give a hang about the guying. And she had the stamina to go on, the stamina.' In fact it's not quite true that she simply ignored her critics. 'They are so ignorant, ignorant!' she was heard to say, denouncing the 'hoodlums' and 'spiteful enemies' who mocked her from the back of the stalls.

Meanwhile she expanded her repertoire and, allegedly, her range. She was travelling in a taxi one day when the driver was forced to slam hard on the brakes. His passenger was hurled forward and emitted a high-pitched squeal – higher in pitch, she suspected, than she'd ever reached before. When she got home to the Seymour Hotel she marched over to the Steinway, hit a high F above C and confirmed, at least to herself, that the accident had given her a new top note a semitone higher than her previous personal best. She'd only ever reached a high E before.

For Florence's next cacophonous visit to the recording studio she made a stab at merriment with 'Adele's Laughing Song' from Johann Strauss's *Die Fledermaus*, a fluttering waltz with a repeated refrain of chortled 'ah ha ha's. For the other side she trampled all over 'Biassy', a poem by Pushkin set to music inspired by a Bach prelude. The composition was attributed to an obscure figure billed as Count Alexis Pavlovich. This proved to be Florence's most surreal foray yet into the outer wastelands of hapless atonality. It presented the sound of someone catastrophically flunking an exam in sight-reading, both of German music and Russian poetry. As ever she concluded with a confidently held yowl before a relieved McMoon crashed out a final chord.

The reviewers were not to be blindsided again by a new release, and didn't expect their readers to be either. 'It will probably suffice to say that here is a new Florence Foster Jenkins record,' said one publication. 'The soprano considers it her best. The recording clearly reproduces all the idiosyncratic touches that have made Mrs Jenkins' record of one of the Queen of the Night's arias from *Die Zauberflöte* a collector's item.' One newspaper counselled that listening to 'Adele's Laughing Song' would provide 'more of a kick than the same amount ($2.50) invested in tequila, zubrovka, or marijuana, and we ain't woofin'!'

If the press in New York could not be persuaded to laud her efforts, Dr James in Washington was there again to serve up contorted paeans of praise. The next time Florence was in the capital he enjoyed a programme which offered 'facets of aesthetic interest for her critically minded hearers'. When she plucked an aria from Bach's St Matthew Passion, he simpered that 'nothing could be more baffling and intricate to anyone not so musically capable as the singer'. There was 'roguishness' in a Mexican number and 'delicacy' in 'Una voce poco fa'.

Washington seemed to hear her singing through a prism which filtered out the awfulness. No wonder she went back in the autumn to share the stage with genuine eminences. The French bass Léon Rothier made his Metropolitan Opera debut in 1910 as Méphistophélès and sang with the company until 1939. Clarence D. Batchelor, a celebrated cartoonist with the *New York Daily News*, was booked as a guest speaker. He had won the Pulitzer Prize in 1936 for an image in which a young European youth is beckoned up the stairs of a boarding house by a barely draped blonde with a skull for a face and 'War' stencilled on her sternum: 'Come on in, I'll treat you right!' she says. 'I used to know your Daddy.' And then there was Florence.

They all gathered in the Hotel Wellington for a patriotic occasion: to celebrate the 2,000th performance of 'America Forever Free', Elmer Russ's stirring popular hit from 1941 which had been learned by glee clubs and church choirs all over the country. Russ, a baritone who composed, had picked up the moniker 'the champion of American song'. He was also a member of Florence's court of composers who dedicated new songs to her. When Florence came back to Washington in April 1943 to perform 'Una voce poco fa' 'by request', Dr B. B. James was once more among the patrons leafing through a handsome programme, its frontispiece printed in a gothic font, a side-on photograph of Madame Jenkins hinting at sly amusement. As an encore she rendered her own fragrant lament, 'Trailing Arbutus'.

For her next visit to the Melotone studios, Florence and McMoon were accompanied by a third party. Her account of 'Charmant Oiseau' – from Félicien David's *opéra comique La perle du Brésil* – called for a flute to accompany the avian calls of the soloist. She had more than one flautist to summon, others having accompanied her in recitals, but on this occasion the fee went to Louis Alberghini, a flautist with the Met. Of all her recordings this perhaps exposed her most cruelly: although technically simpler for the singer, the flute's obbligato fills and several climactic bars called for at least theoretical unison between flute and voice and set in relief Florence's most unbirdlike clumsiness and the erratic nature of her tuning.

As the recording lasted for six minutes it had to be pressed onto both sides of a ten-inch record. Listeners wanting more had to flip the disc. Alberghini stuck around to memorialise another bauble dedicated to Florence by McMoon called 'Valse Caressante'. This dragged on painfully for another six minutes and sailed far beyond the scope of her abilities, as McMoon must have known it would. In a final session Florence closed her recording career with two more staples from her repertoire that were brief enough to occupy one side, the other being given to a re-release of Delibes's 'Bell Song'. For Anatoly Liadov's twinkling *jeu d'esprit* 'A Musical Snuff Box', Florence tiptoed all over the melody in hobnailed stilettos. To complete her Melotone oeuvre, she drew on another of her own poems, this one invoking once again her fantasy that she sang as if borne aloft on the feathered wings of melody. 'Like a bird I am singing,' she sang in 'Like a Bird' (lilting music by McMoon).

> *Like a bird I am singing, like a bird*
> *Joy of the morning,*
> *The river is flowing,*
> *There's a silvery way*
> *O'er the crystalline bay.*

To the notes of thy flute,
The shady groves filling,
My thoughts of thee bring me,
Sweet memories thrilling.

Like a bird I am singing,
Like a bird, like a bird.

Cadences melting
In music divine
Bring a vision so pleasant,
The smile that is thine.

Inspiration comes o'er,
When your music is heard,
In fondest endeavor
I sing like a bird . . .

Like a bird I am singing
Like a bird, like a bird!

It was all o'er in one minute and eighteen seconds. The bird Florence was like was not from the soloists' section of the dawn chorus.

In April 1944 St Clair finally landed a part in a play. *Highland Fling* was a comedy about a ne'er-do-well Scottish ghost who refuses to ascend to heaven. It was directed by George Abbott, whose last big splash on Broadway was *Pal Joey* and whose next would be *On the Town*. 'You would not say it could last a long time,' said one critic, prophetically. It was off within a month. St Clair's lack of employment meant that he had plenty of free time to supervise the engagements of Florence's season. At Sherry's she sang for the Society of New York State Women, who heard several songs from her discography including 'Like a Bird', plus some Liszt. And there was one more date with cathedral organist Malton Boyce in Washington.

But these were private events. At her last ever concert at the Ritz-Carlton, where the audience scrapped for tickets to join in the fun, McMoon now showed ever more overt signs of disloyalty, accompanying Florence with what seemed to one witness 'an impishly satiric touch'. As the audience hollered in approval every time she clambered up to a high note or attempted a trill, he seemed to mistime his chord placement, either coming in too early or too late, for subtly enhanced comic effect. Fans hoping for the Angel of Inspiration's wings to make another appearance for her rendition of 'Like a Bird' were disappointed. (It had become an instant favourite with the Ritz-Carlton crowds when, making her entrance on a previous occasion, one wing had malfunctioned, causing Florence to pause as the rogue appendage was fixed back in place.) 'Mme Jenkins is incomparable,' concluded the *New York Daily Mirror*. 'Her annual recitals bring unbounded joy to the faded souls of Park Avenue and the musical elite.'

Word spread across the Union. Early in 1944 a profile in the Hearst Corporation's *American Weekly*, which had a vast nationwide circulation, was read all over America. Titled 'The Society Songbird Who Sprouts Wings Once a Year', it was syndicated as far afield as Milwaukee and Oregon. A cartoon illustrated the story with Florence in her angel's wings singing to an audience in evening dress that was by turns thrilled and appalled. There was also a photograph of Florence at her Steinway, a bower of blooms filling the rest of the frame. The article was a merciless lampoon. She was hailed as 'the only known diva to achieve fame via the "Bronx cheer" and keep coming back for more' who had removed 'some of the more altitudinous notes' from the classics. McMoon was singled out for notice as 'the only pianist out of twenty tried so far who has been able to play and keep a straight face'. 'Wealthy enough to indulge herself in her amateur career, and cheered on by a group of faithful and flattering sycophants, this ambitious songstress today looks forward to greater and greater triumphs as time goes by.'

Then in August a report surfaced in San Diego which talked of record collectors 'with a taste for the bizarre' who were buying up the discs. 'There should be a new word for what she does with the human throat,' it was suggested. 'She persists in spite of the most caustic criticism. And perhaps she feels vindicated because her recordings are selling briskly. Although they hurt the ears, there is a certain fascination in her vocal escapades.'

Florence had almost lost control of her reputation. But not yet entirely.

11: PRIMA DONNA OF CARNEGIE HALL

'Carnegie Hall has been completely sold out for the recital to be given there tomorrow night by Florence Foster Jenkins, soprano, assisted by the Pascarella Chamber Music Society.'

On 24 October 1944 Florence's final concert was soberly announced in the *New York Times*. The same page featured a review of Stokowski's account of Shostakovich's Eighth with the New York City Symphony and a report from Moscow of the concert premiere of Prokofiev's opera *War and Peace*.

St Clair Bayfield later claimed that he opposed the recital at Carnegie Hall. 'I didn't think a person of her age should take on that strain,' he said. 'There is something in a vast audience that draws the magnetism out of a person. It sucks you dry.' Initially Florence agreed with him. The idea was put to her several times, and she demurred. But having demanded and fed off the praise of her Verdi Club friends for so long, she had no means of resisting insincerity. The profiteer whispering sulphurous encouragement in her ear was George Leyden Colledge, who had set up in artistic management in 1932 and operated out of the RKO Building. He was the one who suggested she switch her annual recital from the relative intimacy of the Ritz-Carlton ballroom (capacity, at a stretch: eight hundred) to the premier concert venue in the entire continent (capacity: three thousand). 'I can do it,' she finally told St Clair. 'I'll show everybody.' Less than two weeks before the concert, Florence's fears visited her in her sleep. 'B told me of a strange dream and was in a nervous condition,' St Clair recorded in his diary for Friday 13 October. Five days later her nerves were back under control and at a rehearsal she 'sang well'. Two days before she was 'in a whirl about seating'. When St Clair delivered some vases to Carnegie Hall on the eve of the concert he saw her picture adorning the frontage of the celebrated venue. Then on the day itself he wrote the word 'recital' in red ink.

The price of admission was set at $3 for the orchestra stalls, $1.80 for the dress circle and 60 cents for the balcony, while lower boxes with seats for eight were $24 and upper boxes $19.20. (Tax was included.) Word spread around the city. Those in the know tipped off others who had never heard of Florence that this was an event which should on no account be missed. By the time the doors opened, the box office had long since run out of tickets. Outside the hall were an estimated two thousand disappointed thrill-seekers. Cosme McMoon had to fight his way through a crowd that teemed down the sidewalk of West 57th Street, past the Little Carnegie Playhouse and round the corner into Seventh Avenue. 'When I approached the hall I could hardly get near it,' he recalled. 'You had to prove your identity to get in.' According to the sculptress Florence Darnault, few of the tickets were actually purchased. St Clair's diary confirms that Florence gave away $3,000 worth of tickets. Newspapers all reported a box-office take of $6,000.

Among those who managed to gain access to the hall were several celebrities from the world of music and entertainment. They included Cole Porter; the great soprano Lily Pons, wearing a hat with a dangling fringe like a lampshade; her husband Andre Kostelanetz, the popular radio orchestra conductor; burlesque star Gypsy Rose Lee; composer-librettist Gian Carlo Menotti; and Marge Champion, the dance model for Snow White and other Disney characters. 'I'd never heard about her,' said Champion. 'I don't think the average audience would flock there. These people must have heard of her through the grapevine.' It is always said that Tallulah Bankhead showed up too, though no newspaper journalist reported her presence. And there were plenty in the house who would not have failed to spot her: from the *New York Sun*, *New York Journal-American*, *New York World-Telegram*, *New York Post*, *New York Herald Tribune*, *Hollywood Reporter*, *Newsweek*, *PM*, the *Los Angeles Times* and *Milwaukee Journal*. There was no more privileged access for the *Musical Courier* alone.

The only photograph that survives of the evening was taken by Adolf Pollitz from the dress circle close to stage left as the clock ticked towards half past eight. One eyewitness reported that many in the audience had donned evening dress for the occasion but, while the photograph contains a few bow ties, most of the men were in suits. A lot of the women wore hats. A few Verdi Club matrons sat in dowdy clumps, dressed to the nines and raising the average age of the gathering. Almost everyone in the photograph is laughing or smiling. Several are clutching or reading the programme, which came with a bright blue cover.

Inside on the front page, lettering in the same bright blue announced the star of the evening, 'Jenkins' in upper case and occupying its own line. Below were printed a trio of attestations from critics who had attended previous concerts. Grena Bennett of the *New York Journal-American* was one of them. Then came Dr B. B. James with his blandishments from the capital. In the *New York Daily Mirror*, Robert Coleman had had a fun night among the orchids and mink at a Sherry's recital: 'she is a personage of authority and indescribable charm,' he confirmed, 'she is incomparable, her annual recitals bring unbounded joy.'

In the auditorium there was barely any standing room left – 'It seemed that the people were hanging on the rafters,' said McMoon – lending some urgency to the notice from the fire commissioner printed just above the details of the recital programme. 'Look around *now* and choose the nearest exit to your seat. In case of fire walk (not run) to *that* Exit. Do not try to beat your neighbor to the street.'

P. B. of the *Herald Tribune* likened the febrile atmosphere, 'both in intensity and unanimity of reaction, to that of *The Voice*, currently drawing the same sort of delighted applause at the Paramount Theater'. The comparison was timely because twenty-four hours earlier the Carnegie Hall stage was occupied by the selfsame Frank Sinatra. The venue had been crammed to the ceiling with bobbysoxers, a hysterical phalanx of teenage fans who showered him with love the way, a generation earlier, their mothers had hot flushes at Valentino. Sinatra was not there to sing – he pleaded laryngitis – but to take part in an electoral rally in support of President Franklin D. Roosevelt.

The contrast between the slim hip young crooner and the solidly constructed tone-deaf soprano of seventy-six could not have been greater. And yet, according to McMoon, Florence didn't see it that way. 'At that time Frank Sinatra had started to sing, and the teenagers used to faint during his notes and scream,' he explained, 'so she thought she was producing the same kind of an effect, and when these salvos of applause came, she took them as great marks of approval of some tremendous vocal tour de force, and she loved that. She would pause altogether and bow, many times, and then resume the song.'

By the time of the concert McMoon had joined Edwin McArthur in Florence's bad books, having lately developed a vaudevillean style of accompaniment which favoured the audience with winks and nods behind Florence's back. 'She was very unhappy with him,' said Pollitz, 'but it was too late to do anything about it, even though she had it in mind to fire him.'

The stage was empty but for the seats for the musicians, a bench, the concert grand piano and a floral display of considerable height which, over the course of the evening, expanded into a botanical bower. At the side of the stage was the pass door through which the evening's performer was about to emerge.

Almost none of the three thousand people knew anything about the inner life of the woman whose entrance they awaited. Many knew that she couldn't sing but believed she could, that she translated catcalls and whistles into sincere gestures of appreciation for her art. Some had seen her podgy frame squeezed into fancy dress that made her look perfectly ridiculous. But if any of them wondered what inspired this baffling relic of another age to cast herself as an entertainer, none had an answer.

However nonsensical her appearance at Carnegie Hall, everything in Florence's previous seventy-six years had a role in delivering her onto its hallowed stage. Even if the story she told of her own life was not all true, Florence believed it to be so. That she was a child prodigy thwarted by her father. A bereaved sister who eloped with a man twice her age from a family of brutes and knaves. An innocent wife infected with a disease which permanently disfigured her. A new music graduate who triumphed over nerves in front of a vast festival audience. An impoverished piano teacher who believed herself disinherited. A New Yorker who reinvented herself as an opera producer. A widow liberated to put her married name to work. A fundraiser energised by a world war. A club founder who gave opportunities to ambitious young musicians. A respected friend of the giants of opera. A president who laid on and starred in the most remarkable parties. Who just wanted to sing. Who, when no one minded, sang some more. Who fed off the applause she had been denied for decades. Who as a little indulgence decided to sing every year in one venue, then another, and another and another. Who after twenty-five years was so silted up with praise and adulation that there was no possibility of self-awareness. Who was abetted by a gentle, collusive dependant she first saw smiling up at her on the stage. Who was deaf to the mocking of audiences, which only increased as her voice enfeebled with age and the gap between what she and they heard grew wider and wider.

The lighting for the show, designed by St Clair, kindly aimed soft pastel shades from the footlights. When Madame Jenkins entered she was greeted by a tumultuous ovation which accompanied her on the Via Dolorosa from the pass door to the piano. Now an undeniably stout old woman, her movements were slow and unsteady, and some feared she might never reach her destination. Florence was decked out rustically in the style of a shepherdess, brandishing the crook she always had with her for the March of the Roses, now helpful for maintaining her in the vertical. Her bosom, recalled Marge Champion, was bedecked with the kind of medals usually pinned on chests by Latin American potentates. Such was the uproar that five minutes had passed before calm was sufficiently restored for her to begin. McMoon, seated at the Steinway and possibly nervous, found it impossible to suppress a rictus.

As was her wont, Florence began with a set of songs all from the same part of the world, in this case a sentimental trio from England: hence the bucolic costume. The programme advertised 'Phyllis' by Young, then two from prolific early-nineteenth-century composer Sir Henry Bishop (best known for 'Home, Sweet Home'): 'Love Has Eyes' and 'Lo, Here the Gentle Lark'. This last called for a busy flute obbligato. It was supplied by the burly Oreste De Sevo, formerly of Toscanini's orchestra in Italy, who contrived against the odds to maintain his embouchure. 'For the gentle lark was having no less than a hell of a time,' explained Richard S. Davis of the *Milwaukee Journal*. Florence had trouble projecting her bat-squeak voice in smaller halls. Here some said she was barely audible to an audience which rushed to smother the last notes of every song with cheers. Others found her all too audible. Al Hubay, a young usher at the Met, was near the rear of the stalls. Her voice 'was kind of icy. It was audible, it wasn't big. I think that was probably the problem. I think the people upstairs heard it too well. Especially in the upper reaches of her voice, it got sharper-sounding as it went up.' Marge Champion remembered a voice that 'wasn't big but it was very very penetrative. I'm very sure that I heard every off-note that she sang. And that was consistent. There was nothing inconsistent about her technique.'

Florence departed the stage while the Pascarella strings sawed through a pleasant Haydn quartet. This gave the audience a chance to recover and Florence enough time to shed the shepherdess outfit and pull on a gown variously described by onlookers as either rose pink or pale peach. As she re-entered, jewels glittered on her bust and neck and rings glinted on her fingers. In her hand was a sizeable fan of orange-and-white ostrich feathers which, after waving it at the audience, she placed on the piano, before leaning on the instrument herself for support. Next to pass through the prism of Florence's larynx was a pair of regular favourites from her repertoire: Gluck's 'Divinités du Styx', a roaring romantic aria in which Queen Alceste offers to lay down her life for love, then the Queen of the Night's furious coloratura howls.

Florence's manner throughout was 'an elegant blend of *sang froid* and studied simplicity', according to the *Tribune*. Her impassivity was baffling to Marge Champion: 'I was just totally unprepared for the fact that it did not seem to bother her in the least that everybody in the audience was convulsed with laughter nor was she in any way thrilled by it. I don't know what she did with it. I don't know how she processed that laughter.' The audience now girded itself into a fresh fit of collective hysteria. Some being familiar with her *Magic Flute* recording, listeners drowned her own trills with laughter. Not everyone appreciated this. Connoisseurs of Lady Florence's art wanted to hear every bum note, every error of pitch. Earl Wilson of the *Post* was in Row T. 'Around me I heard people saying, "Ssssh, don't laugh so loud; stick something in your mouth."' Such was the atmosphere of giddy irony that when a stagehand came on to move a chair even he was applauded.

At the intermission ushers and stage crew swarmed onto the stage bearing vast baskets of blooms which were arranged around the piano so that McMoon returned as if to a greenhouse. One critic was reminded of an expensive mortuary. Florence was greeted by a standing ovation as she re-entered to embark on the Russian section of the evening in a gown Slavic in flavour with a tall jewelled headdress. 'Biassy', the international mulch she had memorialised on disc, was trailed in the programme: 'A band rides through the sky, where snow is falling fast. The moon as a coquette smiles fitfully between the clouds. The horses are lost in a trackless waste, lured by an evanescent devil, who is also a friend of the house devil and many other imps who join in the carnival. The question is, is this the funeral of a great king, or the marriage of a beautiful witch?' This helpful exposition was lost on the audience as Florence fumbled uncertainly into a double maze laid on by the language of Pushkin and the music of Bach. Then Rachmaninov was granted two opportunities to rotate in the grave where, only the previous year, his mortal remains had taken up occupation just up the Bronx River Parkway in Valhalla. Yearningly in 'In the Silence of the Night', brightly in 'The Floods of Spring', Florence's Russian repertoire supplied the audience with further insights into her unique properties as a singer.

As the recital continued the reporters listened to audience reaction and described their own. 'She didn't hit three notes in that one,' one spectator commented. 'She hit only a few notes; the rest were promissory,' snarked Irving Hoffman of the *Hollywood Reporter*. 'Her notes range from the impossible to the fantastic,' reported an anonymous critic from *Newsweek*, 'and bear no relation whatever to any known score or scale.' Robert Bager of the *New York World-Telegram* congratulated Madame Jenkins for having 'perfected the art of giving added zest to a written phrase by improvising it in quarter tones, either above or below the original notes'. It was the noisiest audience McMoon ever encountered anywhere. 'I have never seen such a scene,' he recalled, 'either a bullfight or at the Yale Bowl after a winning touchdown.' And yet he had the presence of mind at the end of several songs, as the decibels of mock approval rose in another crescendo, to spring to his feet and kiss Florence's hand.

The Pascarella ensemble performed another quartet, this time from Schumann, and stayed onstage to accompany Florence. The young composer Daniel Pinkham, who snuck in at the interval having failed to gain entrance earlier, remembered the oddity of the players all seated with their backs to one another. Florence returned in high style as a Spanish temptress in a shawl, her wig ornamented with a jewel-encrusted comb and a red flower. In this garb she proceeded to sing a poem by Rabindranath Tagore translated from Bengali, which had been set to music by American composer Edward Horsman: the altitudes explored in 'Bird of the Wilderness' found Florence in imprecatory mode as she claimed kinship with her winged friends one last time: 'Let me but soar in that sky, In its lonely immensity! Let me but cleave its clouds, And spread wings in its sunshine.' Kostalenetz was the only composer present at the recital (apart from McMoon) to hear his work interpreted by Florence. But if his song 'Interlude' made an impact it was instantly occluded by what was widely agreed to be the night's highlight.

For 'Clavelitos', the high-speed tongue-twisting zarzuela by Valverde, Florence delivered a party trick that had long been a popular staple with her audiences. Equipped with a basket full of red rosebuds, she proceeded to lob them towards the audience in time to the rhythmic pulses of the music. This interaction met with such approval that, carried away, Florence eventually let the empty basket follow its contents into the auditorium. The unison of whistles convinced her of the need for an instant encore, but she couldn't embark on it without the requisite props. The dutiful McMoon, supported by a couple of ushers, trooped down into the stalls to retrieve the basket and the buds. As she started again, the first petal stuck to her finger and she had to make strenuous flicking gestures to fling it off. 'It cracked me up to the point where I could almost not stand it,' said Marge Champion. As McMoon remembered it, during 'Clavelitos' one celebrated actress in the audience had to be carried out of her box in a state of hysteria. She didn't miss much. It only remained for Florence to croon McMoon's 'Serenata Mexicana' and, finally, another dose of Hispanic high jinks: Chapi's 'Las hijas del Zebedeo', the zarzuela which once prompted her to compare herself to Luisa Tetrazzini.

Afterwards, as an audience drugged on hysterics filed out into the New York night, Marge Champion spoke for them all: 'We had sore muscles in our stomachs the next day as we laughed so hard and so long.' Meanwhile Florence's friends and associates clambered onto the stage, where Florence and Verdi Club officers were receiving, to rain praise down on her head. Among them was Mera Weinstock of Melotone Recording Studios. Before she could open her mouth the soloist spoke: 'Don't you think I had real courage to sing the Queen of the Night again after that wonderful recording I made of it at the studio?' On his way out Earl Wilson of the *Post* caught the eye of St Clair Bayfield. 'Why?' he asked him. 'She loves music,' St Clair replied. 'If she loves music, why does she do this?' St Clair explained about the money raised for charity.

Later he took Florence home and, before he turned in at the conclusion of a momentous day, composed a brief, bathetic diary entry: 'Took B up to her recital – capacity house – half of them scoffers but half adoring B. Luckily, a fine day.'

America awoke to thrilling news. 'U.S. DEFEATS JAPANESE NAVY,' ran the headline across the front of the *New York Times*. 'ALL FOE'S SHIPS IN ONE FLEET HIT; MANY SUNK; BATTLE CONTINUES.' At the bottom right-hand corner of page nineteen was a six-line item titled 'Florence F. Jenkins in Recital'. 'Florence Foster Jenkins, soprano, gave a recital at Carnegie Hall last night, assisted by the Pascarella Chamber Music Society quartet; Cosme McMoon, pianist, and Oreste De Sevo, flutist [sic].' The *Times* hadn't sent a critic. Others had. Some filed copy while still intoxicated by the mood of celebration. 'She was exceedingly happy in her work,' said Robert Bager in the *New York World-Telegram*. 'It is a pity that so few artists are. And the happiness was communicated as if by magic to her hearers.' Grena Bennett, a previous encomium of whose was quoted in the programme, found merit in measuring success by markers other than vocal accuracy. 'She was undaunted by either the composers' intent or the opinions of her auditors,' she wrote in the *New York Journal-American*. 'Her attitude at all times was that of a singer who performed her task to the best of her ability.'

A couple of reporters wondered if the fools and gulls weren't actually the audience who had stumped up all that money. Others were more inclined to draw attention to the chasm between the audience's perception of Florence and her own. It was 'the funniest, saddest of all concerts,' said the headline in the *Milwaukee Journal*. 'The blissful dowager on the platform seemed completely unaware that 3,000 persons were laughing at her – not politely, mind you, but uproariously and in gales,' wrote its music critic Richard S. Davis. 'She delivered line after line of her ballad with nothing but her moving lips as evidence that she was singing.' Earl Wilson observed 'snickering, squealing and guffawing at her singing, which she took very seriously'. O. T. (the byline of Oscar Thompson) in the *New York Sun* found an 'infantile quality' in her voice, and barely heard a thing. What he did hear 'was hopelessly lacking in a semblance of pitch, but the further a note was from its proper elevation the more the audience laughed and applauded'. She was spared the verdict of Isabel Morse Jones of the *Los Angeles Times* who didn't file a review, but later she dubbed the concert 'the most pathetic exhibition of vanity I have ever seen'. The prospect of Florence singing folk music in costume prompted her to walk out, disgusted also at the part played by the audience. 'There was something indecent and barbarously cruel about this business,' she wrote. In *PM*, Henry Simon described the audience's frenzied laughter as 'the cruellest and least civilized behavior I have ever witnessed in Carnegie Hall. But Mrs Jenkins met it all with pleased smiles.'

It was perhaps the sympathetic note struck by *PM*'s review that persuaded St Clair to give them an interview the following year. 'I think my wife knew her voice was passing,' he told his interviewer Betty Moorsteen when she visited him in the fourth-floor apartment on West 37th Street. 'But she loved singing so much she determined to continue with it. Perhaps she kept on a little too long, but it was her pleasure, her way of expressing herself.' When St Clair was asked about it years later, he recalled that Florence was already distressed as they made their way back to the Seymour Hotel apartment that night after the concert. His worst fears were confirmed when they both read the newspapers. 'It turned out the fiasco I expected. Afterward, when we went home, Florence was upset – and when she read the reviews, crushed. She had not known, you see.'

St Clair went so far as to claim that the critical reception broke Florence's heart. On a deeper level what it really shattered was her defences. Independent witnesses had no stake in shoring up the potent image of herself she had projected for so many years to all those women's clubs and her own fiefdom in the Verdi Club. And so they destroyed it.

In due course, even the *Musical Courier* deserted Florence after a quarter of a century of hoodwinking its readers in return for money. Being a periodical it limped in late with a report published on 15 November. The critic could not be persuaded to comment on her singing at all. Instead the Pascarella ensemble was singled out for praise. 'The quartet also played with the singer in Mr McMoon's "Mexican Serenade", written for the soprano,' it concluded. 'The vast audience roared bravos at every gesture of the glamorously garbed singer.' Four days later the *San Diego Union*, which reported in July on the brisk trade in her recordings, piled in again with a belated compilation of the critics' raspberries from Carnegie Hall ('Tone-Deaf Coloratura Makes Bad Singing Pay').

But by then Florence wasn't reading her reviews. She was so exhausted by the occasion that on 28 October she sent St Clair to a dinner in her stead where he said he 'felt somewhat persona non grata'. On the final day of October she was 'at last able to relax', he recorded in his diary, and then two days later was 'much recovered'. She was well enough to pay a visit to Danbury, seventy miles north of New York in Connecticut, on 4 November, but on the drive home she had a heart seizure. She refused to let St Clair summon a doctor and they went out to dinner. Re-entering the Seymour he noted that 'she stood still by the door then walked with difficulty'. The next day a physician diagnosed heart strain and complications and prescribed medicine and rest. A couple of days later she presided at a Verdi Club musicale at the St Regis Hotel, whereafter her health fluctuated for a week until, on 16 November, St Clair thought her 'exceedingly ill', a fear confirmed the next day by a heart specialist called Dr Hertz.

Florence's illness was brought on by either the strain of the performance or the trauma of the reviews. Or both. Or, perhaps, she intuited somewhere deep in the labyrinth of her psyche that the span of her life should end on a major chord of resounding, unrepeatable finality. Confined to bed, where she mostly dozed, she was attended by a nurse, her housemaid of seventeen years, Mildred Brown, and St Clair. He was unable to be there constantly as he was rehearsing a play called *Hand in Glove*, which was due to open in early December, so he visited before rehearsals and after. On 22 November he took her flowers. Dr Hertz suggested she go to hospital but she refused, and to St Clair she seemed to be through the worst. 'Dr reports acute stage is past,' he wrote.

In the last meaningful act of their long liaison, at some

point Florence gestured to her briefcase. 'In there is my will,' she said to St Clair, 'and I am leaving everything to you.' On 26 November she agreed to her doctor's demand that a hospital bed be hired. Her conversation was bright in the morning, then she slept in the afternoon, and St Clair felt confident enough to go out to dinner with Prince Galitzen. It was in St Clair's absence that, at about half past seven, Madame Jenkins, Lady Florence, the prima donna of Carnegie Hall, took her final, shallow breath.

12: LIKE FATHER, LIKE DAUGHTER

'After 36 years of happiness in Love, B. leaves me.' St Clair Bayfield returned to the Seymour Hotel and the long face of Dr Hertz, who imparted the news that Florence was dead. The diary, which for many years contained no more than a series of brief jottings, became almost wordy with grief.

At 9 p.m., St Clair rang Arthur Moritz, an attorney who had handled her affairs in Wilkes-Barre and elsewhere for the previous ten years, to inform him and suggest that he take on the administration of her estate. Moritz immediately phoned Campbell's in Madison Avenue, where the funeral of Florence's mother took place in 1930. The *New York Times* was also contacted.

The following morning was a Monday. The *Times* announced the death of Mrs Florence Foster Jenkins, soprano, founder and president of the Verdi Club. The briefest details of her life were offered. She was the widow of Dr Frank Jenkins of Washington, DC and gave a recital at Carnegie Hall on 25 October. Of her accompanists that night, the flautist's name was given as Oeste [sic] De Sevo. The final paragraph consisted of four words: 'No immediate relatives survive.'

St Clair was excused rehearsals that day. Moritz came in from Scarsdale just to the north of the city in order to locate the will. An initial search proved fruitless so he gave orders for the building management to seal the apartment and spent the day arranging for the opening of a box kept at a safe deposit company on Third Avenue in the hope that it would contain the will. The news travelled to Dallas, Pennsylvania, where Florence's next of kin was George Bulford, a second cousin who was descended from Charles Dorrance Foster's older half-brother. His permission was sought for the removal of the body and the arrangement of the funeral. This he gave on the understanding that neither he nor any of his relatives would incur any of the cost. Later that day Moritz and St Clair met the funeral director to choose a coffin. 'The sky shed tears,' wrote a mournful St Clair before adding, 'No will to be found.'

On Tuesday the safe deposit box was opened and also found to contain no will. Instead there were savings bank books, leases affecting Wilkes-Barre properties including Florence's parents' home in South Franklin Street, a cache of her jewellery, two wristwatches initialled F. F. J. and one initialled S. C. B., an eleven-page genealogical document and a four-page typewritten sketch of Florence's life and activities. Moritz applied to the Surrogate's Court of New York, which handled probate and estate proceedings, for sanction to exceed a limit of $250 for expenditure on a funeral to reflect Florence's wealth and social standing. He was granted an upper tariff of $500 including the cost of shipping the body to Wilkes-Barre and interment. St Clair attended a dress rehearsal of *Hand in Glove* and didn't get to bed till four in the morning.

For the funeral on Wednesday he had printed a memorial card showing an elderly Florence beaming brightly under a substantial hat. 'In Loving Memory,' it said in a gothic font. 'Florence Foster Jenkins who passed away with a smile November 26th 1944.' The funeral took place at 11 a.m. It was conducted by St Clair. A harpist played two tunes and a baritone sang 'Going Home' and the Lord's Prayer over an open coffin. 'B. looked lovely,' St Clair wrote. 'I felt some comfort after I had kissed her and held her little hand. The heavens wept.' That night Florence's remains were taken to Wilkes-Barre, accompanied by her old home-town friend Miss Mae Black, with whom she'd stayed on the night of her father's death in 1909.

Moritz arranged with the office of the public administrator for the Seymour Hotel apartment to be searched more thoroughly in the presence of an attorney representing the next of kin. They found Florence's home forbiddingly stuffed with papers in every imaginable cranny. 'There were drawers upon drawers, full to the brim,' recalled Moritz later in an application to retrieve his unpaid fees; the sheer profusion of documents caused him to slip briefly out of formal legalese. It was agreed that a single day was insufficient to complete the search; the maid Mildred Brown, who expressed her certainty that Florence had left a will, was asked to take on the job. She was still looking for it eleven days later, and most days St Clair's diary noted that it had not yet been located.

Twenty-four hours on from her funeral, Florence's body was interred at the Foster family mausoleum in Hollenback Cemetery in Wilkes-Barre. Officiating was the rector of St Stephen's Episcopal church, which burned down in 1897 and in which a stained glass window in memory of her younger sister Lillian Blanche was endowed by her father. The local newspaper's obituary mentioned Florence's many concerts in New York, including her climactic recital; also the deep American ancestry of her parents and her late husband. Finally it alluded to 'H. Clair Hayfield, who handled Mrs Jenkins's musical affairs' and, it was reported, 'was unable to come here for today's service'.

St Clair was stuck in New York, denied a second chance to skip rehearsals of *Hand in Glove*. A psychological murder mystery about Jack the Ripper, the production was directed by James Whale, the maker of several screen horror classics who had been lured from Hollywood by the subject matter. When it opened on 4 December, the *Times* critic found the play diverting if full of holes and underwritten characters, one of them played by St Clair who had 'trouble with a retired school teacher'. It was the first time in many years that a review had deigned to notice him.

In the meantime St Clair was being written out of Florence's life story. His sorrows began even before the funeral when he tried to retrieve some paintings of his from the Seymour Hotel apartment. As it was sealed he needed a lawyer's assistance. He applied to Nathaniel Palzer, an attorney whom he had known via Florence for a dozen years and trusted implicitly. Palzer had drawn up Florence's missing will. When he said he'd need a signature on a document, St Clair provided it without looking too closely at what he was signing. What St Clair didn't know was that the day after the funeral Palzer was appointed to act as the New York attorney for a large body of second cousins from the Bulford clan. St Clair's diary entry of 8 December refers to him as 'friend Palzer', with whom he discussed 'making a claim on B's estate'. (To distract himself St Clair also cleaned his golf clubs that day.) Later St Clair was told by an attorney he instructed that his signature consented to Mrs Ella Bulford Harvey becoming the administrator of the estate. In effect, he had inadvertently surrendered any prospect of inheriting Florence's fortune. According to a later entry in St Clair's diary, Palzer's deception was motivated by professional jealousy. Incensed that it was Moritz rather than him who was instructed on the night of Florence's death, and knowing the missing will left everything to St Clair, Palzer contacted the Bulfords and told them that unless they appointed him their attorney he would make the contents of the will public. St Clair's attorney theorised that Palzer's desertion was the 'result of Jewish incapability of realizing that with a gentleman Honor is not just a ping-pong ball'.

Ella Bulford Harvey was the granddaughter of John Jacob Bulford and Florence's second cousin once removed. Born in 1888, she had been widowed in her mid-twenties and left with a single daughter. She remarried at nearly forty, was now fifty-six, and was chosen as the Bulfords' representative presumably because her life experiences had made her resilient. There were a lot of Bulfords to represent: unlike the Fosters, they had bred busily and Mrs Bulford duly submitted a list of twenty second cousins. One each was from New York state, Virginia and West Virginia; two were from Nebraska, three from New Jersey; the majority from Dallas, Luzerne and Trucksville, Pennsylvania.

Palzer passed on to his new clients the information that Florence had left $70,000 in jewellery and securities and $30,000 in cash. Over the next few days Moritz kept him abreast of his search for the will in Wilkes-Barre banks and half a dozen lawyers' offices in New York and Washington with whom Florence had had dealings as far back as 1913 and as recently as 1940. One of the lawyers, it emerged, had died thirty years earlier. None knew anything about a will. In the apartment a trunk and a cabinet had their locks broken, but nothing was found. On 11 December Mildred Brown, whose rummaging in the apartment had also turned up nothing, mentioned a bag with valuable papers which had not yet been located. She suggested Moritz apply to look for it in a warehouse where Florence rented storage space. A day later she finished her own search, which she calculated had taken her ninety-nine hours and for which she billed Moritz $88. Moritz, getting desperate, took a final peek behind the many paintings in the apartment, including the two portraits of Florence over the Steinway. The next day, which was three days before Christmas, Ella Bulford Harvey filed a petition for letters of administration on the estate – asking the court to appoint her as the official distributor of Florence's assets. The Bulfords were evidently confident of success because on Boxing Day Palzer confirmed to Moritz that he would receive from them a fee for his services in organising the funeral and searching for the will.

Afterwards, theories about the disappearance of the will – and the bag or briefcase in which Florence kept it – laid the blame on two quite different parties. Florence Darnault and Adolf Pollitz believed the thief was Cosme McMoon acting in concert with Mildred Brown. Both, went their theory, had expected to be named in the will. When they discovered they weren't, they attempted to alter it and, making a hash of it, destroyed it instead. 'He was a rotter through and through,' said Pollitz. 'A terrible person,' agreed Darnault. Their low opinion stemmed from their disapproval of McMoon's disloyal stage antics towards the end of Florence's singing career. It is true that her accompanist was expecting something from the will. 'This was a part of the background why I was associated with her,' McMoon said. 'She had spoken to me about leaving a trust fund for scholarships to talented singers and a musical foundation in a house which she owned in Flemington, New Jersey to be known as the Florence Foster Jenkins memorial.' On 22 December he asked St Clair to join him and Mildred Brown in employing a lawyer, but St Clair was working on his own case. McMoon went on to sue the estate; Pollitz testified against him and the case was dismissed.

St Clair was later adamant that McMoon had never said an ill word about Florence, and he was convinced that the will was stolen by a member of the Bulford clan. Either party would need to have done it before her death or almost immediately after it, because Moritz had the apartment sealed on the morning of 27 November.

But the ultimate responsibility for the chaos which followed her death rested with the decedent herself. Florence's distrust of lawyers and bankers, both professions closely connected with her father, meant that she had calamitously failed to lodge her will in a safe place beyond the reach of interested parties. It was her final manipulation.

The emotional cost was borne by St Clair, whose profound grief took on a bitter flavour. The very year he met Florence, indeed not six weeks after their common-law wedding ceremony, Florence had been plunged into an unpleasant court battle occasioned by her father's missing will. She would have known that the failure to find hers would initiate a second legal scrap with her cousins and that without her money St Clair would be penniless. He was surviving on social security handouts and, unable to afford the rent of $87 a month on the 37th Street apartment that Florence had paid since 1917, he extracted an agreement from the landlord that the payment would be met only after the outcome of his legal challenge to inherit Florence's fortune. In the meantime he sublet half of the apartment to reduce his financial commitment. Florence's friends evaporated. He spent Christmas alone in the apartment where every previous year he had hauled a tree up to the fourth floor and decorated it for a party with Florence and friends, who for one night of the year had enjoyed slumming it in St Clair's cramped quarters with its quaint bare decor. 'A wet cool miserable day in tune with my regrets about darling B,' he wrote. 'It is very lonely without her,' he later told Betty Moorsteen of *PM*. 'But I feel I have no right to be indignant at losing someone who gave me thirty-six years of more happiness than most men ever know.'

After Florence's death St Clair did not immediately write to Kathleen Weatherley. He grieved in silence for a month. On 30 December he finally broke his silence. As soon as she received the news Kathleen cabled her condolences. Two days after *Hand in Glove* closed, St Clair confided to her that only she would be able to understand his complicated feelings. 'My life's entirely circled round hers,' he wrote. 'Whilst Florence lived, if I were in necessity, she would provide for me, and if she died first I was to inherit her personal estate. My statements of her promises are corroborated by three witnesses to whom she said much the same thing, but even if this claim were successful it would produce nothing for twelve months, and then much less than my claim. A mere pittance, yet she intended me to inherit all her estate, of that I am perfectly sure. If a will is found this fact will be proved, but the most expert search has failed to reveal one. We are at a loss.'

Towards the end of January *American Weekly* caught wind of the legal story brewing and had a field day with Florence all over again. 'Discordant Diva's Missing Will', said the title. 'What is to happen,' it asked, 'to the wealth of Florence Foster Jenkins, whose odd operatic career amounted to murder of the undetectable B sharp?' No wonder St Clair confided to his diary: 'Had a burst of emotion which tore me apart, at loss of B. Can't seem to get my balance.' He was also suffering from rheumatism. Two days later Florence's qualities were more generously considered at a luncheon held in her memory at the Shelton. Tributes were paid by Verdi Club members, led by St Clair. A new president was elected: Mrs Owen Kildare, married to an émigré Russian prince who hid his identity behind an Irish name, was a busy broadcaster, ardent Republican and former suffragette who strongly disapproved of stylish fashions. She was a tireless club woman and for years she had taken charge of the pageants at the Silver Skylarks

Ball. Without its founder and figurehead, the Verdi Club sub-
sided into invisibility. It was to be mentioned just twice more
in the *Times*, and then only in passing.

On Valentine's Day ('Dear B of last year was my Valentine')
St Clair submitted a petition to the Surrogate Court that he
and Florence had lived together since 1909 as common-law
husband and wife, which various witnesses could confirm, at
which date he had abandoned his career to manage hers; and
that Florence had made a will of which he was to be the main
beneficiary. He also wished to revoke the consent which,
erroneously and without knowing his legal rights, he gave to
Ella Bulford Harvey, and applied to administer the estate
himself. Plus he wanted his paintings back. He signed the
document 'John St Clair Roberts known as St Clair Bayfield'.
In early March he answered Mrs Harvey's demand for proof
of his marriage to Florence by submitting a long bill of par-
ticulars: it included a description of their meeting and pledge
to each other, a list of the addresses in which they had cohabited and the hotels across the country where she had joined
him on tour in the 1910s. He added, for effect, that the tours
had been with Sir Herbert Tree and George Arliss. A list of
fifteen witnesses was supplied who could confirm that he and
Florence were married, including her Hungarian accompanist, Prince Galitzen, the new president of the Verdi Club and
his landlord. He did not know the date of Florence's marriage
to Frank Thornton Jenkins, but he did claim to know when
they were divorced. Also, he knocked a decade off his own
age. On 5 March St Clair was in court as witnesses gave evidence that he was Florence's common-law husband, though
he complained that his attorney was 'utterly outshone' by
Palzer and 'did not make the most of the excellent witnesses
I had marshalled in our favour'. He took the decision to
appoint a new attorney.

In due course the newspapers caught wind of St Clair's petition to be recognised as her heir. 'The Sour Soprano's Discordant Legacy', ran the *Sunday Mirror* headline in early May. Alongside more of the usual jokes about Florence, the article was unkind about St Clair's career – 'he claims that he acted years ago in Sir Herbert Beerbohm Tree's and George Arliss's Shakespearian troupes' – and lampooned the image of him as her loyal protector in a verse to 'a departed chantoose':

> *Though others howled when Madame yowled,*
> *Rudely tooted when La Jenkins hooted,*
> *Hissed when she missed,*
> *Booed when she mooed,*
> *Groaned when she moaned,*
> *Blatted when she flatted,*
> *Razzed the very pantos*
> *Off her bel cantos,*
> *Mocked her Puccini*
> *With wilted zucchini,*
> *Rewarded with spinach her lieder in Finnish,*
> *With odorous scallion*
> *Her group in Italian . . .*
> *Though others did those discouraging things,*
> *NOT St Clair Bayfield! HE cheers in the wings.*

This was published on 6 May, and syndicated to the *Wilkes-Barre Record* on VE Day. Nazi Germany's unconditional surrender offered no distraction for St Clair who started dreaming that Florence was alive and well and with him. He was soon receiving auditory visitations from her. One night he awoke in his apartment to the sound of knocking. 'I disregarded it and told myself I must not be fooled,' he wrote in a letter to Kathleen on 14 May. 'But when some nights later I awaked [sic] for no reason, and then heard a secret knock, very distinctly, in the north room of 66, I went in the dark and talked to her but gained no response. Thinking this was a wish I should communicate, I went to a spiritualist with a handbag of hers. Aware that these people usually preyed on thought reading, I was only astonished when certain things were mentioned which I myself did not know till afterwards verified. Also the message said, "I'm very unhappy you should be suffering because of lack of care on my part. There was a will but it has been destroyed. I love you and shall always love you as much as I ever did with my whole heart, and I send you my blessings. In three months your financial position will be improved, so do not worry. Attend to your stage work to avoid it. Trust in God more than you ever did before, above all I want you to be happy. Bless you, bless you, bless you." I have written this from memory but have the memo I made immediately after hearing this. The other things mentioned were about her father, and not until I verified them did I know them, so that could not have been thought reading.' The clairvoyant talked of a safe and Chase Bank and a court case, though they might easily have intuited this information by reading a newspaper.

St Clair didn't mention his dealings with a clairvoyant in the sympathetic interview which appeared in *PM*. It was published the day before the hearing to establish his marital status. In the Surrogate Court St Clair professed his love for Florence and produced correspondence between them over the years to prove they had thought of themselves as a married couple. One witness brought from Wilkes-Barre told the court that Florence had introduced St Clair as her secretary ('which is the last thing she would do!' St Clair exclaimed in his diary). Only one witness was called to testify that they were often seen together, but she was the grandest personage on his list. Mrs Edith Bobe Hague's sympathy could be counted on as her name had also been dragged through the papers. In

1925 she was physically assaulted and robbed of $40,000 worth of jewellery by three armed men. Her companion for the evening was Robert Hague, the head of the marine division of Standard Oil. The robbery caused their affair to be revealed, Hague to obtain a divorce from his wife and to marry Miss Bobe, who was described as a 'modiste'. She was widowed in 1939. Her presence in court in 1945 attracted press photographers. A platinum blonde in a fur stole and sunglasses emerged into the early summer gloaming, shielding her face from the camera flashes. St Clair wore a dark suit, a fedora and an anxious smile.

Deliberating his verdict, Judge James Delehanty was unable to overlook the blood ties of Florence's cousins, but he took pity on St Clair and found his claim to have some merit. In Delehanty's chambers St Clair's lawyer negotiated with Palzer and came up with a figure of $22,000. On St Clair's birthday – 2 August – Delehanty publicly delivered his judgment. The letters of administration were granted to Ella Bulford Harvey, who would be appointed administrator 'subject to the payment of $22,000 to John St Clair Roberts in full settlement and payment of his claim of common-law husband of the decedent, including any and all claims for services rendered as secretary or manager, or otherwise'.

In Wilkes-Barre this was reported as a victory for Florence's local heirs. 'It is understood,' said the *Wilkes-Barre Record*, 'the heirs have made a small settlement with Bayfield.' In fact, while St Clair had done worse than he had hoped, he fared far better than any other individual in the distribution of Florence's money. The sum almost exactly matched that granted to the Bulfords by Florence's father in the contentious second codicil to his will. The tax on his award was to be paid by the estate, which also had to cover the costs of the public administrator's legal expenses and costs of more than $2,000.

Another $3,000 had already been withdrawn from the estate to settle the outstanding rents at both apartments, plus paying for the restoration of the Seymour Hotel apartment to the condition in which Florence entered it in 1917 (a bathroom had been turned into a storeroom). The following year Moritz asked for his unsettled bill of $750 for services rendered to be paid out of the estate too. It was a far more demanding task than he anticipated. 'The decedent was advanced in years and regarded as eccentric,' he explained in his petition, 'had no one (except for Mr St Clair Bayfield) in close relationship with her.' He submitted a detailed breakdown of the 34⅞ hours he'd spent on tidying up her affairs. The next of kin argued that the payment should be met by St Clair. 'I was never the attorney for Mr Bayfield,' Moritz said. 'I never acted on his behalf.' The judge ruled that the estate must pay. Thus a sum slightly above $70,000 was shared between twenty Bulford cousins. Mrs Harvey also took charge of Charles D. Foster's considerable portfolio of real estate.

On the day St Clair celebrated his seventieth birthday, at least in prospect he was richer than he had ever been. So were many of his co-beneficiaries. On 7 August George Bulford announced that he would be opening a showroom dealing in farm machinery and hardware. On the 19th the Bulfords held their fifteenth annual reunion picnic in the Luzerne country-side. After they'd opened with the Lord's Prayer, the treasurer had something more momentous than usual to report. The absentee Bulfords serving in the armed forces were enumer-ated, including one seriously wounded on D-Day. Three births were recorded, two marriages and two deaths. Although she'd certainly never attended these gatherings, one of the names of the departed belonged to Mrs Florence Jenkins. A measure of how much her money would mean to her more indigent next of kin came on 28 August when the will of Frank Bulford was probated: he left his home and an acre of land to one daughter and $500 each to four grandchildren, splitting between three daughters and one granddaughter the remainder of an estate valued at $1,900.

St Clair was still wounded by sorrow and self-pity. On the anniversary of his common-law marriage he wrote, 'This day 1909' in his diary. At the end of August he was still hearing Florence's knocks. 'Will see spiritualist and find if B wishes me to get in touch.'

On a more concrete plane he and Kathleen made plans to reunite. She sought release from the War Office but didn't sail to New York until January 1946, arriving just as St Clair was going into rehearsals for a play called *Jeb* about a black soldier returning to the US after three years in the South Pacific. She too had not seen him for three years. In Kathleen's judgement, the hunted look she had known when their affair had to be kept a secret had now disappeared. She attributed the change to Florence's death. Two days before they married St Clair, a keen swimmer till the end of his life, had a serious accident in a pool which meant that for several years he was unable to raise his arms above his head. And yet, said Kathleen, 'After a couple of years' marriage with me, even though he was then seventy-three years old, his face completely changed, he became fatter, was exceedingly happy.'

St Clair and Kathleen bought a house in Westchester, while he invested his money and drew an annuity. A rare colour photograph of the Bayfields dressed up for a smart function shows St Clair still lean and imposing in old age. Kathleen clings to his arm, beaming proudly. Their marriage was not necessarily happy. A young pianist called Bill Brady, who lived at the time in Westchester, was introduced to the Bayfields by Adolf Pollitz and came to know them well. In 2006 he gave an interview in which he expressed the view that St Clair was not in love with Kathleen and would never have established contact with her after Florence's death were he not destitute as he awaited the outcome of the court case. According to Brady, Kay was even more domineering than Florence, and St Clair became animated only when she was not present. As he related it, St Clair's swimming injury rendered him sexually inactive, much to Kathleen's frustration.

The Bayfields returned to England several times in the 1950s, while St Clair kept in touch with grand dames of the English theatre. His correspondents included Edith Evans, with whom he shared a stage in *The Lady with the Lamp* in 1931, and Sybil Thorndike, whom he knew as one of the young Ben Greet Players in 1907. He also wrote to Flora Robson. His obituary in the *New York Times* reported that in 1948 he had gone back to London to join her in the cast of George Bernard Shaw's *Captain Brassbound's Confession*; in fact he was making his last ever Broadway appearance, with former Hollywood starlet Nancy Carroll, in a comedy about a pair of stage actresses called *For Heaven's Sake, Mother!*

On his last trip to England, in 1959, St Clair described himself in the passenger manifest as a writer. The biography of Florence he embarked on was not his only way of memorialising her. Every July for several years he sent flowers to be laid on the Foster mausoleum at Wilkes-Barre on Florence's birthday. He also dedicated a seat with her name in a theatre in Abington, Virginia, assembled a scrapbook of her Verdi Club cuttings and kept his collection of their five hundred letters.

The last words he wrote to Kathleen told a different story: 'To the most adorable woman I've met during my ninety years, my wife.' At his ninetieth birthday celebration he sang shanties he remembered from his long sea voyage to New Zealand in the 1890s. He died on 19 May 1967 at the age of ninety-one. The following year a plaque in his memory was unveiled at the Larchmont Public Library, which in 1922 he had helped to fund by giving up his summer to direct a cast of local amateurs in A *Midsummer Night's Dream*.

His widow took on the manuscript of Florence's biography but failed to find a publisher, one of whom advised her to write more about Florence and less about herself. She worked with two collaborators but fell out with both of them. The book never appeared and the manuscript was lost, along with the correspondence between Florence and St Clair, and a scrapbook of photographs of Florence. Nor did the auto-biographical jottings, found in the safe deposit box after Florence's death, survive.

Kathleen took better care preserving St Clair's memory. In 1973 she endowed an annual award to honour the best per-formance in a supporting role by an actor in a Shakespearean play in the New York area. Until her death in 1988 she enjoyed attending the ceremony at the Actors' Equity Associ-ation, and making the presentation. The winner received a cheque and an engraved crystal plaque. To this day, every year in New York, the St Clair Bayfield Award is presented to a performer who, for all their talent, must cede the limelight to a bigger star.

Epilogue

In 1957, fifty-one years after his arrival in America, **Malton Boyce** was last spotted accompanying a soloist on the organ as she sang 'Ave Maria' at a wedding in St Stephen's church, Washington, DC. The *Evening Standard* in Uniontown, Pennsylvania, reported that 'the service was lovely'.

There are still **Bulfords** in Luzerne County.

Lucile Collette did not fulfil her early promise as a violin prodigy and instead worked as a piano accompanist in New York. In 1953 she was foreman of a federal jury which convicted thirteen secondary Communist leaders of conspiracy to teach and advocate the overthrow of the government. She suffered from failing eyesight and left most of her estate to the New York Association for the Blind.

Florence Malcolm Darnault's bronze portrait bust of Rear Admiral John K. Robison is in the US Naval Academy Museum. Her portrait bust of Giuseppe Verdi is, at the time of writing, available for purchase from Anthony's Fine Art and Antiques, Salt Lake City, for $11,800 (global shipping available).

On 22 August 1924 the Kansas tenor **Ernest Davis** sang at a Prom in Queen's Hall, London. Under the baton of Sir Henry Wood he performed 'Figlia mia' from Handel's *Tamerlano* (arranged by the conductor) and Haydn Wood's 'Love's garden of roses'. He never made it to the Met.

Fleming's Castle in Hunterdon County, New Jersey,

remained the headquarters of the Colonel Lowrey Chapter of the Daughters of the American Revolution until 2005.

Ben Greet ran the Old Vic Theatre in London during the years of the Great War, where he produced and directed twenty-three of Shakespeare's plays (and revived *Everyman*). During his tenure the theatre established links with over four hundred schools.

The literary career of **Thornton Jenkins Hains** did not recover after his acquittal, although a prescient short story of his about an ocean-going liner striking an iceberg was published in the *Popular Magazine* in the same month as the *Titanic* sank. He had three more children soon afterwards, then another three between 1934 and 1941.

Eva Hasell of the Caravan Mission continued to drive around the wildernesses of Canada until 1972, when she was eighty-four. She was made a Member of the Order of the British Empire. A memorial to her can be found in St Andrew's church, Dacre, Cumberland.

Society proctologist **Alcinous B. Jamison** responded to the death of his wife, the president of the Euterpe Club, by adding to a list of publications which already included *Intestinal Ills: Chronic Constipation, Indigestion, Autogenetic Poisons, Diarrhoea, Piles, Etc.* and *Intestinal Irrigation; Or, Why, How, and When to Flush the Colon* with a volume titled *Man: Whence and Whither*. He included a foreword, written not by himself, that described him as 'gifted with a clairvoyant faculty that enables him to see certain things and discern operations of natural law that are at present hidden from more than 99 percent of the human race'.

After his disgrace **Presley Jenkins** stayed on in California. Settling in Alemeda over the water from San Francisco, he and his wife went on to have seven children. The last two were boys called Frank and Presley.

Claudia Libbey's second marriage lasted for fifty-five years. There were no children. In her uncontested divorce from the convicted killer Captain Peter Hains she lost custody of their three children and was never allowed to see them again. Her second son Hamilton was awarded the Legion of Merit for services in the South Pacific by President F. D. Roosevelt in 1944. He retired as Rear Admiral Hains.

After his years as the accompanist of Kirsten Flagstad, **Edwin McArthur** was appointed music director of St Louis Municipal Opera, in which post he remained for twenty-three years; he also conducted the Harrisburg Symphony in Pennsylvania for twenty-four years. In 1976 he conducted *Die Walküre* in Naples, perhaps the least Wagnerian city in the whole of Europe. He was not, despite the rumours, the real Cosme McMoon.

After **Attorney John McGahren** died in 1921 his widow put his farm in Trucksville up for sale. It comprised '100 acres in highest state of cultivation; 10 acres of timber; 2 houses, Manor house improved this Spring; 2 barns filled with a bumper crop just harvested; acres of potatoes and cabbage; orchard laden with fruit; 7 registered cows; 4 heifers, chickens, 3 horses, harness, wagons; all new machinery. No agents.'

Cosme McMoon developed an interest in bodybuilding. In 1974 at the Mr Olympia contest he was photographed being held aloft by Arnold Schwarzenegger and another bodybuilder. He lived in New York until, suffering from pancreatic cancer, he returned to San Antonio, Texas, in 1980, where he died two days later.

For many years **Adolf Pollitz** played the piano for the Ben Cutler Orchestra in New York. In later life he returned to Oyster Bay, where the widowed Kathleen Bayfield was a neighbour who called him 'that fairy' behind his back and demanded he chauffeur her around much as he had once chauffeured her predecessor.

When the **Rev. George Bayfield Roberts** died in 1937, his estate was worth £71 8s 9d.

Sängerfests are still going strong in America.

The tour of *The Prima Donna* reached Salt Lake City where a journalist who saw them together was not confident that the marriage of **Fritzi Scheff** and **John Fox Jr** had legs. 'The highly intellectual and interesting Fox is the last person anyone would associate with people or things theatrical, and Fritzi does not seem of the temperament suited to a studious, literary genius.' The Foxes divorced in 1912. Miss Scheff married a third husband the following year, and divorced him in 1921 on grounds of intolerable cruelty. Out of the blue she received a phone call from St Clair Bayfield on 1 March 1945. His diary does not reveal what they discussed.

In 1908 **Miss May V. Smith** and a companion embarked on a four-month tour of nineteen nations. In 1912 she gave lectures with pictures on Egypt, Turkey and Palestine to audiences in the Methodist Episcopal church in Wilkes-Barre and the Ladies' Missionary Society of the Christian Church of Plymouth in Forty Fort. Later that year she acquired a Cadillac touring car.

Five years after the termination of her engagement to St Clair Bayfield, **Rosalind Travers** married Henry Hyndman, the founder of the British National Socialist party (which was eventually absorbed into the Labour Party, and should not be confused with a similarly named German party). He was thirty-one years her senior and died in 1921. Her book *The Last Years of H. M. Hyndman* was published in 1924, the year of her own death at the age of fifty-one.

Janet Waldorf's career never recovered from her mis-reported death. She continued acting in the early 1900s, and even turned up in Wilkes-Barre in a touring production of *The Three of Us* (advertised as 'the greatest of all American plays'). She returned to Pittsburgh to marry, divorce and keep boarders. Her real name was May Maud Midgley.

The *Wilkes-Barre Record* was absorbed into the *Wilkes-Barre Times-Leader*, itself a merger of the *Wilkes-Barre Times* and *Wilkes-Barre Leader*, in 1939. Between 1923 and 1960 the paper in its various permutations housed its printing and distribution facility in the former Grand Opera House behind the Foster homestead on South Franklin Street. After a bitter strike over wages and working conditions, a group of employees set up the *Citizens' Voice*, which has since become the longest-running strike newspaper in the country. Wilkes-Barre, Pa, is thus an American rarity: a town with two newspapers.

Acknowledgements and Bibliography

In researching this biography I was able to stand on the shoulders of others, from which lofty perch the view of Florence Foster Jenkins's life and career was greatly enhanced. Gregor Benko has conducted a vast amount of research over many years and he was unstintingly generous in sharing the fruits of it, both in documentation and photographs. Donald Collup is the creator of *A World of Her Own*, the authoritative feature-length documentary about Florence, and has been tirelessly supportive of this British interloper constantly soliciting advice. Some of the eyewitness accounts of the Carnegie Hall concert, including his wonderful interview with Marge Champion, come from his DVD. I also had the good fortune to strike up a productive correspondence with Elizabeth Skrapits, a Florence fan and a journalist with the *Citizens' Voice* in Wilkes-Barre who was pricelessly kind in sharing her enthusiasm and her local knowledge. To all three I owe a debt of gratitude the size of Carnegie Hall itself.

I also relied on help from those closer to home. Luke Davis meticulously researched the historical background to Florence's life in New York plus those forays to Newport, Rhode Island. With great generosity Alastair Boag rooted productively around the St Clair Bayfield archive in the New York Public Library. Florence Rees read the book in draft and offered valuable comments. Emily Maitland provided precious insights as a psychotherapist into the deep undercurrents of Madame Jenkins's unconscious. My thanks to them all.

My thanks also to Linda LaPointe of the Moravian College (as Florence's school is now known) for unearthing revelatory details from the school yearbook and Susan Law for information relating to St Clair Bayfield's grandfather, the Earl of Ellenborough.

My final thanks to Nicholas Martin, whose enthusiasm for Florence's story was infectious, to James Gill of United Agents, and to Georgina Morley and Jamie Coleman at Macmillan.

I tracked the movements of the book's dramatis personae via a number of online newspaper archives: the *New York Times* archive, the Library of Congress's Chronicling America archive, the British Newspaper Archive, Newspapers.com, the National Library of Australia's Trove archive and the National Library of New Zealand's Papers Past archive. For information relating to the census in both the US and UK, as well as records of birth, marriage, death and ocean-going travel, I consulted the genealogy websites ancestry.com/co.uk and findagrave.com. There is also an excellent page on Florence's ancestry on wargs.com.

The primary sources I consulted were the St Clair Bayfield archive in the New York Public Library, the New York Surrogates' Court documents relating to the Florence Foster Jenkins estate, the transcript of Bruce Hungerford's unpublished conversation in 1970 with Kathleen Bayfield, Florence Malcolm Darnault and Adolf Pollitz, and Gregor Benko's account of his 2006 interview with Bill Brady.

Other key sources include:

Bendiner, Milton: 'Florence Foster Jenkins: An Appreciation' (New York: Melotone, 1946).

Collup, Donald: *Florence Foster Jenkins: A World of Her Own* (Video Artists International, 2008).

Dixon, Daniel: 'Florence Foster Jenkins: The Diva of Din', *Coronet* (December 1957).

Moorsteen, Betty: 'Around Town: St Clair Bayfield Vs 15 2d Cousins', *PM* (1945).

Robinson, Francis: 'The Glory (????) of the Human Voice' (RCA, 1962).

Stevenson, Florence: 'An Angel of Mirth', *Opera News* (1963).

For background research I consulted the following books and articles:

Anon: *100 Years of Marriage and Divorce Statistics, United States, 1867–1967* (US Department of Health, Education and Welfare Publication, 1973).

—— *Historical Sketch: Moravian Seminary for Young Ladies* (Bethlehem, Pa: Moravian Publication Office, 1876).

—— 'The Position of Women', *North American Review* (New York: Harper & Brothers, 1909).

—— Zeckwer-Hahn Philadelphia Musical Academy School Catalogue (1905–6).

Bibby, Emily Katherine: *Making the American Aristocracy: Women, Cultural Capital, and High Society in New York City, 1870–1900* (PhD Thesis, Virginia Polytechnic Institute and State University, 2009).

Bordman, Gerald and Norton, Richard: *American Musical Theatre: A Chronicle* (New York: Oxford University Press, 1978).

Bradsby, H. C. (ed.): *History of Luzerne County Pennsylvania* (Wilkes-Barre, Pennsylvania: S. B. Nelson & Co., 1893).

Brokaw, Clare Boothe: 'American Society and Near Society', *America* (1932).

Burns, Debra Brubaker, Jackson, Anita and Sturm, Connie Arrau: 'Contributions of Selected British and American Women to Piano Pedagogy and Performance', *IAWM Journal* (2002).

Callan, Jim: *America in the 1900s and 1910s* (New York: Stonesong Press, 2006).

Crouse, Joan M.: *The Homeless Transient in the Great Depression:*

New York State, 1929–1941 (Albany: State University of New York Press, 1986).

Diehl, Lorraine B.: *Over Here! New York City During World War II* (New York: HarperCollins, 2010).

Ellis, John: *One Day in a Very Long War: Wednesday 25th October 1944* (London: Random House, 1998).

Fine, Mark A. and Harvey, John H. (eds): *Handbook of Divorce and Relationship Dissolution* (New York: Routledge, 2006).

Goldsmith, Barbara: *Little Gloria . . . Happy at Last* (London: Macmillan, 1981).

Hahm, Dorothea A. and Sheldon, Robert E.: 'The Virgil Practice Clavier', *The Piano: An Encyclopedia* (Palmieri, Robert, ed.) (New York: Routledge, 2003).

Harvey, Oscar Jewell: *A History of Wilkes-Barre* (Wilkes-Barre, Pa: Raeder Press, 1931).

Hayden, Deborah: *Pox: Genius, Madness, and the Mysteries of Syphilis* (New York: Basic Books, 2003).

Jabbour, Nicholas: 'Syphilis from 1880 to 1920: A Public Health Nightmare and the First Challenge to Medical Ethics', *Essays in History* (University of Virginia, 2000).

Jackson, Kenneth T.: *WWII & NYC* (New York: Scala, 2012).

Kisseloff, Jeff: *You Must Remember This: An Oral History of Manhattan from the 1890s to World War II* (London: Johns Hopkins University Press, 1999).

Kludas, Arnold: *Record Breakers of the North Atlantic: Blue Riband Liners 1838–1952* (London: Chatham Publishing, 2000).

Kulp, George B.: *Families of the Wyoming Valley* (Wilkes-Barre, Pa: George Brubaker, 1885).

Leavitt, Judith Walzer and Numbers, Ronald L. (eds): *Sickness and Health in America: Readings in the History of Medicine and Public Health* (Madison, Wis.: University of Wisconsin Press, 1978).

McGee, Isaiah R: *The Origin and Historical Development of*

Prominent Professional Black Choirs in the United States (Florida State University, 2007).

Montgomery, Maureen E.: 'The Fruit that Hangs Highest: Courtship and Chaperonage in New York High Society, 1880–1920', *Journal of Family History*, Vol. 21 (1996).

Morris, Lloyd: *Incredible New York: 1850–1950* (New York: Random House, 1951).

Quetel, Claude (trans. Braddock, Judith and Pike, Brian): *History of Syphilis* (Baltimore: Johns Hopkins University Press, 1990).

Roberts, Ina B. (ed.): *Club Women of New York, 1910–11*, 6th ed. (New York: Club Women of New York Company, 1910).

Stokes, John H.: *The Third Great Plague: A Discussion of Syphilis for Everyday People* (Philadelphia and London: W. B. Saunders Company, 1917).

Taylor, Frank Hamilton: *The City of Philadelphia as it Appears in the Year 1894: A Compilation of Facts Supplied by Distinguished Citizens for the Information of Business Men, Travelers, and the World at Large* (Philadelphia: G. S. Harris & sons, 1894).

Tomes, Robert: *The Bazar Book of Decorum* (New York: Harper and Brothers, 1870).

Trapper, Emma Louise: *The Musical Blue Book of America* (New York: Musical Blue Book Corporation, 1915).

Van Rensselaer, Mrs John King: *The Social Ladder* (New York: H. Holt and Company, 1924).

Vanderbilt Balsan, Consuelo: *The Glitter and the Gold* (London: William Heinemann Ltd, 1953).

Varicchio, Mario: 'The Wasteful Few: Upton Sinclair's Portrait of New York's High Society', *Public Space, Private Lives* (Amsterdam: VU University Press, 2004).

White, Annie Randall: *Polite Society at Home and Abroad: A Complete Compendium of Information Upon All Topics Classified Under the Head of Etiquette* (Chicago: Monarch Book Company, 1891).

Wilson, Ross J.: *New York and the First World War: Shaping an American City* (Surrey: Ashgate Publishing, 2014).

Young, Anthony: *New York Café Society: The Elite Meet to See and Be Seen, 1920s–1940s* (North Carolina: McFarland & Co. Inc., 2015).

FLORENCE FOSTER JENKINS

by NICHOLAS MARTIN

TITLES:

BASED ON TRUE EVENTS – 1944

INT. COMMODORE HOTEL / BALLROOM – NIGHT

Bayfield, the showman in tails, is on stage before a 150-strong AUDIENCE of well-to-do New Yorkers. To one side of the stage, a small orchestra of about 10 MUSICIANS. To the other, a sign which reads "The Verdi Club". Bayfield, 50s, a macho-camp man of the theatre, is in his element.

BAYFIELD 'Swounds, I should take it, for it cannot be, But I am pigeon-livered and lack gall, To make oppression bitter, or ere this, I should have fatted all the region kites, With this slave's offal. Bloody, bawdy villain! Remorseless, treacherous, lecherous, kindless villain! O vengeance!

The Audience is a little taken aback by his theatrics but applause begins to build.

BAYFIELD Thank you, thank you very much. Thank you. That was of course the speech of Hamlet's, from a play I was lucky enough to perform in on several occasions, though not as yet in the principal role.

(beat)

Our next tableau features someone who has devoted herself to the musical life of this city. Amongst others she is patron of the Euterpe Club, of the Brooklyn Orchestra for Distressed Gentlewomen as well as, of course, our very own Verdi Club. Let us journey back in time to 1850 and the state of Alabama . . .

The plush velvet curtains open to reveal the music room of a grand plantation mansion. Accompanying music.

The Audience gasps at the splendid sight.

A PIANIST, 50s, playing Stephen Foster dressed in frock coat, is tinkling away at the piano.

BAYFIELD (*cont'd*) America's greatest popular songwriter, Stephen Foster, has run out of ideas! He's a desperate man . . .

The Pianist tries to write a few notes on the score but sighs in frustration before screwing up the sheet and tossing it on the floor, where it joins many others. He buries his head in his hands – he's a terrible actor. The Audience laughs.

BAYFIELD (*cont'd*) But wait, what is this?

At the side of the stage, STAGEHANDS heave on ropes.

The Audience gasps as FLORENCE FOSTER JENKINS, 65, dressed in a white gown, pouf hat, and wearing magnificent white wings "descends" from on high holding a golden harp. She really is an extraordinary vision.

BAYFIELD (*cont'd*) It is the Angel of Inspiration, sent from on high!

With her index finger extended, she touches the Pianist on the temple, bestowing upon him the gift of Inspiration. The Audience gasps some more and applauds.

A little hesitantly, Foster begins to pick out the familiar tune of "Oh Susanna!"

BAYFIELD At last! Stephen Foster can write his song!

STEPHEN FOSTER (*singing*) "I came from Alabama with my banjo on my knee . . ."

The Audience love this and clap along. As the song reaches its climax, Foster is joined onstage by actors playing his FAMILY and SERVANTS.

ALL (*singing*) "Oh Susannah, won't you marry me . . ."

The Stagehands struggle with their ropes. Florence is quite a weight!

STAGEHAND # 1 Hold her! Hold her! Keep her steady!

The song finishes with a flourish and Bayfield steps centre stage as the Audience applauds.

BAYFIELD Bravo! Bravo! The Angel of Inspiration – Madam Florence Foster Jenkins!

The curtain falls to loud cheering and enthusiastic applause.

INT. COMMODORE HOTEL / DRESSING ROOM – NIGHT

Bayfield enters Florence's dressing room where JENNY, 40s, her dresser, is helping her prepare for the next scene. Florence wears armour. An old leather briefcase rests on the dresser.

BAYFIELD It's going very, very, very well.

FLORENCE I don't feel I imbued the moment of inspiration with the intensity it deserved, but it was a serviceable attempt.

BAYFIELD Better than serviceable. It was good.

FLORENCE My armlets, please.

BAYFIELD Armlets.

FLORENCE (*cont'd*) Has the impending potato salad catastrophe been averted?

BAYFIELD Even as we speak, the chef has a team out scouring Manhattan for chives.

FLORENCE No chives, what next I wonder?

BAYFIELD Unconscionable, I know, but they tell me there is a war on, Bunny.

SPEAKER (*O.S.*) Valkyries on stage please. The Overture has begun.

FLORENCE What about the sandwiches?

BAYFIELD Ham and tomato, plain cucumber and chicken with a hint of Dijon mustard, actually delicious.

FLORENCE Excellent.

Bayfield passes Florence a winged helmet which she places on her head. She makes a very splendid Brunhilda.

FLORENCE (*cont'd*) How do I look?

Bayfield glows with pleasure.

BAYFIELD *Wunderbar!*

They giggle together, before Florence picks up the leather briefcase and heads for the door.

BAYFIELD Now *schnell, schnell.* Go on quickly. You're a very naughty Valkyrie.

INT. COMMODORE HOTEL / BALLROOM – NIGHT

Bayfield returns to the stage and does his best to quell the thunderous applause.

BAYFIELD And now we come to the finale of our evening. I should warn you that the vision you are about to witness will be both shocking . . . and terrifying.

The Audience sighs in keen anticipation. The orchestra strike up the opening of Wagner's "Ride of the Valkyries". Bayfield milks it.

BAYFIELD (*cont'd*) A battle is raging. Volleys of arrows pierce the air, shields clash and swords do their terrible work. But swooping down from the clouds comes the most terrible spectre of all . . . Ladies and gentlemen, the Verdi Club presents – The Ride of the Valkyries!

The music swells. The curtains open to reveal a spectacular and terrible scene. Florence stands at the top of the "mountain" in her armour, her hair and cape blowing in the wind. Below her MINOR VALKYRIES strike suitably dramatic poses. On the battlefield, the DYING writhe in agony.

The Audience cheers and applauds. Florence remains in character – she is Brunhilda!

INT. COMMODORE BALLROOM / STAGE – NIGHT

Florence, now in evening dress, stands before committee member BRUCE ADAMS, 60s, polished, who steps onto the stage.

ADAMS It is my very great pleasure to present you with this small token of our esteem.

He hands Florence a slim box.

FLORENCE (*thrilled*) Thank you, shall I open it?

ALL Yes!

She opens the box which contains a beautiful bejewelled watch. Florence sighs with surprise and pleasure. The Audience gasps.

FLORENCE Well, this is beautiful! Thank you all so very much.

(*beat*)

You know, years ago when I founded the Verdi Club I never

could have imagined that I'd be here tonight, 25 years on, with my beloved husband by my side.

(*beat*)

Music . . . has been and is my life.

(*beat*)

Music matters.

The Orchestra breaks into spontaneous applause.

BAYFIELD Bravo!

FLORENCE And at this dark moment in history, with our brave boys fighting for civilization itself, it matters more than ever. So I implore you to continue to support the musical life of this city.

Applause and cheers. Florence is deeply moved and bows again. Bayfield kisses her.

INT. FLORENCE'S APARTMENT / HALL – NIGHT

Florence's maid, KITTY, 40s, opens the front door and lets Florence and Bayfield in. Florence is so exhausted that she needs Bayfield's arm.

The walls of the hall are lined with photos and posters featuring Florence.

KITTY Good evening, Madam Florence.

FLORENCE Hello, Kitty.

Kitty takes their coats and Florence's leather briefcase, which she places on a table in the hall.

KITTY How did it go?

BAYFIELD Very, very well, thank you.

INT. FLORENCE'S APARTMENT / BEDROOM – NIGHT

Bayfield helps Florence (now wearing a nightgown) into bed. She's exhausted, but content.

BAYFIELD And now, my bunny, you must sleep.

FLORENCE I don't want this day to end.

BAYFIELD I know, I know. Shut your eyes.

FLORENCE Only if you recite for me.

BAYFIELD Very well.

Bayfield smiles. He thinks for a second then stands and begins to recite Shakespeare's sonnet No. 116. His performance is a little hammed up, but very sincere.

BAYFIELD "Let me not to the marriage of true minds admit impediments. Love is not love which alters when it alteration finds . . .

Florence shuts her eyes and surrenders blissfully to the words and her tiredness.

BAYFIELD (cont'd) . . . Or bends with the remover to remove: O no!"

Bayfield realizes that Florence is already asleep. Kitty enters. He removes Florence's wig. Beneath it she is entirely bald. Kitty takes the wig and places it on a stand. Bayfield then removes Florence's false eyelashes and helps Kitty place a turban on Florence's head. He takes her hand and checks her pulse against his watch before making a note in a little notebook that rests beside the bed.

Finally, Bayfield kisses Florence's forehead.

INT. FLORENCE'S APARTMENT / HALL – NIGHT

Kitty helps Bayfield into his coat.

BAYFIELD Thank you, Kitty.

KITTY Good night, Mr. Bayfield.

EXT. HOTEL SEYMOUR – NIGHT

Bayfield steps through the doors of the hotel and speaks to the DOORMAN.

BAYFIELD A taxi if I may, Jimmy.

The Doorman steps into the street and hails a cab.

EXT. OUTSIDE BAYFIELD'S APARTMENT BUILDING – NIGHT

As the cab leaves, Bayfield climbs the steps of a rather shabby apartment block.

INT. BAYFIELD'S APARTMENT – NIGHT

Bayfield lets himself into his apartment. It's a small but cosy space.

Beautiful KATHLEEN, 34, enters from the bedroom. She wears a cocktail dress and heels. She smiles as she sips a martini.

KATHLEEN Welcome home. I'm a tad drunk.

BAYFIELD Oh, lucky you.

KATHLEEN (*cont'd*) How was Florence?

BAYFIELD Magnificent.

KATHLEEN And you?

BAYFIELD (*with obviously false modesty*) I'd say I gave an adequate performance.

KATHLEEN I wish I could have come.

BAYFIELD How was Augustus's play?

KATHLEEN (*laughing*) Terrible! (*she gives the glass to Bayfield*) Finish it – I'm teaching first thing – the oculist with bad breath and two left hands – both of which tend to wander.

Bayfield laughs and glugs down the cocktail.

Bayfield smiles as he slips his arms around her narrow waist and kisses her tenderly.

KATHLEEN I love you, St Clair.

BAYFIELD With knobs on.

INT. FLORENCE'S APARTMENT / BEDROOM – DAY

Bayfield, wearing jacket and tie and carrying a breakfast tray, enters the bedroom where he finds Florence sitting up in bed reading through the newspapers.

BAYFIELD (*brightly*) Good morning Miss Rabbit.

FLORENCE Have you seen the reviews, Whitey? Carlton Smith in the *Musical Courier* says it was the event of the season.

BAYFIELD (*placing the tray before her*) Well it jolly well was. Now—

FLORENCE (*indicating the tray*) —put it on the table, I'm getting up.

BAYFIELD Now, Bunny, that's not a good idea. Last night, your pulse—

FLORENCE —on the table, please.

Bayfield does as commanded.

FLORENCE We need to plan the Verdi lunch.

INT. FLORENCE'S APARTMENT / LOUNGE – DAY

A PIANO TUNER is at work. He taps the keys as he turns his hammer. The gleaming grand piano stands to one side of Flor-ence's plush lounge. Bayfield and Florence pore over a seating plan. They move names around like generals planning a battle.

FLORENCE (*sighing*) . . . No, no, no. You can't put Mrs. James O'Flaherty next to the Baroness – she slurps her soup.

BAYFIELD (*becoming irritated*) So let's serve smoked trout. I doubt even Mrs. O'Flaherty could slurp a trout.

FLORENCE (*scoffing*) The Verdi Luncheon always begins with a soup, you know that. How could we not begin with soup? There would be a riot.

BAYFIELD (*crossing the room*) In that case let us put her over here on the card table between Mr and Mrs Levi. Perfect.

FLORENCE No. Mrs. O'Flaherty isn't keen on the . . . Jews. (*placing the card*) We'll put her between Prince Galitzer and Mrs. Oscar Gurmunder.

BAYFIELD No.

FLORENCE Yes! They're both as deaf as posts!

BAYFIELD No!

FLORENCE Yes!

Florence rearranges the seating plan with satisfaction as Kitty enters.

KITTY Maestro Toscanini is here.

The Piano Tuner catches the name and immediately stops test-ing the keys.

BAYFIELD Charlie, cup of coffee.

Bayfield leads the Piano Tuner from the room.

FLORENCE (*to Kitty*) Do show him in, Kitty, please.

Kitty nods and leaves. A second later ARTURO TOSCANINI, 70s, appears. He's a wiry and intense man who wears a three-

piece suit and speaks with an Italian accent as thick as puttanesca sauce.

FLORENCE (*cont'd*) Arturo, what a wonderful surprise!

TOSCANINI (*kissing her*) You don't mind me visiting by unannounced?

FLORENCE No. *La mia casa e la tua casa.*

TOSCANINI I 'ave a little gift. (*handing her a record*) My recording ova da Bell Song with Lily Pons.

FLORENCE (*looking at the record*) Arturo, how very thoughtful of you. Thank you. You know we are so looking forward to the concert. Are preparations going well?

TOSCANINI Very well . . . though there are some financial matters that remain . . . problematico.

FLORENCE (*feigning surprise*) Oh?

Toscanini milks it for all its worth.

TOSCANINI (*shaking his head*) Madam Florence . . . withouta your 'elp there will be no concert!

INT. FLORENCE'S APARTMENT / LOUNGE – DAY

Florence slips the record from the sleeve and examines it. Bayfield enters.

BAYFIELD How much did he want?

FLORENCE A thousand. (*cynically*) But he gave me a record.

She puts the disk on the Victrola. After some crackles the introduction to Delibes' "The Bell Song" begins to sound. They listen together attentively. But when Pons takes her first breath and launches into the song . . .

INT. CARNEGIE HALL / RECITAL HALL – NIGHT

. . . she is on stage singing at Carnegie Hall.

LILY PONS, 35, wears a stunning, shimmering dress that shows off her marvellous figure.

PONS (*singing*) *"Ou va la jeune Indoue, fille des Parias . . ."*

Her voice is extraordinary: flawless and powerful. Even unamplified, it fills the huge auditorium where a black-tie audience of 2,800 listen, mesmerized.

Toscanini conducts the NBC Orchestra with intense concentration.

Sitting in the front row of the stalls Bayfield and Florence are both stunned by the beauty of the sound.

Florence breathes in the sound, then slowly looks around. It's as if Pons is touching the souls of every single person in the room. Her voice brings a tear to Florence's eye.

INT. CAB – NIGHT

Florence and Bayfield ride home in the back of a cab, arm in arm. Florence is still mesmerized by the sound of Lily Pons's voice.

FLORENCE I haven't heard a voice that good since Caruso.

BAYFIELD Extraordinary little thing, isn't she?

FLORENCE Can you imagine what that must feel like? To hold nearly three thousand people in the cup of your hand? To share such profound . . . communion?

(*beat*)

Did you see Carlo Edwards from the Met?

BAYFIELD No?

FLORENCE He was seated to our right. I gather he's coaching again.

BAYFIELD (*smiling*) Oh is he now, Bunny?

FLORENCE I would like to take some more lessons with him.

BAYFIELD Then I shall phone him first thing in the morning.

FLORENCE (*earnestly*) I shall need a pianist.

BAYFIELD Yes.

FLORENCE (*imagining*) Someone young . . . someone with passion . . .

HARD CUT TO

INT. FLORENCE'S APARTMENT / LOUNGE – DAY

An incredible sound fills the room. At a grand piano sits ERNST ZEIGLER, late 30s. He's a storm of flying arms and hair as he plays Liszt's Hungarian Rhapsody with great flamboyance.

Florence sits at the table. Bayfield stands nearby. He's enjoying the performance, but it's all too much for poor Florence. He crosses to her.

FLORENCE (*under her breath*) Oh, my hat!

BAYFIELD What? Not passionate enough?

FLORENCE He's raping my ears. Make him stop. Make him stop!

BAYFIELD (*calling out*) Thank you, Mr. Zeigler. Thank you very much . . .

But Zeigler is lost in his performance and doesn't hear him.

BAYFIELD (*cont'd*) (*shouting*) Thank you!

Finally, Zeigler stops and looks up.

BAYFIELD (*cont'd*) Very good. We'll be in touch.

INT. FLORENCE'S APARTMENT / HALL – DAY

Bayfield shows Zeigler to the door.

BAYFIELD Thank you again.

In the hall half a dozen PIANISTS sit reading through scores as they await their audition. Bayfield approaches.

BAYFIELD Gentlemen, the chairs are not for practical use. You have been told.

Surprised, the Pianists get to their feet.

BAYFIELD (*checking a list*) Cosme McMoon?

COSME McMOON, 32, steps forward.

McMOON That's me, Sir.

BAYFIELD Come.

He begins to follow Bayfield, but has to scurry back as he's forgotten his scores.

INT. FLORENCE'S APARTMENT / LOUNGE – DAY

Now seated at the piano, McMoon collects himself before turning to Florence.

McMOON What should I play?

FLORENCE Well I really don't mind, as long as it's not too loud.

McMoon thinks about it and then begins to play Saint Saen's "The Swan" from The Carnival of The Animals.

It's a rather syrupy and sentimental piece, but as soon as he touches the keys Florence sits up. She can't quite believe what she's hearing. Bayfield notices the change in her as she begins to smile.

FLORENCE (*cont'd*) (*under her breath*) What loveliness!

INT. FLORENCE'S APARTMENT / HALL – DAY

The other Pianists hear the tune and become curious.

PIANIST # 1 What is he playing?

PIANIST # 2 (*scoffing*) Some Saint Saen's . . . bullshit.

INT. FLORENCE'S APARTMENT / LOUNGE – DAY

McMoon plays on. Florence is so deeply touched by the tune that she starts to cry a little.

McMoon stops playing, unsure what's going on. Bayfield passes Florence a handkerchief.

FLORENCE (*smiling through her tears*) You know . . . (*drying her eyes*) . . . when I was sixteen years old, my father told me that if I didn't give up music and marry a dull banker, he'd cut me off.

Florence laughs heartily at the memory. Bayfield enjoys seeing her happy. McMoon is a little embarrassed.

BAYFIELD It's true!

FLORENCE Sorry, continue, Mr. McMoon.

McMoon begins to play again.

FLORENCE (*cont'd*) Of course he didn't understand musicians. We'd rather go without bread than Mozart, wouldn't we?

McMOON It's not even a choice for us.

FLORENCE Of course, he did cut me off, but I got a little apartment in Philly and I made a living teaching piano to children. We'd play "The Swan". That was my favourite.

McMOON Wow. Great story.

FLORENCE It is, isn't it? Of course he came round eventually and I was . . . back in the will.

McMoon finishes the piece. Florence beams and sighs with pleasure.

FLORENCE (*beat*) Well, I must say you I think you're absolutely ideal.

McMOON Did I mention that I also compose?

FLORENCE (*to Bayfield*) And he also composes.

BAYFIELD (*cynically*) Yes, I'm sure he does. (*to Florence*) There are some other candidates to hear, Bunny.

FLORENCE (*turning to McMoon*) Do you know any of them?

McMOON I do. (*under his breath*) They're all rather . . . heavy-handed, I'm afraid.

INT. FLORENCE'S APARTMENT / HALL – DAY

Now all the Pianists are craning their necks.

PIANIST # 1 (*under his breath*) Son of a bitch!

INT. FLORENCE'S APARTMENT / HALL – DAY

Bayfield escorts the failed candidates to the door.

BAYFIELD Madam Florence regrets she's unable to hear any more candidates today.

ALL (*very irritated*) What? Why not? I trained at Juilliard.

BAYFIELD I'm so very sorry.

PIANIST # 1 Why?

BAYFIELD You're not her type.

INT. FLORENCE'S APARTMENT / LOUNGE – DAY

Florence and McMoon sit on a sofa taking tea.

FLORENCE Now, I must warn you. I work very hard. I study each morning for an hour, sometimes two. And my father didn't leave me as much money as everybody thinks. I couldn't pay you more than . . . a hundred and fifty?

McMOON A month?

FLORENCE A week. (*scoffing*) I'm not destitute.

McMoon's eyes nearly pop out of his head. Christmas has come early!

INT. HOTEL SEYMOUR / CORRIDOR – DAY

McMoon follows Bayfield down the corridor.

BAYFIELD A few pointers as to how Madam Florence does things. You will note that she carries a briefcase with her at all times. You are not to touch the briefcase or enquire as to its contents.

McMOON Right.

BAYFIELD In the hall Madam Florence keeps a collection of chairs in which people of note have expired. They're not for practical use.

McMOON I understand.

BAYFIELD She abhors pointed objects, so never smoke in her presence or hand her a knife or anything like that.

(*stopping*)

Are you fond of sandwiches?

McMOON (*unsure*) Yes?

They step into the elevator.

BAYFIELD Good. Madam Florence is inordinately fond of sandwiches – and potato salad, too. When we throw a party we make mountains of the stuff. It would serve you to consume both with enthusiasm.

McMOON I shall.

INT. HOTEL SEYMOUR / ELEVATOR – DAY

They step into the elevator.

BAYFIELD (*to the operator*) Good morning, Patrick.

The doors shut.

EXT. HOTEL SEYMOUR / LOBBY – DAY

Bayfield and McMoon step out of the elevator and into the plush lobby of the hotel. Bayfield counts out some twenty-dollar bills from his wallet. He hands them to McMoon.

BAYFIELD So here is a week in advance and a teeny bit extra for a new shirt?

McMOON (*touching his frayed collar with embarrassment*) Thank you.

BAYFIELD (*beat; sincerely*) If you can forgive Madam Florence her eccentricities, you will find her to be a most generous and delightful person. Ours is a very happy world.

(*shaking hands*)

Welcome, Mr. McMoon. (*leaving*) Tomorrow morning at nine. Don't be late.

McMOON I won't, Sir!

McMoon breathes a sigh of satisfaction. He's landed a dream job!

EXT. 45TH STREET – DAY

McMoon heads down the busy street with a new spring in his step.

DISSOLVE TO:

INT. FLORENCE'S APARTMENT / LOUNGE – DAY

Kitty and McMoon enter.

KITTY Mr. McMoon is here.

Florence and Bayfield are chatting with debonair CARLO EDWARDS, 50s.

FLORENCE Do come in, Mr McMoon. (*to Edwards*) This is the talented young man I was telling you about.

EDWARDS (*shaking hands*) How do you do, Mr. McMoon?

FLORENCE This is my vocal coach, Maestro Carlo Edwards, assistant conductor at the Metropolitan Opera.

McMOON (*starstruck*) How do you do, Sir? I saw you conduct *La Bohème* last season—

EDWARDS (*for Florence*) —please! Don't remind me!

FLORENCE (*laughing*) Oh, Carlo!

McMoon panics a little.

FLORENCE (*to McMoon*) He's kidding, obviously.

McMOON (*relieved: producing the scores*) I've learnt everything. I'm virtually off score.

EDWARDS Good! Then let's get started!

Florence giggles with excitement as Edwards flips through McMoon's scores and selects one.

EDWARDS (*cont'd*) Here we are. "The Bell Song".

FLORENCE (*laughing*) Isn't it a little early in the morning for Lakme, Carlo?

EDWARDS Not for a singer of your ability.

He hands the score to McMoon who sets it up.

EDWARDS (*cont'd*) Whenever you're ready, Mr. McMoon.

McMoon prepares himself, then plays the short introduction. He was telling the truth – he is off score.

Florence draws a deep breath in preparation for the tricky a cappella section, but at the very last second, she shakes her head. Something is not quite right.

FLORENCE No, no, no.

McMoon stops.

FLORENCE A little more . . . allegretto, please, if you don't mind, Mr. McMoon.

Bayfield nods to Florence in agreement.

McMoon begins again – this time with a little more bounce.

Once again, Florence fills her lungs and this time she sings. When she does she unleashes a sound so dreadful that McMoon's mouth drops open.

FLORENCE (*singing*) Agh agh agh agh agh . . .

In shock, McMoon looks to Carlo Edwards and Bayfield, but both of them seem unconcerned. Bayfield appears to be actually enjoying the performance. McMoon is completely discombobulated by the sound.

EDWARDS Raise the soft palette!

FLORENCE Agh agh agh . . .

EDWARDS Good.

FLORENCE Agh agh agh . . .

EDWARDS Use the air!

FLORENCE Agh agh agh . . .

EDWARDS On the breath. Project forward.

She howls on just the same.

BAYFIELD (*mouthing the words*) Very good.

McMoon struggles to understand what is going on. When the a cappella section comes to an end, he struggles to pick up the piano part.

Edwards winces and Florence flinches, but McMoon finally finds his spot and Florence begins to howl again.

McMoon struggles on in desperation.

FLORENCE "*Ou va la jeune Indoue, fille des Parias . . .*"

EDWARDS Think of the mask, Florence. The squillo! The voice is in the mask!

FLORENCE "*Quand la lune se joue, Dans le grand mimosas? . . .*"

Florence tries desperately hard to follow Edwards's instructions, but nothing can save her. She howls some more before reaching a terrible climax.

EDWARDS Stop there.

Florence catches her breath as Edwards considers his verdict. He pauses for effect, then plays it tough but tender.

EDWARDS (*cont'd*) There's work to be done.

(*beat*)

But you've never sounded better!

Florence claps her hands with pleasure, as if Edwards's words come as a welcome surprise.

BAYFIELD Hear, hear!

FLORENCE (*shaking her head*) Oh maestro, it is true that most singers my age are on the decline, but I just seem to get better and better.

EDWARDS I know. It's hard to believe, isn't it?

FLORENCE I am so blessed.

EDWARDS (*kissing her hand*) There is no one quite like you.

Florence is flattered and turns to Bayfield to make sure he has noticed the attention she is receiving.

EDWARDS Onwards! (*under his breath to McMoon, snidely*) I thought you were off score?

McMoon lowers his eyes in embarrassment.

CUT TO:

INT. FLORENCE'S APARTMENT / HALL – DAY

Bayfield shows McMoon to the front door.

BAYFIELD Did you enjoy the class?

McMOON Very much so.

BAYFIELD She's remarkable, isn't she?

McMOON She is.

BAYFIELD I thought you played very nicely.

McMOON Thank you.

Bayfield lets him out of the front door.

BAYFIELD Good. Same time tomorrow then?

McMOON Yes. Goodbye.

INT. HOTEL SEYMOUR / ELEVATOR – DAY

McMoon steps into the crowded elevator. The doors shut and the elevator begins to descend. It's only now that the mask slips.

McMoon starts to shake. He tries to control his laughter, but cannot and begins to guffaw. The other PASSENGERS notice but try to ignore him and continue staring ahead or reading their newspapers.

Finally, McMoon manages to get a grip and stops laughing. The elevator reaches the ground floor and the doors open with a ping. The other passengers disgorge, grateful to get away from the madman.

McMoon straightens himself up and steps into the calm of the lobby.

CUT TO:

EXT. 45TH STREET – DAY

Florence wails over the scene.

Bayfield steps out of the hotel carrying an armful of Florence's dresses.

BAYFIELD (*to the doorman*) Morning, Jimmy.

JIMMY Morning, Mr Bayfield.

INT. FLORENCE'S APARTMENT / LOUNGE – DAY

McMoon dutifully accompanying Florence. Edwards and Bayfield are at her side as she sings "Biassy", a song based on Bach's Prelude no. XVI, in a language all of her own.

FLORENCE "*Jedu, jedu chistom pole, stanlee tu-chi . . .*"

EDWARDS Find a breath, Florence.

She lets out a howl that frightens everyone.

FLORENCE "*Ej, poshjo, jamshchik! . . .*"

EXT. 45TH STREET – DAY

Bayfield returns to the hotel carrying an armful of Florence's dresses. They've been dry-cleaned.

INT. FLORENCE'S APARTMENT / LOUNGE – DAY

McMoon continues to accompany Florence as she wails away at the "Biassy".

FLORENCE Agh agh agh!

Edwards offers ever more inane instruction.

EDWARDS Lean into it. Appoggio. Expand your diaphragm, Florence! Breathe! Breathe, Florence! Good.

As Edwards grips Florence around the waist, Bayfield becomes concerned.

INT. FLORENCE'S APARTMENT / LOUNGE – DAY

Edwards continues to give Florence instruction as she sings the "Musical Snuffbox" by Anatoly Lyadov.

FLORENCE "Quaint melodies, bring back old days, faintly the old music box plays . . ."

EDWARDS Soar! Like a bird! Wonderful.

Bayfield enters with a bag of groceries. Florence kisses him in between off-key notes.

Florence lets out a final and very dramatic burst before McMoon strikes the final chord. The room falls silent.

Florence sighs with satisfaction, then turns to Edwards for the verdict. The great man pauses as he attempts to sum up his very profound feelings.

EDWARDS (cont'd) One word: authenticity.

FLORENCE Maestro. Do you think I'm ready for a concert?

McMoon is gobsmacked. His mouth drops open.

EDWARDS You'll never be more ready.

BAYFIELD You have been absent from the stage for far too long, Bunny.

FLORENCE (*turning to McMoon*) Mr. McMoon? Do you think I'm ready?

McMoon stares back like a stunned mullet. Finally he squeezes out a reply.

McMOON (*beat*) Sure . . .

BAYFIELD (*enthusiastically*) And perhaps I shall perform a monologue.

Florence doesn't like this idea. Bayfield takes the hint.

BAYFIELD (*cont'd*) (*masking his disappointment*) Or not. Or not. I shall start to make arrangements.

Florence giggles with pleasure. McMoon swallows hard.

INT. HOTEL SEYMOUR / LOBBY – DAY

Bayfield and Edwards step out of the elevator and head towards the hotel entrance.

EDWARDS (*anxiously*) Obviously, I'll do my utmost to attend the concert, but I'll be away in Florida at some point.

BAYFIELD Oh? When?

EDWARDS Let me know when you've fixed a date.

Bayfield doesn't like Edwards's disloyalty, but remains gracious.

EDWARDS One other thing . . . (*confidentially*) . . . since I've been working so intensively with Florence, I've rather neglected my other students. It might be best if we were discreet about these classes. I'd be mortified if Madam Florence became the focus of any envy.

BAYFIELD (*biting his lip*) Well, thank you so very, very much.

Bayfield hands over an envelope.

EDWARDS Oh, she spoils me. (*patting Bayfield's shoulder*). But then she spoils us all. Doesn't she?

BAYFIELD Enjoy Florida.

EDWARDS (*leaving*) I will.

With Edwards gone, Bayfield heads back towards the elevator. He is then approached by an anxious McMoon who follows him.

BAYFIELD (*surprised*) Mr. McMoon?

McMOON Could we speak, Mr. Bayfield?

BAYFIELD Yes, of course. What is it?

McMOON (*nervously*) Well . . . I thought I was being hired to accompany Madam Florence's lessons.

(*treading carefully*)

I'll be honest with you, Mr. Bayfield. I think Madam Florence might need a little more preparation before she sings in public.

The doors of the elevator open. Bayfield steps inside. McMoon follows.

INT. HOTEL SEYMOUR / ELEVATOR – DAY

They ride up together.

BAYFIELD But we've been rehearsing for a month?

McMOON (*really struggling*) I know, but from time to time she can be a little . . . a little . . . flat.

BAYFIELD (*surprised*) Flat?

McMOON A tad. Just a tad.

BAYFIELD (*apparently perplexed*) Carlo Edwards didn't mention any flatness, and he is the leading vocal coach in the city.

McMOON (*perspiring*) Gees, Mr. Bayfield . . . we can't be talking about the same singer. I mean, her vocal cords, they don't phonate freely . . . her phrasing is haphazard, as for her sub-glottal pressure . . . it defies medical science—

BAYFIELD (*starting to lose his patience*) —it is true that her instrument is not what it was, but as Beethoven said, a few wrong notes can be forgiven, but singing without feeling – cannot.

The doors of the elevator open. Bayfield steps out. McMoon follows.

INT. HOTEL SEYMOUR / 7TH FLOOR CORRIDOR – DAY

McMOON (*unconvincing*) Mr. Bayfield, is there any way I could do the lessons – but not the concerts?

BAYFIELD No, I'm afraid not.

McMOON (*in desperation*) But I have my reputation to think of!

BAYFIELD Oh really? . . . What reputation is that? (*coldly*) If you want to go back to playing for tips in a steak house – be my guest.

McMoon is cut to the quick.

BAYFIELD (*cont'd*) (*more gently*) Cosme, Florence is very fond of you. She's paying you well and she wants to help you. She knows . . . everyone.

McMOON But Mr. Bayfield—

BAYFIELD —and she has sung in dozens of sell out concerts. She has a magnetism that her followers adore.

McMOON I understand that . . . but what if less educated members of the public show up?

BAYFIELD (*beat; earnestly*) You're right, we must exclude the hoodlum element and ensure that only true music lovers gain entry. These kinds of events take all kinds of careful preparation.

EXT. BACK STREET – DAY

Bayfield and McMoon in a back street. Bayfield offers a wad of money to a smart GENTLEMAN. He takes the money and leaves with a smile for Bayfield.

Bayfield steps over to McMoon and takes out a little notebook.

CLOSE UP: A list of publications, some already struck out. Bayfield crosses off the Musical Courier. Only two remain.

BAYFIELD So, two to go.

HARD CUT TO:

INT. FLORENCE'S APARTMENT / LOUNGE – DAY

Bayfield and McMoon sit at a desk in the lounge selling tickets. A line of patient TICKET BUYERS stretches out of the door of the apartment. Most are Verdi Club ladies, with a few WEALTHY-LOOKING COUPLES here and there.

Bayfield is discreetly interviewing a MAN, 30s, who has too much of a twinkle in his eye.

BAYFIELD Have you attended one of Madam Florence's concerts before?

MAN No. But I heard all about her.

Bayfield recoils inwardly. This chap is not the right type at all.

BAYFIELD Yes, well, I'm afraid we're giving priority to Verdi Club members at the moment.

MAN But I came all the way from Brooklyn!

BAYFIELD (*looking down*) I'm so sorry. Next, please. (*to McMoon*) *Not* a music lover.

A phone in the hallway rings. Bayfield gets up to answer it.

BAYFIELD (*to McMoon*) You take over. Two dollars a pop.

INT. FLORENCE'S APARTMENT / HALL – DAY

He passes PHINEUS STARK, 50s, a businessman who is with his young wife, AGNES, 20s, a brassy showgirl.

BAYFIELD Mr Stark, very nice!

Bayfield answers the phone.

BAYFIELD (*on phone*) Yes, thank you for calling back. The poster. President and founder, Florence Foster Jenkins, that should be larger, 28 point.

PHINEUS (*to Agnes; under his breath*) If asked, your favourite composers are Mozart, Verdi, and Beethoven.

AGNES (*through chewing gum*) Phineus, try to get this through your fat head. I'm not interested in your bullshit music club, OK?

PHINEUS Agnes, please! (*getting a surprise*) My God!

Florence walks into the hall, arm-in-arm with Toscanini.

FLORENCE On the 4th, Saturday night at 8 p.m. I do so hope you can be there.

TOSCANINI Well, unfortunately we're rehearsing.

FLORENCE Oh, on Saturday night?

TOSCANINI Well, yes, we rehearse all the time.

Florence shows Toscanini out.

PHINEUS (*under his breath*) Oh my God. That's Toscanini, the conductor.

AGNES And I thought it was Toscanini – the anchovy paste salesman.

Bayfield's still on the phone.

BAYFIELD (*on phone*) And finally, the line below that should read: "Directed by St. Clair Bayfield, eminent actor and monologist" . . . Eminent, yes.

After leaving Toscanini at the door, Florence returns and spots glamorous Agnes. Clearly, she takes a dim view. She approaches Bayfield.

FLORENCE (*under her breath*) St. Clair, who is that vulgar woman?

BAYFIELD The new Mrs Phineus Stark, I imagine.

FLORENCE (*scoffing*) Huf! What happened to the last one? Who is that man, anyway?

BAYFIELD Phineus? Sells meat – in cans. Very wealthy. Very generous.

Florence scoffs again before returning to the lounge.

INT. FLORENCE'S APARTMENT / LOUNGE – DAY

Phineus and Agnes have reached the front of the line. Phineus is trying to persuade McMoon to sell him a pair of tickets. Agnes couldn't care less.

PHINEUS (*anxiously*) I understand that Agnes isn't a member . . . she's new to the world of classical music . . . but she is very keen to learn.

McMoon turns to passing Bayfield for guidance. Bayfield gives him a nod of approval.

McMOON (*under his breath*) Well, in that case I think we can make an exception. Four dollars, please.

PHINEUS (*thrilled*) Thank you so much.

McMOON (*handing over the tickets*) A whole world of pleasure awaits you, Mrs. Stark.

AGNES You can never get too much pleasure. Right?

McMOON Right!

CUT TO:

INT. FLORENCE'S APARTMENT / LOUNGE – DAY

The Verdi luncheon is taking place. Guests are seated around a few different tables eating sandwiches and potato salad. McMoon plays Verdi's "Chorus of the Hebrew Slaves" on the grand piano.

Shameless Bayfield hands over a pair of tickets to Mrs. Levi and takes cash in return.

BAYFIELD So, that is two tickets for the Levis and a dollar change.

Bayfield turns to MRS. VANDERBILT.

BAYFIELD Now then.

MRS. VANDERBILT Oh, Mr. Bayfield. I am so excited.

BAYFIELD Well, we all are. I have put you in row E, Mrs. Vanderbilt – E for elegance.

At another table Florence holds court. She rises and beckons to Bayfield.

BAYFIELD Four dollars, if I may. (*noticing Florence*) Excuse me?

Bayfield sidles over to an anxious Florence.

FLORENCE (*under her breath*) They're getting through the potato salad like gannets. Is there any more?

BAYFIELD Let me check.

INT. FLORENCE'S APARTMENT / BATHROOM – DAY

Bayfield enters the bathroom.

BAYFIELD How's it going, Kitty? Running low?

Cut to reveal that KITTY is spooning potato salad onto a silver platter with a ladle from the bathtub – it's full to the brim with the stuff.

KITTY I think we should be fine, Mr. Bayfield.

BAYFIELD (*reassured*) Very good. I'll take that.

Kitty hands him the dish of potato salad.

KITTY Thank you, Mr. Bayfield.

INT. FLORENCE'S APARTMENT / HALL – NIGHT

The guests have gone. Bayfield tots up the cash. Kitty enters.

KITTY There's an Earl Wilson here.

BAYFIELD (*hesitant*) Send him in. Thank you.

For some reason Bayfield is immediately on his guard. He gathers up the cash and puts it in the desk drawer.

BAYFIELD Earl Wilson of the *New York Post*.

EARL WILSON How do you do, Mr. Bayfield?

BAYFIELD I read your column, it's great fun.

EARL WILSON Thank you.

BAYFIELD What brings you here?

EARL WILSON I was hoping I could get a ticket for the concert?

BAYFIELD Well, I'm afraid we're all sold out.

EARL WILSON Oh? Carlton Smith from the *Musical Courier* has got one. So has Stubbs from *World Bugle*.

BAYFIELD I'm really not sure that it's an event that would interest the readers of the *New York Post*.

EARL WILSON My editor would disagree. There's quite a buzz around town about it – he sent me down here, himself.

(*beat*)

So, can I get that ticket?

BAYFIELD (*very unsure*) Why not?

EARL WILSON Thank you.

Bayfield reaches into the drawer of his desk. He stuffs a fifty into an envelope together with a ticket and offers it to Wilson.

BAYFIELD (*cont'd*) Voila.

EARL WILSON (*cont'd*) I just need the ticket.

BAYFIELD It's both or neither, Mr. Wilson.

EARL WILSON (*ignoring the envelope*) Then I'll trouble you no more. Good evening.

BAYFIELD Good evening.

EXT. BAYFIELD'S APARTMENT – NIGHT

A taxi pulls up.

INT. BAYFIELD'S APARTMENT / HALL – NIGHT

Tired Bayfield enters his apartment. He hears voices.

KATHLEEN (O.S.) Darling. Augustus is here.

BAYFIELD Ah, what a surprise. How are you, Augustus?

CORBIN (*O.S.*) Couldn't be better.

BAYFIELD I hear your play was a triumph.

INT. BAYFIELD'S APARTMENT / LOUNGE – NIGHT

Bayfield enters the lounge where he finds flamboyant AUGUS-TUS CORBIN, 50s, drinking a cocktail. Kathleen sits on the arm of his chair. She gets up to kiss Bayfield.

CORBIN I am a second-rate playwright and we all know that but a first-rate friend. The latter outweighing the former, I feel.

KATHLEEN (*kissing Bayfield*) With knobs on!

Bayfield begins fixing a drink for himself.

CORBIN (*cont'd*) So, is it really true?

BAYFIELD What's that?

CORBIN Madam Florence is taking to the stage once more?

BAYFIELD Yes.

CORBIN It's been too long! How much are the tickets?

BAYFIELD I'm afraid we're all sold out.

CORBIN (*shocked*) You can't be sold out.

BAYFIELD I'm so sorry.

KATHLEEN St. Clair, don't be a silly arse.

CORBIN (*imitating her Britishness*) Yes, don't be a silly arse, St. Clair!

Kathleen laughs.

BAYFIELD The concert is for true music lovers – not mockers and scoffers like you and your artistic friends.

CORBIN When have I ever mocked or scoffed? (*sincerely*)

The lady is an eloquent lesson in fidelity and courage and that's why we love her. Please, St. Clair, do you want to see a grown man cry?

KATHLEEN Be a sport . . . (*kissing him; turning it on*) . . . I'll make it up to you.

BAYFIELD No, I'm sorry.

KATHLEEN Please?

BAYFIELD No. *Non. Niet.*

INT. RITZ-CARLTON HOTEL BALLROOM – NIGHT

The ballroom is filling up fast.

INT. RITZ-CARLTON BALLROOM / LOBBY – NIGHT

Kathleen, Corbin and their ARTISTIC FRIENDS approach Bayfield.

BAYFIELD You're very lucky to be here. You've made some promises and I'm holding you to them.

CORBIN I've brought some friends. Music lovers.

BAYFIELD We'll see. I'm watching them carefully.

Kathleen, Corbin and their Friends head into the ballroom.

Journalist CARLTON SMITH, the man who took the cash in the back alley, arrives with fellow journalist, STUBBS.

BAYFIELD Carlton Smith and Mr. Stubbs. We're greatly honoured. I hope you enjoy the evening.

SMITH We will, St. Clair.

BAYFIELD Fingers crossed.

Bayfield crosses to the main door where a pair of USHERS are checking tickets.

BAYFIELD (*under his breath*) Tell the ushers downstairs that absolutely no one gets in without a ticket. No exceptions. And if Earl Wilson turns up, they politely show him the door.

USHERS Yes, Mr. Bayfield.

Mr. and Mrs. Stark arrive.

BAYFIELD Mr. and Mrs. Stark, how very nice. Will you forgive me? I have an important nose to powder.

PHINEUS (*sighing*) Just beautiful.

INT. RITZ-CARLTON HOTEL / BALLROOM / WINGS – DAY

McMoon, wearing a tuxedo, peeps out from the wings and surveys the audience. He's sweating with anxiety.

McMOON (*under his breath*) God.

Bayfield joins him on the stage.

BAYFIELD They're going to adore you, you have my word.

His words don't settle McMoon.

Florence appears wearing an extraordinary outfit of shimmering silk and feathers; it's splendidly kitsch.

FLORENCE Too many feathers, you think?

BAYFIELD The perfect number of feathers. Restrained and elegant.

FLORENCE (*laughing*) I'm so nervous, Whitey! Are you nervous, Mr. McMoon?

McMOON Somewhat.

BAYFIELD We've a full and very warm house and you are both going to be sensational. Ready?

FLORENCE Yes!

Bayfield kisses Florence.

BAYFIELD Break a leg.

He signals to the LIGHTING GUY.

BAYFIELD House lights, please.

Florence smiles at McMoon.

FLORENCE This is what we live for, isn't it? This moment.

The curtains open. The Audience applauds.

McMoon takes his seat at the piano and strikes up the opening chords of "Adele's Laughing Song" from Die Fledermaus. *Florence begins to sing.*

FLORENCE (*cont'd*) (*singing*) "Oh noble sir, how far you err, you're really not discreet . . ."

The Verdi Club members listen in reverential silence, but at the back of the hall, Corbin and his friends are already in convulsions, though they are very careful not to make a sound.

FLORENCE "My little white hands so fine, agh agh agh agh agh! . . ."

But Agnes can't believe the sound Florence is making. Her mouth drops open with incredulity. She looks around and is astonished to see that the Verdi Club members seem to be unfazed, indeed enraptured. She attempts to stifle a giggle. Phineus shoots her a warning look but this only makes matters worse.

FLORENCE "Your blunder almost takes the cake . . ."

Agnes laughs more loudly – the sound distracts others. A couple of the Verdi ladies shoot her irritated looks.

PHINEUS (*hissing under his breath*) For God's sake woman – be quiet!

FLORENCE "Pray excuse me, aha ha ha . . ."

But it's too late. Agnes can no longer control herself.

McMoon notices that Agnes is laughing and struggles to maintain his composure.

Bayfield spots the trouble and moves in as Agnes is gripped by a full-blown laughing fit.

BAYFIELD (*under his breath*) Is she unwell, Mr. Stark?

PHINEUS (*under his breath*) A coughing fit.

BAYFIELD (*under his breath*) She needs fresh air. This way, Mrs. Stark.

All the fuss just makes things worse for poor Agnes.

INT. RITZ-CARLTON HOTEL / OUTSIDE BALLROOM – NIGHT

Bayfield and Phineus half carry Agnes into the corridor outside. With the door shut behind them, Agnes collapses on the floor with tears of laughter streaming down her face. She forces her knees together as a precaution.

PHINEUS Control yourself, Agnes! (*turning to Bayfield*) I am so sorry, Mr. Bayfield.

BAYFIELD Not at all. (*to Agnes*) I wish you a speedy recovery, Mrs. Stark.

AGNES (*fighting for breath*) She is the god-damned worst singer in the whole, entire world!

PHINEUS Why must you always embarrass me?

INT. RITZ-CARLTON HOTEL / BALLROOM – NIGHT

Bayfield returns to the ballroom where Corbin and his friends are struggling to remain silent. Kathleen, too, is fighting to stay in control. Bayfield shoots them an angry look.

ON THE STAGE: McMoon does his best to stay in time with Florence, but she's sliding around and it's a real struggle. To his huge relief, Florence reaches the end of the song with a final and terrible howl.

It all becomes too much for Corbin, whose muffled laughter is becoming audible. To mask the sound, he breaks into applause . . .

CORBIN Bravo, Madam Florence! Bravo!

The ballroom fills with cheers and applause.

McMoon takes a deep breath then turns to the audience. Florence takes a bow.

A smile of relief comes over McMoon's face. Not only have they survived, they have triumphed. He joins Florence and takes a bow.

Finally, Bayfield has had enough of Corbin.

BAYFIELD That's enough. Sit down!

CUT TO:

INT. RITZ-CARLTON HOTEL / FLORENCE'S DRESSING ROOM – NIGHT

WAITERS serve sandwiches and potato salad from silver platters. Florence is surrounded by well-wishers. Bayfield talks to some Verdi ladies.

BARONESS St. Clair, congratulations. What a wonderful evening.

BAYFIELD Thank you, Baroness.

MRS. OSCAR GURMUNDER Oh, Mr. Bayfield, I don't hear very well but I just think Madam Florence is magical!

BAYFIELD (*raising his voice*) Well, I know how very grateful she is for your friendship and your support. (*noticing Florence*) I'm so very sorry, just one moment.

BARONESS That little McMoon. What a find.

Bayfield makes his way through the crowd, accepting congratulations as he goes. He reaches Florence's side and notices that she's looking exhausted.

MRS. JAMES O'FLAHERTY Darling, darling, the *Die Fledermaus* was thrilling! Absolutely thrilling!

Florence soaks up the praise.

BAYFIELD Everything all right?

FLORENCE (*under her breath*) I don't feel very well, Whitey.

INT. FLORENCE'S APARTMENT / HALL – NIGHT

Kitty opens the door. Bayfield guides Florence in, she's unsteady on her feet. Kitty takes the leather briefcase from Bayfield.

KITTY Dr. Hertz is in Washington, but he sent his colleague, Dr. Hermann.

INT. FLORENCE'S APARTMENT / BEDROOM – NIGHT

Florence in bed in her nightgown with Bayfield at her side. DR. HERMANN, 60s, listens to her heart with a stethoscope. He removes the earphones and checks the glands in Florence's neck.

DR. HERMANN If I may, please.

He then checks her back. He spots something and pauses.

DR. HERMANN I didn't have time to look at your medical notes.

FLORENCE The scarring is from syphilis.

DR. HERMANN When did you contract the disease?

FLORENCE On my wedding night. My first husband, Dr. Frank Thornton Jenkins, was something of an alley cat.

DR. HERMANN How old were you?

FLORENCE Eighteen.

DR. HERMANN Where did the chancre first appear?

FLORENCE On my left hand. Right here.

He examines Florence's limp hand.

DR. HERMANN (*beat*) Are you taking any medication?

FLORENCE Just mercury – and arsenic, of course.

DR. HERMANN Any other symptoms?

FLORENCE No.

BAYFIELD She has seizures from time to time.

(*gently scolding*) When she has over-exerted herself.

DR. HERMANN I see.

(*the examination over*)

Well, there is a murmur and some palpitations, but no indication that the disease is entering the tertiary phase.

(*ironically*)

The two hours of coloratura you performed this evening might account for the tiredness.

Florence and Bayfield laugh politely as Dr. Hermann packs up his bag.

DR. HERMANN (*cont'd*) Bed rest until your strength returns. I'll speak to Dr. Hertz and let him know.

FLORENCE Thank you, Doctor.

Bayfield follows Dr. Hermann out of the room.

INT. FLORENCE'S APARTMENT / LOUNGE – NIGHT

Bayfield accompanies Dr. Hermann to the door.

DR. HERMANN I've known patients survive twenty years with syphilis, but never nearly fifty. I'm amazed. What is her secret?

BAYFIELD Music. She lives for music.

DR. HERMANN And no doubt your love has proved to be a panacea, too.

BAYFIELD We were fortunate to have found each other.

DR. HERMANN Clearly.

(confidentially)

I don't mean to pry, Mr. Bayfield, but . . . how is your own health?

BAYFIELD *(under his breath)* Florence and I have always abstained.

DR. HERMANN Very wise. I have several patients who observe the five-year rule but it's no sure prophylactic.

BAYFIELD From the start, Florence felt that my health was paramount.

DR. HERMANN Excitement stimulates the disease. She needs rest, Mr. Bayfield. Rest.

INT. FLORENCE'S APARTMENT / BEDROOM – NIGHT

Bayfield returns to Florence's bedroom. He can see that the examination has upset her.

BAYFIELD Rest, my love.

FLORENCE I can't help wondering what my life would have been, if I had never met Frank Jenkins.

BAYFIELD He is in his grave now. Forget him.

FLORENCE But I could have given you a child. We could have been a family—

BAYFIELD (*tenderly*) —we *are* a family. A great and devoted family – united by our love of music. Are we not happy, Bunny?

Florence does her best to nod, but the pain of her childlessness is very great. Bayfield turns to Keats for help.

BAYFIELD Shut your eyes. I'll recite for you.

(*beat*)

"Bright star, would I were steadfast as thou art, Not in lone splendour hung aloft the night, And watching, with eternal lids apart—"

FLORENCE (*thoughtlessly*) —I think I'll read.

Bayfield stops. He stands and kisses her cheek.

BAYFIELD Good night, my love.

FLORENCE Night night.

Florence nods. Bayfield leaves.

EXT. BAYFIELD'S APARTMENT – NIGHT

A tired Bayfield steps out of a cab and heads up the steps of his rather shabby apartment building.

INT. BAYFIELD'S APARTMENT / HALL – NIGHT

Bayfield lets himself in. From the lounge we hear a jazz trio playing the Fats Waller song "It's a Sin To Tell a Lie".

Near the door, journalist Carlton Smith is calling in his copy on the telephone.

SMITH (*reading from a notebook*) —and the consensus was that she'd never sung better—

Carlton spots Bayfield and gives him a friendly wave.

SMITH (*cont'd*) —her grace and brilliant personality only added to the remarkable quality of her voice. By the end of her performance, the stage was a bower of blooms, and Madam Jenkins retired to affectionate applause . . .

Bayfield gives him a look.

SMITH (*correcting himself*) . . . make that "thunderous" applause.

INT. BAYFIELD'S APARTMENT / LOUNGE – NIGHT

Bayfield enters the lounge where a party is taking place. Many of the characters from Florence's concert are there. Corbin and his artistic crew are having a fine old time.

KATHLEEN (*to all*) Everybody, look who's here!

A great cheer goes up as the party guests recognize Bayfield and applaud.

KATHLEEN (*kissing Bayfield*) Darling!

Bayfield recognizes Agnes.

KATHLEEN (*indicating Agnes*) You don't mind? I invited the showgirl. She's simply adorable. Darling, the concert was wonderful. How is Florence?

BAYFIELD She's absolutely f—

Bayfield spots McMoon who is standing alone in the kitchen.

KATHLEEN Well, I couldn't not invite him. Would you like a drink?

BAYFIELD (*heading away*) In a minute.

INT. BAYFIELD'S APARTMENT / KITCHEN – NIGHT

McMoon straightens himself up as Bayfield enters.

BAYFIELD Cosme.

McMOON Good evening, Mr. Bayfield.

Bayfield offers him a cigarette from an elegant cigarette case.

BAYFIELD Cigarette?

McMOON No, thank you . . . I hope you don't mind me being here, your friend Kathleen was most insistent that I stop by.

Bayfield takes a cigarette for himself and lights it.

BAYFIELD You're very welcome. Do you have a drink?

McMOON Yes.

He sucks on his coke through a straw and makes a little noise.

McMOON (*shifting about*) Maybe I should get home?

BAYFIELD No no no. You stay where you are.

McMOON This is all . . . a little awkward. I mean, I thought that you and Madam Florence were married?

BAYFIELD We are.

McMOON But you live here with . . . Kathleen. Is she . . . your sister?

BAYFIELD She's my girlfriend. It's a little complicated.

McMOON Yes, it is.

BAYFIELD Cosme, you have nothing to worry about. Florence and I have an understanding.

McMOON (*wide-eyed*) Madam Florence, she . . . knows about Kathleen?

BAYFIELD (*beat*) Well, she . . . understands that love, love . . . takes many forms. Believe me, there is no shortage of love between any of us. Surely you can see I'm devoted to Florence? Our marriage is a thing of the spirit, it transcends this realm.

(*beat*)

I am very fond of you, Cosme. I think of you as a chum.

McMOON That's kind of you, Mr. Bayfield. Seeing as we're talking in a familiar fashion . . . could I possibly ask what it is that Madam Florence carries in that briefcase?

BAYFIELD No.

McMOON No!

Bayfield guides Cosme out of the kitchen.

BAYFIELD Now, what do you say we grab a couple of Manhattans and go and join the hepcats?

INT. BAYFIELD'S APARTMENT / LOUNGE – NIGHT

Bayfield and McMoon rejoin the party. McMoon is admired by a passing MALE GUEST.

McMOON Mr. Corbin's friends are all so personable.

BAYFIELD (*cynically*) Yes, I bet.

He hands McMoon a drink.

BAYFIELD There you are. To friendship. In one. Go!

They down the cocktails.

Whooping and cheering. Tom-tom drums. "Sing! Sing! Sing!" begins to play on the record player.

AGNES Hey! Mr. Bayfield, I want to see you dance!

BAYFIELD No, no . . . my dancing days are done.

Kathleen drapes herself around Bayfield and kisses him.

KATHLEEN Dance, St. Clair! I wanna see you dance!

BAYFIELD No, I really shouldn't.

Suddenly, Bayfield cuts loose and goes mad with Agnes – he's a great dancer! Kathleen whoops and claps – it's so much fun.

McMoon loves it and is surprised to find his drink being refreshed by his admirer.

Bayfield throws Agnes into the air.

The guests love it! They all join in.

DISSOLVE TO:

INT. BAYFIELD'S APARTMENT / LOUNGE – DAY

The following morning.

McMoon sleeps fitfully on the sofa in a state of some dishevelment.

There's a knock at the door. Then a slightly louder one. McMoon stirs and sits up, trying to get his bearings. He looks around. The room is a mess. Empty bottles, half-full glasses and ashtrays litter the tables and floor.

FLORENCE (O.S.) St. Clair. Are you there? St. Clair? Wake up! There's something I simply have to show you.

McMoon recognizes Florence's voice and leaps up. Only now do we see that he's not wearing trousers. The bell sounds again.

FLORENCE (O.S.) (cont'd) St. Clair, are you in there?

McMoon fights his way into his trousers and dashes into the bedroom . . .

INT. BAYFIELD'S APARTMENT / BEDROOM – DAY

. . . where he finds a very naked Bayfield asleep in bed with a very naked Kathleen. McMoon taps Bayfield's shoulder.

McMOON (*under his breath*) Oh golly. Mr. Bayfield! Wake up! Mr. Bayfield.

Bayfield stirs.

McMOON (*cont'd*) (*under his breath*) Madam Florence is here!

BAYFIELD (*shocked*) What?

McMOON That's her at the door.

Bayfield sits bolt upright in panic. He jogs Kathleen violently.

BAYFIELD (*under his breath*) Wake up!

KATHLEEN (*stirring*) Huh? What's the matter?

BAYFIELD It's Florence. She's here.

KATHLEEN What's she doing here?

BAYFIELD (*to McMoon*) Stall her! (*to Kathleen*) Get out of bed. Get out.

INT. BAYFIELD'S APARTMENT / LOUNGE – DAY

McMoon returns to the lounge. Florence is becoming increasingly frustrated and begins banging on the door.

FLORENCE (*O.S.*) St. Clair, are you there?

McMOON Just a moment, Madam Florence.

She stops banging.

FLORENCE (*O.S.*) (*beat*) Who is that?

McMOON It's me. Mr. McMoon. How are you?

FLORENCE (*O.S.*) Mr. McMoon? What are you doing here? Open this door at once!

McMoon has no option. He opens the door and Florence strides in carrying an armful of newspapers.

FLORENCE Where's Mr. Bayfield?

Florence trips on an empty bottle before taking in the mess with disgust.

FLORENCE Oh, my hat!

Florence strides past McMoon and reaches for the door handle of Bayfield's bedroom. Fearing the worst, McMoon tries to stop her –

McMOON Madam Florence! Please!

– but he's too late. She throws open the door . . .

INT. BAYFIELD'S APARTMENT / BEDROOM – DAY

. . . and discovers Bayfield sitting up in bed wearing a dressing gown and glasses as he reads a book.

FLORENCE Whitey?

BAYFIELD Bunny. How very nice. I was just reading a little early Austen. Quite fun.

He puts down the book and gets out of bed.

BAYFIELD (*cont'd*) Could I offer you some tea?

FLORENCE What is going on? Why is Mr. McMoon here?

BAYFIELD He lost his house key, so I put him up for the night.

FLORENCE But what about the mess?

BAYFIELD (*playing confused*) There's a mess?

INT. BAYFIELD'S APARTMENT / LOUNGE – DAY

They step into the lounge where McMoon awaits, nervously. Bayfield takes in the chaotic sight; he's "horrified".

BAYFIELD Good God. (*turning to McMoon*) When I said help yourself to a nightcap, I meant ONE! Just look at the place!

He turns to Florence, who, for once, is speechless.

BAYFIELD (*cont'd*) Look what he's done. Bunny, aren't you going to chastise him?

FLORENCE (*stumbling*) Well, I am very disappointed in you, Mr. McMoon. I do not approve of drinking. What got into you?

McMOON (*bewildered*) I'm very sorry.

BAYFIELD Never again, Mr. McMoon. Do you understand?

Bayfield notices that Florence is carrying a wad of newspapers under her arm.

BAYFIELD (*cont'd*) (*brightly*) The reviews! What do they say?

Florence returns to the purpose of her visit. McMoon's transgressions are suddenly forgotten.

FLORENCE Well, they're simply marvellous! Come, come, come.

They sit down on the sofa.

FLORENCE (*cont'd*) Page seven. Here. Down below.

Bayfield searches through the paper for the review with great urgency. He finds it and reads aloud:

BAYFIELD . . . the consensus was that she'd never sung better. Her grace and brilliant personality only added to the remarkable quality of her voice . . .

Florence soaks up the praise like a sponge. Suddenly, McMoon's eyes widen as he sees Agnes stagger out of the bathroom behind Florence's back. She wears just a slip, her hair is like a bird's nest, and mascara is smeared all over her face.

BAYFIELD (*cont'd*) . . . by the end of her performance, the stage was a bower of blooms, and Madam Jenkins retired to thunderous applause!

Bayfield sees Agnes but keeps his cool. Florence is so distracted that she doesn't notice McMoon slip behind her and escort Agnes back into the bathroom.

BAYFIELD (*shouting*) Bravo! Bravissimo!

FLORENCE And I've had a simply darling idea for the Christmas gift for the members.

BAYFIELD Really?

FLORENCE We're booked in for eleven o'clock.

BAYFIELD Booked for?

FLORENCE It's a surprise. (*giggling with excitement*) So continue your ablutions – quickly. I've got a cab waiting downstairs. And bring McMoon with you. I've been looking for him all morning!

Bayfield shows Florence to the door.

BAYFIELD I shall.

FLORENCE Just hurry.

BAYFIELD Yes, yes! In a tiny demi-quaver.

Bayfield lets Florence out and shuts the door behind her before taking a deep breath.

INT. BAYFIELD'S APARTMENT / BEDROOM – DAY

Bayfield enters the bedroom and opens the closet door.

BAYFIELD She's gone.

Kathleen steps out with a sheet around her.

KATHLEEN (*fuming*) This is just ridiculous.

BAYFIELD I'm sorry.

KATHLEEN I shouldn't have to hide in my own home. It's humiliating and there are rules.

BAYFIELD I think she was just overexcited.

KATHLEEN You are to speak to her.

BAYFIELD Yes, that's a very good idea and I shall say, "Florence, although you pay the rent on my apartment would you mind not visiting it."

KATHLEEN Oh, shut up. I won't go on living like this. Do you understand?

(*getting dressed*)

What am I doing here? I'm willing to share you, St. Clair, but . . . I need some dignity.

BAYFIELD Of course, of course. I am so sorry. I'll make sure it doesn't happen again. I don't know how.

Kathleen sighs and sits on the bed. Bayfield sits beside her.

BAYFIELD (*beat*) Why don't we go away for a few days. Golf? Hamptons? Good idea?

Kathleen nods.

KATHLEEN (*sighing*) Yes.

To cap it all, from the bathroom we hear the sound of McMoon vomiting.

INT. BAYFIELD'S APARTMENT / HALL – DAY

Bayfield steps out of the bedroom and sees Agnes holding McMoon's hair as she smokes a cigarette in the bathroom.

AGNES There you go.

BAYFIELD Oh, good Lord.

EXT. STREET OUTSIDE MELOTONE RECORDS – DAY

A New York street. Excited, Florence climbs out of a cab and points at a sign in the window of a shop which reads "Melotone Records".

FLORENCE Here we are!

Bayfield and McMoon follow.

FLORENCE We're going to make a recording and give a copy to the members for Christmas. I'm so excited!

BAYFIELD It's a lovely idea but Bunny, Dr. Hermann was very, very specific about excitement—

FLORENCE —oh phooey! Come along.

McMoon stands hesitantly at the side of the road as Florence bounds into the studio. Bayfield snaps his fingers at McMoon.

BAYFIELD Come on. Come on!

INT. MELOTONE RECORDS / RECORDING STUDIO – DAY

Florence stands before a microphone and shrieks her way through McMoon's song "Like A Bird". McMoon does his best to stay with her.

In the adjoining control room, the ENGINEER struggles to understand what's going on. He turns to Bayfield for help, but receives only a supercilious smile.

To one side, the needle of a recording machine cuts into a disc of shellac.

As Florence hits the big note at the end, the Engineer is forced to lift his earphones away from his ears. Mercifully, the song comes to an end.

BAYFIELD Bravo! That was wonderful, Bunny.

Florence giggles with pleasure.

EXT. BEACH ROAD – DAY

To cheerful music, Bayfield's little sports car clips along a seaside lane.

EXT. GOLF COURSE – DAY

Amid glorious sand dunes and with a splendid view of Long Island Sound, Bayfield and Kathleen are having a marvellous time together. Kathleen looks sensational as she plays the flirt for Bayfield's entertainment. She swings the club erratically.

KATHLEEN Oh flipping hell!

A group of fellow GOLFERS are appalled by the spectacle.

BAYFIELD Try this one. I did suggest this earlier. It's a little shorter and a little easier.

KATHLEEN Oh yes, I like this one.

BAYFIELD (*holding her hips*) And slightly to the left and swing – as if through molasses.

She hits it! She's so excited and jumps into Bayfield's arms.

DISSOLVE TO:

INT. FLORENCE'S APARTMENT / LOUNGE – DAY

Bach's heartbreaking Sarabande in D Minor for violin plays over.

Boxes of records sit on the table. Florence is hard at work. She's wrapped a hundred records but it's a Sisyphean task. On the radio, the Sarabande comes to an end.

RICHARD CROOKS (O.S.) (*on radio*) You're listening to the Firestone Hour with me, Richard Crooks, on the NBC Radio network. We have a caller on line one, Mrs. Edna Hoffman of New Jersey. Go ahead, Edna.

EDNA HOFFMAN (*O.S.*) (*on radio*) Mr. Crooks, would you play Brahms' Lullaby?

RICHARD CROOKS I'd love to. For anyone in particular?

EDNA HOFFMAN (*beat*) My son, Samuel. He's a flight navigator . . . He's missing in action over Germany.

Florence sighs in sympathy with the poor woman and stops wrapping.

FLORENCE Oh my hat.

RICHARD CROOKS (*O.S.*) (*on radio*) Our hearts go out to you today, Edna. We'll all be thinking of Samuel.

Florence listens to the sound of Brahms' heartbreaking tune sung in a sweet soprano voice.

SINGER (*on radio*) "*Guten Abend, gute Nacht, mit Rosen bedacht . . .*"

EXT. HOTEL SEYMOUR – DAY

Florence walks out and hands a wrapped record to the Doorman.

FLORENCE Jimmy, I'd like you to have that hand-delivered please and I'm going to grab one of these cabs.

DOORMAN (*showing her to the cab*) Sure. This way, ma'am.

EXT. CRUMMY STREET – EVENING

A block in a humble neighbourhood. CHILDREN play. A yellow cab picks its way through the streets and pulls up at a doorway. In furs and hat, Florence seems out of place.

INT. McMOON'S APARTMENT – EVENING

McMoon lifts weights. Suddenly there is a loud knock on the door. He stirs.

NEIGHBOUR (*O.S.*) Hey! McMoon! You got a visitor.

McMOON Alright!

FLORENCE (*O.S.*) Hope I'm not disturbing you, Mr. McMoon?

Florence climbs the stairs to McMoon's messy apartment. McMoon is shocked to see her.

McMOON Madam Florence.

FLORENCE I was out and about and suddenly realized that I was in your neighbourhood.

McMOON What a . . . happy coincidence.

FLORENCE Indeed.

McMOON Is Mr. Bayfield with you?

FLORENCE No. May I come in?

McMOON (*unsure*) Sure.

Very reluctantly, McMoon lets Florence in. He's consumed with embarrassment.

FLORENCE (*cont'd*) I've brought you our recording.

She hands a copy to McMoon.

McMOON Gee, thank you, Madam Florence.

FLORENCE You're very welcome.

She notices that the kitchen area is a mess.

FLORENCE (*laughing*) You haven't done your dishes, Mr McMoon! (*sighing*) Would you like me to do them for you?

McMOON (*anxiously*) No, you don't need to do that, Madam Florence.

FLORENCE Well, they'll not wash themselves, will they? I'll make you a deal. I'll wash your dishes if you play something for me. How about that?

Florence takes off her coat and begins rolling up her sleeves.

McMOON (*shaking his head*) Madam Florence, I can—

McMoon stands watching as Florence gets to work.

FLORENCE (*brightly*) —Do we have a deal, Mr. McMoon?

McMoon realizes that he has no choice but to play. He takes his seat at the piano.

McMOON What should I play?

FLORENCE Anything you like.

McMoon settles, then begins playing a sweet little song.

FLORENCE That's such a pretty melody. Is it yours?

McMOON (*smiling*) Yes.

Florence starts to sing along to McMoon's despair.

FLORENCE You inspire me. I shall write some lyrics for you.

McMOON Oh. Wonderful.

Florence tries to come up with some lyrics but they don't really make much sense.

FLORENCE (*singing*) "The birds . . . in the trees . . ."

McMOON Madam Florence, do you mind if I ask how you met Mr. Bayfield?

FLORENCE (*thrilled*) Oh! I was performing in a musicale at the Waldorf, 1919, and I was wearing a violet, velvet gown. I looked into the audience and saw a man with the most beautiful smile I had ever seen. (*beaming*) He had such an aristocratic bearing. That was that. (*laughing gently*) Of course, his grandfather was an earl, you know?

McMOON Doesn't that make him an earl, too?

FLORENCE (*shaking her head*) He wasn't on the legitimate

line. There was nothing for him in England, so he came here and became an actor. He wasn't always successful. I had to hide the reviews occasionally.

(*beat*)

You play so beautifully, Mr. McMoon. You know, I played for the President when I was eight years old?

McMOON Really?

FLORENCE Yes! I played at the White House. Little Miss Foster, they called me. I had very high hopes of becoming a concert pianist . . .

(*massaging her hand*)

. . . but then the nerves were damaged in my left hand, that was not to be.

McMOON That's too bad. What happened to your hand?

Suddenly, Florence knocks a knife onto the floor. She jumps back, very startled and struggles to control her breathing. McMoon jumps up from the piano and hides the knife beneath a tea towel before removing it.

FLORENCE (*recovering*) I'm sorry. I am a silly woman.

McMOON No . . . would you like a glass of water?

Florence nods. McMoon rinses a glass and fills it from the tap. Florence gulps it down.

FLORENCE When Mr. Bayfield is away playing golf, the days can seem awfully long.

(*beat*)

I understand that he needs his sport, but I miss him terribly.

McMOON He'll be back soon, Madam Florence. He's devoted to you. He told me so.

Florence nods, a little reassured. Florence massages her weak hand.

McMOON You OK?

FLORENCE The change in temperature . . . It can be very painful.

Florence pauses then nods nervously. She joins McMoon at the piano.

FLORENCE Do you know the Prelude in E minor? Chopin?

McMoon nods. With only his left hand McMoon begins to play the bass notes intro. Florence joins him with her right hand and they begin to play together as one.

FLORENCE That's it.

Florence is overcome with agony and joy.

DISSOLVE TO:

EXT. FIELD – DAY / DUSK

Kathleen and Bayfield lie together on a picnic blanket. Bayfield rolls over and kisses Kathleen who giggles.

EXT. WOOD – DAY / DUSK

Kathleen and Bayfield walk hand-in-hand through the woodland.

INT. BAYFIELD'S APARTMENT / HALL – DAY

Bayfield and Kathleen return from their happy weekend away. They drop their bags and golf clubs in the hall.

INT. BAYFIELD'S APARTMENT / LOUNGE – DAY

Kathleen flops down on a chair.

BAYFIELD Drink?

KATHLEEN Rather!

BAYFIELD Let me just take your bags, Madam. And may I say what lovely legs you have, Madam.

As Bayfield disappears into the bedroom, Kathleen turns on the radio. We hear a singer performing "Like A Bird". Gradually, Kathleen recognizes Florence's voice and becomes increasingly alarmed.

KATHLEEN (*standing up*) St. Clair. Come in here.

BAYFIELD (O.S.) One moment.

KATHLEEN St. Clair!

Bayfield returns to the room.

BAYFIELD What?

Bayfield recognizes Florence's voice. He is horrified.

KATHLEEN How did she get on the radio?

The song comes to an end.

RICHARD CROOKS (O.S.) (*on radio*) That was Florence Foster Jenkins singing "Like a Bird" by Cosme McMoon.

(*beat*)

We're getting quite a few calls on that one. We have Ed calling from the military hospital in Queens. Ed, you're on the air.

KATHLEEN How did Richard Crooks get—

Bayfield cuts her off.

ED (O.S.) (*on radio*) Mr. Crooks, the guys here, we all love that record! I lost my left leg and half my face at Guadalcanal, but that dame's got me feelin' happy to be alive! Can you play it again? And please tell us where we can find her records!

RICHARD CROOKS (O.S.) (*on radio; laughing*) I don't think it's for sale. It's a private recording . . .

INT. FLORENCE'S APARTMENT / HALL – NIGHT

Kitty lets Bayfield into Florence's apartment. She's very agitated.

KITTY Thank goodness you're here, Mr. Bayfield. Things have been goin' crazy. It's difficult when you're away.

BAYFIELD Yes, I'm very sorry, Kitty. Tell me, how did Richard Crooks get the record?

Bayfield heads towards Florence's bedroom.

KITTY She gave it to him – he's been playing it all weekend. The phone's been ringing off the hook with people wanting a copy – Cole Porter called. It put Madam Florence into one of her excited moods.

BAYFIELD I'll talk to her.

KITTY (*shaking her head*) She's not here. She's at a meeting.

BAYFIELD With?

KITTY (*anxiously*) Mr. Totten.

BAYFIELD Thank you very much.

The alarm bells ring in Bayfield's head. He hurries out . . .

EXT. CARNEGIE HALL – DAY

Bayfield jumps out of a taxi and hurries through the door of the hall.

INT. CARNEGIE HALL / FOYER – DAY

Bayfield enters the foyer where he runs into JOHN TOTTEN, 50s, the General Manager.

TOTTEN (*shaking his hand warmly*) Mr. Bayfield, how good to see you.

BAYFIELD And you, Mr. Totten. Is Madam Florence here?

TOTTEN She's in the hall.

BAYFIELD (*hurrying on*) Thank you.

TOTTEN You have a moment?

BAYFIELD Yes, in a jiffy.

INT. CARNEGIE HALL / RECITAL HALL – DAY

Bayfield finds Florence sitting alone in the middle of the stalls.

Bayfield joins Florence and sits with her. She's calm, but not entirely in the room.

BAYFIELD Do I see a pair of rabbit ears?

FLORENCE Oh, Whitey.

BAYFIELD Bunny!

FLORENCE (*a little tartly*) How was the golf?

BAYFIELD (*slightly shamefaced*) It was nice enough, thank you.

FLORENCE Good. (*moving on*) This is my favourite place in the whole world. (*beat*) And I'm going to sing here. I've booked the hall for October 25th. I'm going to give a thousand tickets to the soldiers because we must support our boys.

BAYFIELD (*beat*) Well . . . I applaud your courage and no one would enjoy seeing you triumph here more than I, obviously, but this place . . . it's just so big. It's almost three thousand people.

FLORENCE Well, Lily Pons's voice filled it. And she's a little bird.

BAYFIELD Yes, but she is a young woman, with a young woman's strength and perfect technique—

FLORENCE (*affronted*) —my technique isn't perfect?

BAYFIELD No, it is. It is, I just think it might be too much for you.

FLORENCE (*scoffing*) Well, if Mr. Churchill had adopted that attitude, why, Herr Hitler would be standing on the balcony of Buckingham Palace, howling like a Doberman as we speak!

BAYFIELD You're not strong enough, Bunny. (*very anxiously*) What if it kills you?

FLORENCE Then I shall die happy!

(*beat*)

Death has been my constant companion for the last fifty years. I have lived from day to day, never knowing when my body will succumb or my reason desert me.

(*beat*)

But I have fought and fought – and I am still here. And I'm going to sing here.

BAYFIELD Have I not stood by you?

FLORENCE If you truly love me, you'll let me sing here.

INT. BAR – NIGHT

Kathleen and Bayfield sit in a booth drinking cocktails. Bayfield is in reflective mood. Kathleen takes Bayfield's hand, warmly.

KATHLEEN It was a lovely weekend.

BAYFIELD It was. We must do it again.

KATHLEEN We must.

(*beat*)

Darling, please don't look so out of sorts.

BAYFIELD I'm sorry.

KATHLEEN She might change her mind, you know?

BAYFIELD I very much doubt that.

Kathleen begins to lose patience.

KATHLEEN Let's try to be happy tonight, eh?

BAYFIELD Well, I'm trying.

Kathleen sighs and sits back.

KATHLEEN You certainly are.

BAYFIELD I just feel, if we had not gone away, none of this would have ever happened, but that's completely my fault.

Nearby, at the bar, WAGGISH YOUNG MEN drink and do their best to interest a group of YOUNG WOMEN. Jazz plays on a record player. A YOUNG MAN runs in. He puts a record on the player.

YOUNG MAN Guys, Guys! I got it! Wait 'til you hear this.

We hear an excruciating burst of very off-key singing. It's Florence murdering "The Bell Song". The Wags fall about laughing.

Kathleen recognizes the sound.

KATHLEEN It's Florence, they've got her record.

Bayfield is livid.

KATHLEEN Darling, ignore them.

BAYFIELD I shall not ignore them.

KATHLEEN This is our night out, St. Clair.

BAYFIELD Oh? So you think I should just sit here and have a jolly drink with you while human vermin laugh at my wife? Is that what you think?

KATHLEEN You will sit down or, so help me God, I will leave you, St. Clair. Do you understand?

Bayfield ignores this and begins to stand. He springs from the table and pushes his way through the guffawing drinkers to the record player, where he pulls the needle from the record and snatches it.

BAYFIELD Excuse me, excuse me. You have no right to have this, this is a private recording. It is not yours.

The Wags are furious and begin jostling Bayfield violently. The record is snatched from him. One of the girls pulls Bayfield's handkerchief from his pocket and tosses it on the floor.

GIRL You dropped your mouchoir, Mr Fancy Pants!

BAYFIELD Get your Philistine hands off me. Give it to me or I will call the police.

Bayfield tries to fight off the attackers but he's quickly roughed up. The record is torn from his grip and he's tossed back towards the booth.

SOLDIER Beat it, you hinty old sap!

Humiliated, Bayfield tries to straighten himself up as best he can. But the final humiliation is yet to come. When he turns into the booth . . . Kathleen is gone.

Bayfield draws a breath, then dashes towards the door.

EXT. MANHATTAN STREET – NIGHT

He bursts out of the bar and catches a glimpse of Kathleen as she gets into a cab at the far end of the street. Bayfield dashes towards her.

BAYFIELD Kathleen! Wait!

But he's too late. The cab disappears into the night.

DISSOLVE TO:

INT. McMOON'S APARTMENT – DAY

Bayfield, looking unshaven and rough, talks with McMoon, who sits on the end of his bed.

McMOON (*shaking his head*) I cannot play Carnegie Hall with Madam Florence!

(*beat*)

Maybe you could speak to Mr. Totten – tell him it's not such a great idea. Surely he'd understand?

BAYFIELD (*shaking his head*) It's too late: she's given a thousand tickets to the War Veterans' Association.

McMOON What did Kathleen say?

BAYFIELD (*mournfully*) Kathleen . . . has left me.

McMOON (*shocked*) Gees. I'm so sorry. That's awful.

BAYFIELD Please, Cosme. Will you do it?

McMOON (*striding around*) Mr. Bayfield, I am a serious pianist. I have ambition!

BAYFIELD (*angrily*) You think I didn't have ambition? I was a good actor, but I was never going to be a great actor. It was very hard to admit that to myself, but once I had, I felt free from the tyranny of Ambition. I started to live!

(*beat*)

Is ours not a happy world, Cosme? Do we not have fun?

McMOON Please, Mr. Bayfield—

BAYFIELD —you see, we have to help her because without loyalty there's nothing.

McMOON We'll be murdered out there.

BAYFIELD You think I'm not aware of that? For twenty-five years I have kept the mockers and scoffers at bay. I'm very well aware of what they might do.

(*beat*)

But Florence has been my life. I love her and I think you love her too. Hmm? Singing at Carnegie Hall is her dream and I'm going to give it to her. The only question is whether you will stand by your patron and friend, in her hour of need, or whether you'll focus on your . . . ambition?

McMoon sighs. He's torn.

BAYFIELD Please, Cosme. Will you play for your friends?

McMOON Okay.

BAYFIELD Thank you.

(*beat; kisses McMoon's head*)

Come on. You're going to play Carnegie Hall. How many people can say that?

McMOON (*unconvinced*) Oh, boy. We're gonna die out there.

EXT. CARNEGIE HALL – NIGHT

A crowd presses around the famous "upcoming concerts" board on the wall outside Carnegie Hall. The board carries a poster of Florence. The word "tonight" has been slashed across the corner.

INT. CARNEGIE HALL / FOYER – NIGHT

Manager John Totten anxiously surveys the scene. SOLDIERS in excited mood are packing in and most have been drinking.

Flashbulbs pop as TALLULAH BANKHEAD and COLE PORTER make their entrance.

SOLDIER # 1 It's Cole Porter – and Tallulah Bankhead.

SOLDIER # 2 Hey, Tallulah!

Bankhead smiles sweetly for the excited Soldiers.

TOTTEN Miss Bankhead, Mr. Porter. What an honour!

Totten buttonholes an USHER.

TOTTEN (*under his breath*) Don't let anyone in who's drunk!

USHER They're all drunk.

BANKHEAD Me included!

The crowd laughs uproariously.

INT. CARNEGIE HALL / DRESSING ROOM – NIGHT

Florence's dressing room is filled with costumes, including her magnificent wings. Jenny is fussing around. Bayfield helps Florence make her final vocal preparations.

BAYFIELD And lower – from the diaphragm. Blow the candles, Bunny.

FLORENCE Agh! Agh!

BAYFIELD Blow the candles out. Hate the candles.

FLORENCE Where is Cosme? He's very, very late.

BAYFIELD Bunny, you must relax.

FLORENCE What if he's dead?

BAYFIELD He's never been late.

There is a knock on the door.

FLORENCE Oh, here he is!

Bayfield answers it and finds a COLONEL, 40s, outside. He's smartly turned out in uniform and much decorated.

BAYFIELD Colonel.

COLONEL Could I speak to Madam Florence for a moment, Mr. Bayfield?

BAYFIELD Of course. Bunny, it's the Colonel.

The Colonel hobbles in with the aid of a stick.

FLORENCE Ah, Colonel. Is the house warming up nicely?

COLONEL It sure is, Madam Florence. I'm not surprised, you're the talk of the town.

BAYFIELD She sold out faster than Sinatra.

COLONEL I don't doubt it. On behalf of the Marine Corp I just wanted to say thank you so much for the free tickets. The boys are very grateful.

FLORENCE Given the sacrifices you've made it's the very least I can do.

COLONEL Some things are worth dying for.

FLORENCE (*with a look to Bayfield*) You take the words right out of my mouth. (*apologetically*) Colonel, you'll forgive me, I must prepare.

COLONEL (*bowing*) Of course. Break a leg, that's what you say, isn't it?

FLORENCE Yes, I'll try.

Bayfield shows the Colonel out.

BAYFIELD Thank you, Colonel. Those were kind words.

FLORENCE Now, we are ten minutes from going on stage, where is he?

BAYFIELD Bunny, you must relax.

FLORENCE Where is Cosme? (*shouting*) Cosme!

INT. CARNEGIE HALL / RECITAL HALL – NIGHT

Tallulah Bankhead walks down the aisle to many whistles and cheers. A rowdy atmosphere is beginning to build.

More drunken soldiers flow into the hall and fight for seats. They whoop and cheer with excitement.

Some of the Verdi Club ladies turn and scowl. This is not the way to behave at a recital!

Totten has never seen anything like it and becomes increasingly anxious.

INT. CARNEGIE HALL / BACKSTAGE – NIGHT

Florence storms along. Bayfield and Jenny do their best to calm her down.

FLORENCE Where is that silly, silly boy?

BAYFIELD Well, I don't have an answer, Bunny, I wish I did. We know the traffic is terrible and I'm sure he'll be here any moment.

Florence hands Jenny her briefcase.

FLORENCE Hold this. Keep it close.

Totten appears; he's close to panic.

TOTTEN Mr. Bayfield, half the audience is drunk!

BAYFIELD Well, you were told about the soldiers, what did you expect?

TOTTEN But this is Carnegie Hall!

BAYFIELD You took the money, though, I notice.

TOTTEN Listen to that! They're hoodlums. Hoodlums.

FLORENCE Hoodlums, as you call them, Mr. Totten, who have been risking their lives for our country and I'd be grateful if you showed them the respect they deserve.

TOTTEN Madam Florence, they're tearing the place apart. You must go on!

FLORENCE (*wailing*) But my pianist hasn't shown!

TOTTEN Then you'll have to sing a cappella!

Suddenly, McMoon appears in the wings. He's dishevelled and a little traumatized.

FLORENCE Cosme, where have you been?

McMOON I got jumped by a bunch of sailors – they were most disrespectful.

BAYFIELD Straighten yourself up. (*to Totten*) Five minutes, Mr. Totten.

TOTTEN Not a second longer, PLEASE!

FLORENCE Shush!

Bayfield gets to work straightening McMoon up. Behind him, Totten disappears through a door.

INT. CARNEGIE HALL / RECITAL HALL – NIGHT

Agnes enters the hall with her husband Phineus.

The Soldiers immediately begin whistling lasciviously, to the great embarrassment of Phineus. But Agnes responds by slipping her fur down her shoulders, revealing quite a bit of flesh.

The Soldiers go mad. They begin to whoop and clap as Agnes sashays down the aisle in a deliberately provocative manner, with a smile on her face.

PHINEUS For God's sake, Agnes, cover yourself up!

Agnes ignores him.

PHINEUS (*under his breath*) Oh, nuts!

Eventually Agnes rejoins him.

PHINEUS Behave yourself!

AGNES (*angrily*) What!

They take their seats amongst the Verdi faithful.

PHINEUS Sit down!

AGNES (*sighing*) What a grouch.

PHINEUS Read your programme.

IN THE WINGS:

Bayfield peeps out into the auditorium through a spyhole. He's surprised to see Cole Porter in the front row.

McMoon and Florence join him.

BAYFIELD Well, it's quite a house, Bunny. I spy Cole Porter in the front row, no less!

McMOON (*shocked*) Cole Porter?!

BAYFIELD And Tallulah Bankhead is here!

Florence peeps through the spyhole and sees the enormous sea of faces.

FLORENCE (*shaking her head*) Oh my hat! What have I done? I can't. I can't do it, Whitey. I can't go on that stage. I've made a terrible mistake.

Totten appears from the auditorium. He sees that Florence has lost her nerve. He draws Bayfield to one side.

TOTTEN (*under his breath*) She has to go on!

BAYFIELD (*firmly*) A moment please, Mr. Totten. Goodbye!

A chair is found for Florence.

Bayfield turns to Florence. Her nerves are in pieces, but Bayfield takes her hands.

BAYFIELD (*cont'd*) Listen to me, Bunny. Those men out

there, they have seen horrors. Their bodies have been smashed, their minds have been torn – they need joy. They need . . . music. You can heal them. That is your purpose. Believe it.

FLORENCE I'm afraid.

BAYFIELD Don't be. They're going to love you.

As the audience grows increasingly impatient and begins to stamp its feet and whistle, Florence turns to McMoon, who suddenly finds his courage.

McMOON You'll be great, Madam Florence.

Florence nods and takes McMoon's hand.

McMOON (*cont'd*) We can do it.

Florence manages a smile.

FLORENCE Jenny, may I have my briefcase, please.

Jenny passes her the briefcase. Florence opens it and takes out a thick document. She turns to the back page.

FLORENCE (*cont'd*) A pen?

Bayfield gives her a pen. She sits and begins scribbling a note.

Totten reappears – he's desperate.

TOTTEN You must go on – NOW!

FLORENCE (*ignoring Totten*) I'm adding a codicil to my will. I'd like you to have a little something when I die, Cosme.

McMOON (*very touched*) Thank you, Madam Florence.

FLORENCE (*passing him the pen*) Mr. Totten, would you mind witnessing? Right here.

Exasperated, Totten takes the pen and scribbles his signature as quickly as possible.

FLORENCE (*taking back the pen and will*) Thank you very much.

TOTTEN Not at all, now will you PLEASE go on!

BAYFIELD (*smiling*) Ready?

Florence nods as she hands the bag to Jenny.

BAYFIELD (*cont'd*) (*to Totten*) House lights down please, Mr. Totten.

Totten gives the signal to his LIGHTING TECHNICIAN and the lights begin to dim in the hall.

Bayfield gives Florence a final kiss of reassurance.

BAYFIELD (*cont'd*) Now then, Little Miss Foster, make me proud.

IN THE HALL:

Suddenly, the audience begins to cheer and clap with excitement as darkness envelops them.

The lights come up on McMoon. He bows to the applauding audience.

A huge cheer goes up as Florence appears.

McMoon strikes up the opening bars of "Valse Caressante", then Florence unleashes a blast of ungodly notes that reverberate around the hall.

FLORENCE (*singing*) Agh, agh, agh, agh, agh . . .

The dreadful sound stuns the entire audience into silence.

But as Florence continues a wave of laughter rises up.

FLORENCE *"Valse caressante, verse ancient . . ."*

The laughter becomes almost deafening. Soldiers convulse, unable to sit straight in their seats.

IN THE WINGS:

Bayfield watches on, unable to do anything.

ON STAGE:

Florence falters. She's shocked by the laughter – her confidence begins to collapse. McMoon struggles on.

IN THE WINGS:

Totten approaches Bayfield.

TOTTEN Good job, Mr. Bayfield.

Bayfield sees it all but is powerless to help. He looks to McMoon, but he is catatonic with shock and stops playing.

ON THE STAGE:

Florence stands alone, facing the huge audience who are laughing harder and harder.

She turns to Bayfield. For a moment the two are locked together. Their world is collapsing around their ears, but they are united by their 35 years together.

IN THE HALL:

Corbin and his friends are laughing, too, but he begins to sense danger and realizes that Florence is about to crack. This is not Corbin's idea of fun at all. He stops laughing and becomes increasingly anxious for Florence. But the Soldiers just can't control themselves.

Agnes too realizes that Florence is in trouble. She stops laughing and becomes increasingly concerned. Desperate to save the day, AGNES gets to her feet and whistles loudly.

AGNES (*crying out*) Hey! Give the dame a break! She's singing her heart out!

One of the drunken soldiers answers her.

CORPORAL Yeah, and her heart sounds like a dying cat.

AGNES A cat dying?

CORPORAL Hey, she can't sing!

AGNES You kiss your mother with that mouth? Sit your ass down. Shame on you. Shame on all of you! You better cheer, assholes. Cheer! Cheer!

Corbin turns to the Soldiers and joins in.

CORBIN Bravo, Madam Florence! Bravo!

IN THE WINGS:

Bayfield begins to clap wildly. He turns to Totten and spits words.

BAYFIELD Clap! Clap!

Totten obeys.

IN THE HALL:

AGNES Up on your feet! Cheer!

Agnes turns to Florence and smiles her stunning smile.

AGNES (*applauding*) Sing, Madam Florence!

Agnes beams with pleasure as she applauds. Phineus finally stands and cracks a smile: this is why he loves Agnes. He kisses her cheek tenderly.

PHINEUS You're beautiful. I love ya!

AGNES (*pushing him away*) Alright. Enough.

Finally, the Soldiers get the message. They stop hooting and howling and begin to applaud and cheer.

ON THE STAGE:

Florence begins to recover from her panic.

AUDIENCE Sing! Sing! Sing!

IN THE WINGS:

Bayfield senses the change of mood and smiles.

BAYFIELD Sing, Bunny! Sing.

ON THE STAGE:

Finally, Florence smiles, then bows to the audience reverentially.

Florence's confidence returns as the cheering intensifies.

She turns to McMoon and smiles. McMoon recovers his wits and strikes up the next section of the song.

FLORENCE (*singing*) "Valse carresante, verse ancient . . ."

The audience is a sea of happy faces. When Florence hits a particularly hilarious bum note, even the Soldiers do their best to mask their laughter.

Suddenly, McMoon finds himself having a good time.

IN THE WINGS:

Bayfield is relieved and begins enjoying the show.

Everyone in the audience is smiling and applauding – everyone except Earl Wilson.

Bayfield's face hardens as he recognizes the critic.

IN THE HALL:

Earl Wilson shakes his head with contempt and heads for the exit.

IN THE WINGS:

Bayfield watches, then slips away.

INT. CARNEGIE HALL / FOYER – NIGHT

As Earl Wilson heads through the foyer, Bayfield catches up with him.

BAYFIELD Mr. Wilson. Are you leaving already? She's only just started.

Wilson collects his coat and hat.

EARL WILSON I've heard enough.

BAYFIELD She just needs a little warming up, that's all. Listen to her.

EARL WILSON (*scoffing*) I have never seen such a pathetic, vain-glorious display of egotism in my life. That you encouraged Mrs. Jenkins to make a spectacle of herself is quite simply unforgivable.

BAYFIELD Will you be writing something?

EARL WILSON Yes. And it will be the truth.

BAYFIELD Isn't it the truth that a lot of hurt people are having some fun – did you not notice?

EARL WILSON Music is important, it should not be mocked.

Bayfield takes Wilson's arm and stops him.

BAYFIELD How dare you. She's done more for the musical life of this city than anyone and that includes you.

EARL WILSON (*beat; coldly*) Do you mind?

BAYFIELD (*lets him past*) You're nothing but a jumped-up hack.

Wilson is shocked by Bayfield's anger. Bayfield produces a wad of cash and starts counting out twenties with contempt.

BAYFIELD Name your price, Mr. Wilson. A hundred? Two hundred?

Wilson heads for the door.

BAYFIELD (*calling after him*) Three hundred, that's my limit!

EARL WILSON You're insane.

BAYFIELD Listen! Listen to them, hack!

INT. CARNEGIE HALL / RECITAL HALL – NIGHT

Florence, now dressed as The Queen of the Night, fights her way through the tricky second aria.

FLORENCE (*singing*) "Ti lascio, t'abbandono, piu madre tua non sono . . ."

The audience is loving it.

Florence reaches the last few bars of the aria and gives it all she's got. The sound is excruciating, but unforgettable.

As McMoon strikes up the final chords, the audience rise to their feet. The cheering and applause is deafening.

HARD CUT TO:

INT. FLORENCE'S APARTMENT – NIGHT

Kitty lets Bayfield and Florence into the apartment. McMoon follows carrying a huge armful of roses.

KITTY (*beaming*) Congratulations, Madam Florence. The phone hasn't stopped ringing!

FLORENCE Thank you very much, Kitty.

BAYFIELD You're pooped, Bunny. Straight to bed or I shall be very, very cross.

FLORENCE (*to McMoon*) Well, Mr. McMoon, we did it!

McMOON We did it!

FLORENCE (*thoughtlessly*) And good night!

MCMOON Good night.

FLORENCE (*to Bayfield*) And you'll come kiss me good night?

BAYFIELD Of course I will.

Kitty takes Florence's coat and the leather briefcase which she places on the table, then leads her into the bedroom.

Bayfield follows McMoon into the lounge.

INT. FLORENCE'S APARTMENT / LOUNGE – NIGHT

McMoon places the roses on the table, then collapses on the sofa, exhausted. He loosens his tie and smiles with deep satisfaction. Bayfield takes off his coat and sets about pouring whiskies.

McMOON (*laughing*) I played Carnegie Hall.

(*beat*)

Goddarnit, Mr. Bayfield, Cosme McMoon from San Antonio, Texas, played Carnegie Hall!

BAYFIELD And he was brilliant. Utterly brilliant.

McMOON We did it!

BAYFIELD I think we did!

He hands McMoon a glass and toasts him.

BAYFIELD Mud in your eye.

They drink.

McMOON (*moved*) Thank you, Mr. Bayfield. Thank you for everything.

BAYFIELD No, don't thank me. I had the night of my life.

(*beat*)

Down in one!

They down their drinks.

INT. FLORENCE'S APARTMENT / HALL – NIGHT

McMoon sleeps on a sofa. Bayfield steps into the hall from the lounge where he finds Kitty.

BAYFIELD Kitty, would you mind fetching a blanket for Mr. McMoon? He's staying the night.

KITTY Of course. Madam Florence is already asleep.

BAYFIELD Good, I'll get on then.

KITTY Good night, Mr. Bayfield.

As Kitty heads off to find a blanket, Bayfield heads to the end of the hallway where he begins putting on his coat. To his surprise, he hears the door of Florence's room open.

He turns and sees Florence standing in the doorway.

BAYFIELD Kitty said you were asleep.

FLORENCE No. You will buy the papers in the morning, won't you?

BAYFIELD Yes, of course.

FLORENCE (*hesitantly*) Stay the night.

CUT TO:

INT. FLORENCE'S BEDROOM – NIGHT

Florence and Bayfield kiss as they lie together, Bayfield on top of the covers.

FLORENCE (*cont'd*) I love you so, St. Clair.

BAYFIELD And I love you, my bunny rabbit.

They hug each other tenderly . . .

DISSOLVE TO:

EXT. 45TH STREET – DAY / DAWN

But soon the dawn has come . . .

A NEWSPAPER VENDOR is opening up his stand.

INT. FLORENCE'S APARTMENT / BEDROOM –
DAY / DAWN

Florence and Bayfield lie in bed asleep. Florence wears her nightgown and Bayfield his shirt. Bayfield's eyes open.

Suddenly he remembers that there is business to be taken care of. As gently as possible he eases out of bed so as not to disturb Florence. We see that he's still wearing his trousers.

INT. FLORENCE'S APARTMENT / LOUNGE –
DAY / DAWN

McMoon, still dressed, sleeps on the sofa with a blanket wrapped around him.

Bayfield touches his shoulder.

BAYFIELD (*softly*) Wake up, Cosme.

Bayfield throws open the curtains.

McMoon stirs and sits up.

EXT. OUTSIDE HOTEL SEYMOUR – DAY

Bayfield and McMoon scuttle across the street to the newsstand. Bayfield buys a copy of the New York Post.

BAYFIELD *Post*, please.

Nervously, he burrows through it until he finds Earl Wilson's review. He reads a few lines of the harrowing write-up, then cannot read more.

He hands the paper to McMoon, who reads a few words. McMoon is shocked by the viciousness of Earl Wilson's review.

McMOON Oh God.

BAYFIELD She must never see this. (*to the Vendor*) I want every copy of the *Post* you have, please.

VENDOR But I got regular customers—

Bayfield hands the Vendor a twenty-dollar bill.

BAYFIELD I'm sure they'll manage.

The Vendor shrugs and takes the cash.

VENDOR I think so, too.

BAYFIELD I'd also like the *Bugle*, the *News*, and the *Correspondent*.

VENDOR Thank you, Sir.

BAYFIELD Thank you.

Bayfield picks up the copies of the Post, *then carries them over to a trash can, where he dumps them.*

INT. FLORENCE'S APARTMENT / BEDROOM – DAY

Florence lies in bed surrounded by newspapers. As Kitty reads from the Herald Tribune, *Florence glows with pleasure.*

KITTY (*reading*) "Madam Jenkins's performance conquers Carnegie Hall . . ."

FLORENCE (*clapping her hands*) Oh, my hat!

KITTY (*reading*) ". . . only the night before at Carnegie Hall, Sinatra entertained three thousand of his bobbysocks followers . . ."

INT. FLORENCE'S APARTMENT / HALL – DAY

As Kitty continues to read glowing reviews in the bedroom, Bayfield speaks on the telephone in a hushed but very forceful tone.

BAYFIELD (*on phone*) . . . the piece was spiteful, vicious and wholly inaccurate and has caused a great deal of upset . . . Well, do I need to remind you that Madam Florence is a very close personal friend of Arturo Toscanini? It would be a pity if the *Post* was excluded from Carnegie Hall . . .

McMoon lets himself into the flat and shuts the door. He stands by as Bayfield listens on the phone.

BAYFIELD (*cont'd*) (*on phone*) . . . Thank you for your understanding, Mr. Thackrey. Thank you so much. Thank you.

Bayfield replaces the receiver.

McMOON (*under his breath*) I bought up every copy of the *Post* within two blocks.

BAYFIELD (*relieved; under his breath*) Well done. And I very much doubt the piece will be in the afternoon edition. So, a few more hours and we're in the clear.

FLORENCE (*O.S.*) St. Clair!

INT. FLORENCE'S APARTMENT / BEDROOM – DAY

Bayfield enters the bedroom where Kitty is still reading to Florence.

KITTY "Madam Jenkins wore a series of extraordinary costumes of great elegance and beauty."

FLORENCE Whitey, Whitey! (*to Kitty*) Read the thing about the simultaneous . . . something.

KITTY "But even their simultaneous reflections were nothing compared to the applause and community spirit afforded Madam Jenkins."

Florence laughs with delight. Kitty leaves them to it.

FLORENCE All the reviews are just terrific – but no *Post*.

BAYFIELD I don't think they covered the concert.

Florence gets out of bed.

FLORENCE The *Post* always covers Carnegie Hall.

BAYFIELD Well then, I shall find you a copy.

(*beat*)

Are you sure you should be getting up? You must be so tired.

FLORENCE (*walking away*) The Baroness and some of the others are gathering for lunch downstairs. I'm going to join them.

BAYFIELD Now, Florence, that really is not a good idea.

FLORENCE (*firmly*) What on earth is the matter with you today?

INT. HOTEL SEYMOUR / DINING ROOM – DAY

Florence and Bayfield eat lunch with Baroness La Feyre and other Verdi Club members in the sparsely filled dining room. The ladies gush with praise for Florence.

FLORENCE . . . After the first half, I was pooped!

BARONESS Your voice was as fresh as morning dew 'til the very last, Florence!

McMoon is doing his best to listen, but, like Bayfield, he's keeping a nervous eye on everyone who enters the dining room.

PATSY SNOW People were fighting for tickets outside. I was offered twenty dollars for mine!

Suddenly, Bayfield spots a man behind Florence's back carrying a copy of the New York Post *under his arm. McMoon spots him too and gets up.*

McMOON Excuse me.

Bayfield is distracted watching McMoon.

BARONESS What was the high point of the evening for you, Mr. Bayfield?

BAYFIELD (*comes to*) I'm sorry, Baroness?

MRS. JAMES O'FLAHERTY What was the high point of the evening for you?

BAYFIELD Well, there were so many—

PATSY SNOW No, it was your Queen of the Night aria, Florence!

Bayfield watches McMoon try desperately to get the paper from the Diner without success.

BAYFIELD Excuse me, ladies.

He slips away and approaches McMoon and the Diner who are arguing.

BAYFIELD I realize this is absurd but is there any way we could persuade you to part with your newspaper?

DINER Well, no, you couldn't. This one's mine.

BAYFIELD (*getting out his wallet*) How much?

DINER (*pompously*) What's going on? I'm not taking your money!

BAYFIELD Fifty bucks?

DINER (*beat*) Well, if you insist.

BAYFIELD Thank you so very much. It's very nice of you.

Bayfield hands the Diner the money and takes the paper, which he hands to McMoon.

BAYFIELD Get rid of it.

Bayfield then heads towards Florence's table, but gets a shock – Florence is missing.

BAYFIELD (*anxiously*) Where's Florence?

MRS. OSCAR GARMUNDER She's gone to powder her nose.

He dashes off.

MRS. JAMES O'FLAHERTY (*surprised*) She's gone to powder her nose, Mr. Bayfield.

BAYFIELD (*sitting at the table*) Oh, quite.

INT. HOTEL SEYMOUR / LOBBY – DAY

Florence exits the powder room and is met by two young men, CUNNINGHAM and THORNTON.

CUNNINGHAM Madam Florence? It is you? We saw your show at Carnegie Hall last night.

THORNTON It was wonderful!

FLORENCE (*thrilled*) Thank you! Thank you very much.

CUNNINGHAM We've never laughed so hard.

THORNTON My ribs are still aching!

Florence is rattled by this.

CUNNINGHAM (*smiling*) You have an enormous comic talent, Mrs. Foster Jenkins.

THORNTON It was so funny.

FLORENCE (*beat; shaken*) Thank you very much. I must be on. Good afternoon to you.

She walks away from them.

CUNNINGHAM And don't pay any attention to that review.

THORNTON That hack knows absolutely nothing.

Rattled, Florence heads for the front door.

INT. HOTEL SEYMOUR / DINING ROOM – DAY

Bayfield sits anxiously as the Verdi ladies gossip.

VERDI CLUB LADIES Is everything all right, Mr. Bayfield?

BAYFIELD I think I just need some air. Excuse me, ladies.

He escapes the table.

EXT. OUTSIDE HOTEL SEYMOUR – DAY

Florence crosses the sidewalk and approaches the newsstand where the Vendor is still at work.

FLORENCE The *Post*, please.

VENDOR Sorry, Lady, all sold out.

FLORENCE Already? How come?

VENDOR (*laughing*) You won't believe it, but this guy comes by this morning, takes all the copies I got. An Englishman.

Florence's interest is piqued.

FLORENCE (*beat*) What did he look like?

VENDOR Oh, tall. Your gentleman type.

FLORENCE Why did he buy all of them?

VENDOR I dunno. Twenty bucks, he gives me – then he dumps them in the trash.

He indicates the nearby trash can.

INT. HOTEL SEYMOUR / LOBBY – DAY

Bayfield goes into the Powder Room. He reappears and picks up the phone in the lobby.

BAYFIELD (*on phone*) 708, please.

EXT. OUTSIDE HOTEL SEYMOUR – DAY

Florence approaches the trash. She digs out a copy of the Post *and begins looking through it.*

Finally, she finds Earl Wilson's review and begins to read. The words are too shocking for her to take in. She begins to struggle for breath as a full-blown panic attack grips her.

Gasping for air, she stumbles across the road.

INT. HOTEL SEYMOUR / LOBBY – DAY

Florence re-enters the lobby carrying a copy of the Post. *She is very distressed and unsure on her feet.*

Suddenly, she collapses. A general exclamation of shock. HOTEL GUESTS gather around.

Bayfield rushes forward and cradles Florence's head in his arms.

BAYFIELD (*to Florence*) Bunny? Bunny? It's me. It's Whitey. (*to the doorman*) Get a doctor – quickly! (*to Florence*) Darling, it's me. It's me, my precious. I'm going to turn you over. Speak to me, Bunny, please.

Florence's face remains unresponsive.

DISSOLVE TO:

INT. FLORENCE'S APARTMENT / LOUNGE – NIGHT

A copy of the Post *rests on the piano. The headline reads: "Foster Jenkins Gravely Ill".*

McMoon plays "The Swan". He is incredibly upset but, out of duty, struggles on.

INT. FLORENCE'S APARTMENT / BEDROOM – NIGHT

Florence lies in bed unconscious. Bayfield sitting beside her holding her hand.

Finally, Florence stirs.

BAYFIELD Bunny, it's me. I'm here. Can you hear me?

Florence opens her eyes a fraction. She panics and tries to sit up but Bayfield settles her down.

BAYFIELD Rest, my beautiful.

FLORENCE Was everyone laughing at me the whole time?

BAYFIELD I was never laughing at you. Yours is the truest voice I have ever heard.

McMoon begins to play Charles's "When I Have Sung My Songs For You". Florence perks up.

INT. CARNEGIE HALL / RECITAL HALL – NIGHT (DREAM)

Florence stands in a spotlight wearing a dazzling headdress and angel wings. She sings . . . beautifully.

FLORENCE (*singing*) "When I have sung my song to you, I'll sing no more . . ."

INT. FLORENCE'S APARTMENT / BEDROOM – NIGHT

Florence's singing continues over. Florence looks to Bayfield.

FLORENCE Listen . . .

BAYFIELD I love you, my Bunny.

FLORENCE The audience, they were applauding and cheering.

INT. CARNEGIE HALL / RECITAL HALL – NIGHT (DREAM)

Florence and McMoon take their bows on stage as the audience cheers and applauds.

Florence looks to the wings and reaches out for Bayfield. He's hesitant but eventually he joins them on stage.

The three take their bow.

INT. FLORENCE'S APARTMENT / BEDROOM – NIGHT

Kitty and McMoon approach the bedroom door, both upset.

FLORENCE People may say that I couldn't sing, but no one can say that I didn't sing.

BAYFIELD Bravo, my love. Bravo.

Florence smiles, enigmatically, and then she is gone . . .

DISSOLVE TO:

INT. CARNEGIE HALL / RECITAL HALL – NIGHT (DREAM)

Bayfield releases Florence's hand for her to take her final bow.

FADE TO BLACK:

END CARD:

FLORENCE FOSTER JENKINS
1868–1944

One of the most requested programmes from the Carnegie Hall archive is for the concert given by Florence Foster Jenkins.

The records she made for Melotone became their biggest seller.

Cosme McMoon's career as a pianist never surpassed his performance with Florence.

He developed an interest in bodybuilding and judged a number of competitions before his death in 1980.

St. Clair Bayfield devoted the rest of his life to celebrating Florence and her passion for music. He died in 1967.

CREDITS